Reinventing American Jurisprudence

Reinventing American Jurisprudence

Law through the Lens of Value

George David Miller
With Laura Brown

LEXINGTON BOOKS
Lanham • Boulder • New York • London

Published by Lexington Books
An imprint of The Rowman & Littlefield Publishing Group, Inc.
4501 Forbes Boulevard, Suite 200, Lanham, Maryland 20706
www.rowman.com

86-90 Paul Street, London EC2A 4NE, United Kingdom

British Library Cataloguing in Publication Information Available

Library of Congress Cataloging-in-Publication Data

Names: Miller, George David, author. | Brown, Laura, 1986– contributor.
Title: Reinventing American jurisprudence : law through the lens of value / George Miller, Laura Brown.
Description: Lanham : Lexington Books, [2022] | Includes bibliographical references and index. | Summary: "Using value analysis, the authors uncover the undercurrents of famous United States Supreme Court rulings. Value inquiry reveals surprising and alarming agendas while opening up a fertile ground for debate, scholarship, and an assessment of the values at the heart of a country"—Provided by publisher.
Identifiers: LCCN 2021036848 (print) | LCCN 2021036849 (ebook) | ISBN 9781793639400 (cloth) | ISBN 9781793639417 (epub)
Subjects: LCSH: Political questions and judicial power—United States—Cases. | Law—Political aspects—United States—Cases.
Classification: LCC KF5130 .M544 2022 (print) | LCC KF5130 (ebook) | DDC 347.73/12—dc23
LC record available at https://lccn.loc.gov/2021036848
LC ebook record available at https://lccn.loc.gov/2021036849

[Although] originality is a valuable element of human affairs . . . [it] is the one thing which unoriginal minds cannot feel the use of.

—John Stuart Mill, *On Liberty*

Yet some people are as fearful as making a grammatical mistake as of committing a vital error. How stupid to waste our lives in infinite details.

—Lao Tzu, *Tao Te Ching*

Contents

Acknowledgments

We are grateful for the timely and vital support of the team at Lexington Books throughout the process of birthing this text. Thank you, Becca Beuer, for giving us an opportunity to publish this text and your constant encouragement. Thanks as well to Carter Moran for his helpful advice and for his work on the front and back covers. We also appreciate the assistance of Monica Sukumar for guiding us through the final production stages and for the oversight of Catherine Herman.

Introduction

According to John Stuart Mill, original people are valuable because they discover new truths, point out the falsity of what were once considered truths, initiate new practices, model enlightened conduct and more refined taste and sense, introduce good things that had previously not existed, and prevent human life from becoming a stagnant pool and people from degenerating into robots by using their genius to animate established practices.[1] These are good reasons and probably deserve a B—without adding in grade inflation. The more important truth about originality is this: originality is rarely welcomed in the arena of scholarship and is generally regarded as a trespasser. Originality is the Other in the business of scholarship. Originality is a disvalue—original people ridiculed. The original person as the Original Other always has an uphill battle, working against tradition and habit and clannishness and incuriosity and insecurities. If the universe in its first moments were as unambitiously unoriginal as these scholars, it would have remained a single point forever. While the unoriginal are enmeshed in trifling matters, original people, unencumbered by petty details, aim at the sublime. The third-century CE philosopher Cassius Longinus captures this sentiment in his essay, *On the Sublime*:

> A mind always intent on correctness is apt to be dissipated in trifles; but in great affluence of thought, as in vast material wealth, there in must needs be an occasional neglect of detail. And is it not inevitably so? Is it not by risking nothing, by never aiming high, that a writer of low or middling powers keeps generally clear of faults and secure of blame? whereas the loftier walks of literature are by their very loftiness perilous? I am well aware, again, that there is a law by which in all human productions the weak points catch the eye first, by which their faults remain indelibly stamped on the memory, while their beauties quickly

> fade away. Yet, though I have myself noted not a few faulty passages in Homer and in other authors of the highest rank, and though I am far from being partial to their failings, nevertheless I would call them not so much wilful blunders as oversights which were allowed to pass unregarded through that contempt of little things, that "brave disorder," which is natural to an exalted genius; and I still think that the greater excellences, though not everywhere equally sustained, ought always to be voted to the first place in literature, if for no other reason, for the mere grandeur of soul they evince.[2]

The quest for originality appears to be a foolish, over-romanticized, and supercilious fetish performed by Icarus wannabes. Against the advice of counsel warning them not to fly too close to the sun lest the wax on their wings melt and they crash to the earth, original people fly upwards. Yet Icarus inspires original people because many of us want to reach the brightest and highest values in our lives. We, too, aspire toward the sun, but learning from Icarus's misfortune instead of using wax on our wings, we invent a nonmelting adherent and redeem ourselves. Those who value originality also value redemption, not as a one-time thing but as routine and repetitive. In the same vein, original people would give Eve another chance with the serpent and not immediately expel her from Paradise for one lousy error of judgment. Original people repurpose boilerplates and templates, promising deliverance from drudgery and drivel. They possess an aesthetic sense for reassembling and reengineering the world into raw reorientations of reality. Absent always, in unoriginal people, is such an aesthetic sense. They prefer to check off the boxes and draw the same dry conclusions from the same dreary arguments. For the box checker, reorientation is seen as overreach. For the box checker, originality is seen not looking before leaping. Contrary to conventional wisdom, the original person looks before leaping, but at where to land and not at the dismay and disapproval of onlookers. Yet it might well be a rough landing as the landing point shifts during flight. As in most cases when a value emerges, it emerges in concert with other values, as does the value of originality. Other values accompanying, adjoining, or buttressing originality include process, ambiguity, risk-taking, and redemption. The original person does not prematurely use Ockham's razor, but grows out ideas even in wild and incongruous ways to allow new ideational strands to emerge. Ockham's razor has the positive value of simplicity, but has the negative quality of obstructing new ideas from emerging. Allowing to grow out a tangled weave of complexity to emerge often reveals ideas that would have been shaved according to the value of simplicity. Ockham's razor, while valuable, must be counterbalanced by Bubba's beard to maximize ideation. Finally, originality is not to be mistaken with oddness or eccentricity, although those values often appear with it. Oddness or eccentricity is not the point of the originality we are pursuing here. We are pursuing originality in the service of opening up new ways of encountering a whole host of philosophical issues, including those in the philosophy of law.

For every sacred cow, there is correspondingly an equally peculiar type of goat called a scapegoat. In the language of values, for every hyper-value, a value that is considered absolute or near the zenith of a value hierarchy (a sacred zenith value), there is correspondingly a nadir value, also an absolute, at the bottom of the value hierarchy (a profane nadir disvalue). The sacred cow-scapegoat value scheme is at the core of a Manichean outlook. A common attitude of the person embracing the hypervalue looking down at the nadir value is contempt. Taking instant offense is common among the contemptuous. The contemptuous box checkers in particular take instant offense to any form of originality. Similarly, people committed to diversity look contemptuously at absolutism. When diversity is positively hyper-valued, correspondingly absolutism is negatively hyper-disvalued and scapegoated and in a great irony excommunicated from diversity.

This preamble clarifies the approach of this book. Our approach points people to the original texts for the purpose of examining Supreme Court rulings in original ways. It sees jurisprudence not as ethereal pronouncements or talking points from political agendas, but as value judgments made by flesh and blood human beings in real time. More than that, it teaches students to trust their instincts about what they see. Thinking for oneself means trusting one's self. One of our big issues with *Say Yes to the Dress* is the bride-to-be not trusting her own instincts on what dress looks good on her, but wholly depending on others for their judgments. Original persons trust their insights and regard the interjections of others as the frame around a painting. Otherwise, thinking devolves into glorified groupthink.

Fueled by the value of originality, this inquiry reinvents American jurisprudence. It impacts legal scholarship and adjudication. In addition to originality, we value the elegant over the baroque, the poignant over the ponderous, and the explicit over the implicit. To accomplish our task, we initially establish a clear ontological and axiological grounding. Then, we demonstrate that values underlie each of the major theories of law. From this grounding, we assess notable Supreme Court cases. We identify leading value-complexes in play and offer a unique way of fleshing out authorities in something akin to a logical proof—for the purpose of realizing the values of coherence and transparency.

Our approach challenges some basic beliefs about jurisprudence. For example, the analogy that judges are umpires or referees is misleading in two respects. First, what counts as a foul or a penalty often depends upon the interpretation of judges or umpires. What one official sees as a foul or penalty another may not. Interpretation plays a role in aspects of officiating.

Second, umpires and referees judge the action in front of them based on a single rulebook and not a complex of primary authorities such as constitutions, legislative statutes and codes, case opinions from the courts, and regulations or secondary authorities such as articles, treatises, hornbooks, or legal encyclopedias.[3]

Lest we forget: laws are created by fallible beings, interpreted by fallible beings, adjudicated by fallible beings, abided or not abided by fallible beings. There is nothing ethereal about law. It is a human machination. In a free society or something that resembles a free society, citizens should be wary of the origin of laws, their interpretation, and their implementation. Citizens must be the watch guards of law and not just accept it as fait accompli. Part of being a watch guard is to demand and request a full value justification for laws and all legal decisions. As a watch guard citizenry, we must demand to see the value ingredients that go into laws as much as we demand them on food or drug labels. This is full disclosure.

In a society valuing fairness, adjudicators must be above reproach. Above reproach does not mean adjudicators make their decisions outside the human condition. All people make their decisions from the confines of their own values. This doesn't mean that values can't evolve or change, but it does mean that we make our decisions according to those values. To be beyond reproach is to acknowledge personal values as those that go into decision-making. Jurists are not neutral: their values lead them by their noses. They have things they want to come to fruition and those they don't. Don't we all?

Our approach differs from many others because of our emphasis on insight and its close cousin, essentialism. In recent scholarship, over-contextualizing and hyper-pluralizing reign supreme. Rather than lead to clarity, this just leads to more obscurity. In effect, dizzying detail has replaced insight. Overvaluing intellectual pluralism has led to a diminishment of the value of insight as well as the actual power of insight. Insight aims toward the essential always, and intellectual over-pluralization resists a unification crystallized in insight. The penchant for ever-more context and plurality and the devaluation of essence and unity culminates in a genre of inquiry that in touching on everything never seems to get to the point of anything. To this point, Machiavelli identifies three types of intellects: those who grasp the matter, those who know what others said about the matter, and those that neither grasp the matter nor know what others say about it.[4] Over-contextualizing falls under the second category of gathering viewpoints instead of exercising insight. Even Deconstruction, the champion of over-contextualization, smacks of essence because each act of deconstruction begins and ends for a reason.[5] Furthermore, being temporarily undecided in the Deconstructionist sense disrupts any attempts to use standards to assess texts or bring interpretation to closure.[6] But this bold foray, once unmasked, can only be seen as smoke and mirrors, which in the end does not eradicate an essentialism at the heart of Deconstructionist mission—in which nonclosure becomes essentialized. We will argue for an ineradicable value essentialism, which will probably be met by consternation at best and condemnation at worst. Essentialism has been canceled in many intellectual circles due to the hypervaluing of pluralism (making it an essence—but no matter). If it makes any difference to cancellation queens, our *e*s*s*e*n*t*i*a*l*i*s*m* in which sometimes values protrude and at other times they are recessed. Yet to touch on any meaning is to be cut by the sharp edge of values and disvalues.

Under the black light of axiological inquiry, values can be detected. Some values protrude while others are recessed. Just as a black light detects blood and other body fluids, so philosophical black light detects values and disvalues. This black light comes about by reorienting our perspective toward identifying preferences, or the valuing of one thing over another.

This is not that amazing a discovery, like the discovery of another plane of existence. In their lives, humans make innumerable choices. Those choices are always preferences, and those preferences consist of selecting one item over another or valuing them. The oft-repeated assertion of Protagoras that "man is the measure of all things" implies that humans measure—and we measure according to our values.

We understand law according to its value. We can think of a society in which law does not exist, where good people make decisions according to their best intentions and everybody trusts everyone else to do so. In such a society, there would be no competing interests or differences about the Good. In such a society, law would not be a necessity. In all others, in which there are competing interests, people act selfishly and with little or no regard to others, law becomes a necessity. Even if all people saw the Good, they would see it differently and then law would be a necessity. Less than a strict necessity, but nearly necessary if a functional society is to come about. A possible criticism of this approach would be that it would delegitimize jurisprudence. Any ruling can be said to be arbitrary and subjective and therefore not legitimate. What is the basis of the legitimacy of the law? Its legitimacy comes from respect of law as a near positive necessity[7] for the operation of a complex society. Jurisprudence is a continuum in which laws are legitimized and delegitimized. Legitimization and delegitimization rest in the hands of human beings who can marshal support for this agenda or that. In the end, the justification for any agenda of legitimization or delegitimization is value-oriented.

In the second part of the book, we will use our philosophical black light to identify the values in play in pivotal Supreme Court cases, the values behind the legal reasoning. Not every analysis will be done in the same way, mainly to avoid boredom on our parts and more importantly on the part of the readers, and also because we want people to understand there are many ways to do value analysis. At the beginning of each case, we will set forth what are usually considered the fundamental facts of it. We will address the majority opinion and dissent (if applicable) and for many cases, concurrences will be analyzed. In general, for each majority opinion, concurrence, or dissent, we will demonstrate an arc of authorities as a means to clearly show the legal lay of the land. Sometimes this will be exhaustive, other times more selective. Subsequently, we articulate the legal reasoning and identify the operating values. In many cases to promote clarity, we segregate our analyses of the majority opinion, concurrence, and dissent for each case. In some cases, we blend them. At the end of each case, we offer the perspective of what we call "Reckoning of the Rogue Justices." The Rogue Justices come to their own decision in each case, using black light value analysis.

We prioritize original texts to actualize originality. Our focus is to show the operative values in each case. For this endeavor, our focus has to be unrolling the new theory on what specific Supreme Court justices stated. The interjection of other views in midst of this process would complicate an already difficult task. As part of the introduction of each Supreme Court case, we include diverse scholarly perspectives as a way of showing connections with our work. But this is to round out our project and is not the animating force. We do not consider secondary sources anathema, but they are not the crux of our project. They help frame our project. Our project is phenomenological axiology: using our philosophical black light to reveal and pinpoint value narratives in U.S. Supreme Court cases. We utilize a version of what Husserl and Co. call bracketing or Epoché. Bracketing creates a kind of gated community that excludes or pushes out assumptions and biases in order to create space for essences, including value essences. Yet bracketing also has value context. It values what is within the brackets more than what is outside the brackets. The essences within the brackets are more significant or important than the less significant or less important elements outside the brackets. Values then inform the inclusionary-exclusionary process of bracketing. Bracketing *evaluates*.

It can be argued our approach, by adding a value dimension, adds an unnecessary layer to jurisprudence, and in so doing increases confusion rather than promoting clarity. Any kind of new approach introduces confusion at first, but like driving on the right-hand side of the road when you're used to driving on the left in your country, it can be managed with practice.

Be not bemused by this seemingly glib approach. It is only different.

NOTES

1. John Stuart Mill, *On Liberty* (London, Felling-on-Tyne, New York, Melbourne; Project Gutenberg, January 10, 2011), Chapter III, http://www.gutenberg.org/files/34901/34901-h/34901-h.htm.

2. Longinus, *On the Sublime* (London and New York, 1890; Project Guttenberg, March 10, 2006), Chapter XXXIII https://www.gutenberg.org/files/17957/17957-h/17957-h.htm.

3. "Legal Research Tip: Types of Legal Authority," https://www.law.du.edu/documents/lawyering-process/types-of-legal-authority.pdf.

4. Nicolo Machiavelli, *The Prince* (Project Guttenberg, March 1998), Chapter XXII https://www.gutenberg.org/files/1232/1232-h/1232-h.htm. A similar three-fold division can be found in Aristotle, *Nicomachean Ethics of Aristotle* (Project Gutenberg, July 10, 2003), Book 1, Chapter II, https://www.gutenberg.org/files/8438/8438-h/8438-h.htm. "He is best of all who of himself conceiveth all things;/Good again is he too who can adopt a good suggestion;/But whoso neither of himself conceiveth nor hearing from another/Layeth it to heart;—he is a useless man." Aristotle attributes this to Hesiod. See also Immanuel Kant, *Critique of Pure Reason*, trans. Norman Kemp Smith (New York: St. Martin's Press, 1965), 78. "Deficiency in judgment is just what is ordinarily called stupidity, and for such a failing there is no remedy. An obtuse or narrow-minded person to whom nothing is wanting save a proper degree of understanding and the concepts appropriate thereto, may indeed be trained through study, even to the extent of becoming learned. But as such people are commonly lacking in judgment (*secunda Petri*), it is not unusual to meet learned men who in the application of their scientific knowledge betray that original want, which can never be made good."

5. Jack M. Balkin, "Tradition, Betrayal, and the Politics of Deconstruction," *Yale Law School Repository*, May 20, 2021, 15. https://digitalcommons.law.yale.edu/cgi/viewcontent.cgi?article=1282&context=fss_papers.

> Yet if one always deconstructs for a reason, then there is a logos or rationale behind such a decision, a method to this textual madness. The deconstructionist may appear crazy, but she is crazy like a fox. Her practice is a logocentric practice at its inception—even as it seeks to subvert the logocentrism of the particular text:

Thus: "Not only does a deconstructionist begin deconstructing for a reason, she also ends her deconstruction for a reason." Those "reasons" are actually values.

6. Alan C. Hutchinson, "Identity Crisis: The Politics of Interpretation," *New England Law Review* 26, 4 (1992): 1185. Osgoode Digital Commons, May 20, 2021. https://digitalcommons.osgoode.yorku.ca/cgi/viewcontent.cgi?referer=https://www.google.com/&httpsredir=1&article=1452&context=scholarly_works.

7. Necessity and probability have traditionally been regarded in Manichean terms with necessity regarded as a zenith value and contingency as a nadir disvalue. Two issues emerge. What if necessity and probability were not the two poles? What if possibility played a role in establishing some kind of spectrum of degrees of

actualization? Two bolts of lightning have hit us at once. First, there is one kind of necessity that can be seen as positive, for example, a square necessarily having four right angles. Another kind of necessity can be seen as negative, for example, a bachelor being married. This is where possibility plays a role. In both negative and positive necessity, there is no room for possibility. In negative necessity, something can never be, while in positive necessity, something must always be. There can be degrees of possibility that more resemble what can never be and types of possibility that more resemble what must always be. A person walking on water resembles negative necessity, while a rock dropped from a mountain and falling to a ground resembles a positive necessity. The more possible something is regarded, the more it trends toward positive necessity; the less possible, the more it trends toward negative necessity. Laws being a part of human civilization can be seen as a near-positive necessity.

Part I

INTRODUCTION TO A NEW THEORY OF LAW

Chapter 1

The Primacy of Value

Value as the Sharp Edge of Meaning

TWO EXAMPLES AS A WINDOW INTO AXIOLOGICAL ANALYSIS

Two examples from famous films introduce our axiological analysis.

In the iconic film *It's a Wonderful Life*, a despondent George Bailey wishes he had never been born. George's guardian angel, Clarence, fulfills George's wish and according to this what-if scenario, in the absence of George Bailey the world is turned upside down. In George's absence, his brother Harry drowns and, deprived of Harry's heroic actions, dozens of soldiers die on an aircraft carrier during World War II. Without George to stop him from filling a prescription with a lethal chemical, the druggist Mr. Gower accidentally poisons a child and, unable to deal with this guilt, is imprisoned for his crime and ends up as an alcoholic. George's absence means that Mary will live an unfilled life as a stereotypical bespectacled and timid old-maid librarian. George also won't be able to save the Building and Loan, which means that it will be left to the well-meaning, but bumbling Uncle Billy to wreck. Uncle Billy ends up in a mental health facility and the Building and Loan falls into the hands of Plutocrat Potter. Instead of offering affordable homes to working families, Potter relegates them to shanties while the town is filled with angry people, lurid entertainment, and trigger-happy police officers who open fire on Main Street. Idyllic Bedford Falls is no longer and becomes seedy Pottersville.

In this saga, the values of the adversaries protrude. Mr. Potter values efficiency and wealth maximization and as an extreme individualist feels no responsibility to lift others to better lives. He has contempt for the common man and favors a social system where wealth and power are concentrated rather than redistributed. On the other hand, George Bailey values people and places them over profit-efficiency. He is a communitarian who sees his family's business as a means to improve the standard of living in the community by making housing loans affordable to working people.

Not only does an axiological investigation lay bare the core values of films like *It's a Wonderful Life* but also all avenues of human existence, including jurisprudence. Jurisprudence can be demystified by understanding the basic values behind the laws.

The value dimension of jurisprudence becomes clear when a science fiction film like *Planet of the Apes* (posing a what-if scenario in which apes evolve from humans) performs a role reversal, casting human beings as soulless animals and simians as rational beings in the image of God. Simian law reflects the values of simian culture:

> My case is simple. It is based on our first Article of Faith: that the Almighty created the ape in his own image; that He gave him a soul and a mind; that He set him apart from the beasts of the jungle, and made him the lord of the planet.[1]

The value of personhood belongs to apes; the disvalue of bestiality belongs to human beings. From this valuation, the subjugation of humans is justified and the simians' version of speciesism affirmed. Humans can be caged, experimented on, hunted, and after their deaths exhibited in museums.

From both films, we recognize the impact of values. Going beyond the films and what little we said about value in our "Introduction," we will now articulate a more cogent defense of the pervasiveness of value in the human experience.

VALUE: A PHENOMENOLOGICAL APPROACH

Intellectuals love to criticize the general public for its rampant consumerism and falling prey to the dubious spokespeople. But intellectuals exhibit the same type of consumerism and fall prey to the same type of mindlessness by buying into notions of equally dubious spokespeople without really vetting their ideas. When phenomenology comes to mind, Husserl, Heidegger, Sartre, and Merleau-Ponty stand as its giants and the ideas of horizons, intentionality, bad faith, *Dasein*, and the Other their picked-over conceptual merchandise. Hidden behind these once-compelling but by-now devoured ideas stands the seminal work of Max Scheler on value. Scheler's insight on value becomes our launching pad for our own critique of values as they pertain to jurisprudence.

The first few pages of Scheler's 1916 essay *Ordo Amoris* supply the staples for his view on values. The first sentence of the essay illustrates how values stand at the forefront of human experience: "I find myself in an immeasurably vast world of sensible and spiritual objects which set my heart and passions in constant motion."[2] "[T]he objects I can recognize through perception and thought," Scheler continues, "as well as all that I will, choose, perform, and accomplish, depend on this movement of the heart"[3] or emotive intuition. The essence of a person, family, age, or nation can most fully be understood in light of its value-preferences, how in each case the ordering of love and hate, or what Scheler calls the *ordo amoris*[4] (order of love), structure our valuations. Investigation of the *ordo amoris* could offer a descriptive dimension to see the value reality behind "wishes, customs, needs, and spiritual achievements."[5] Thus, Scheler proclaims: *Whoever has the ordo amoris of the man has the man himself.*[6]

Scheler emphasizes the primacy and objectivity of values. Even before "the unity of perception, a value-signal experienced as *coming from things* [our emphasis], not from us, announces, as though with a trumpet flourish, that 'Something is up.'"[7] We experience our world through a lens of values:

> Man is encased, as though in a shell, in the particular ranking of the simplest values and value-qualities which represent the objective side of *ordo amoris*, values which have not yet been shaped into things and goods. He carries this shell wherever he goes and cannot escape from it no matter how quickly he runs. He perceives the world and himself through this shell, and perceives no more of the world, of himself, or anything else besides what these windows show him.[8]

Only through acts of preferring do we intuit higher and lower and positive and negative values. We grasp higher and lower and positive and negative values by acts of preferring and placing after within the context of a spectrum of values:

> Since all values stand essentially in an order of rank—i.e., since all values are, in relation to each other, higher or lower—and since these relations are comprehensible only "in" preferring or rejecting them, the "feeling" of values has its foundation, by essential necessity, in "preferring" and "placing after."[9]

Scheler criticizes the predominant worldview that the emotional life consists of a subjective whirlwind that must be tamed so that the work of rationality could be done: "Rather, they [modern people] take our emotional life to consist of a serious of totally blind happenings which run their course in us like any natural processes; happenings which eventually one must have a technique for managing in order to get some use from them and avoid harm."[10] Our emotional lives are seen as "dumb, vague, or without direction or objective necessity."[11] Modernity fails to see that love and hate and their noematic correlates (values) "*govern the sense and meaning of our lives*," because "[t]he heart possesses a strict logic of its own domain that it does not borrow from the logic of the understanding: laws are inscribed on it . . . which correspond to the plane on which the world is constructed as a world of value."[12] There exists an "eternal architecture and scaffolding"[13] that manifests higher and lower and positive and negative values. The heart sets "before our eyes a strictly *objective sphere* of facts which is the most objective, the most fundamental of all possible spheres of fact; one which remains in the universe even if *Homo sapiens* is destroyed, just as does the truth of the proposition 2 x 2=4."[14] Acts of love and hate (the heart) possess an ordered logic just as reason possesses a different, but ordered logic and just as there are ordered objects of reason, there are ordered objects of the heart.

VALUE AS THE SHARP EDGE OF MEANING

Inspired by Scheler, we see that the intrinsic nature of values has been ignored and dismissed by a devaluation pushing values out of our intellectual purview and concealing them under a cloud of scientific quantification. As Thomas Kuhn points out, values impact the practice of science:

> Perhaps they [scientists] interpret simplicity differently or have different convictions about the range of fields within which the consistency criterion must be met. Or perhaps they agree about these matters but differ about the relative weights to be accorded to these or to other criteria when several are deployed together.

Some scientists place more premium than others on originality and are correspondingly more willing to take risks; some scientists prefer comprehensive, unified theories to precise and detailed problem solutions of apparently narrower scope.

> But they [the values of accuracy, consistency, and scope] do specify a great deal: what each scientist must consider in reaching a decision, what he may and may not consider relevant, and what he can legitimately be required to report as the basis for the choice he has made.[15]

If science, reputed to be the most rigorous and objective of knowledge is so impacted by values, then jurisprudence—unless we say jurisprudence rises above the rigor of scientific knowledge—must be similarly impacted.

Since a good portion of jurisprudence depends upon precedents, it would be a sage idea to understand what happens when people historicize. No matter how careful and allegedly even-handed we claim we are, we must choose from innumerable facts. Such choosing involves judgments on the part of the historian on the level of which facts to include and which to exclude. Historicizing demands interpretation directed by the interests of particular historians, or their values:

> By the time I began teaching and writing, I had no illusions about "objectivity," if that meant avoiding a point of view. I knew that a historian (or a journalist, or anyone telling a story) was forced to choose, out of an infinite number of facts, what to present, what to omit. And that decision inevitably would reflect, whether consciously or not, the interests of the historian. . . . But there is no such thing as a pure fact, innocent of interpretation. Behind every fact presented to the world—by a teacher, a writer, anyone—is a judgment. The judgment that has been made is that this fact is important, and that other facts, omitted, are not important.[16]

We are as wary as anyone of becoming so attached to a theory that it dictates that we see instances of it everywhere, just as the believer sees that will or hand of God everywhere. We can become oversold on a theory and so carried away that it speaks from all corners of the universe and speaks to us so incessantly that it drowns out other voices. We recall the sage advice of Karl Popper:

> I found that my friends who were admirers of Marx, Freud, and Adler were impressed by a number of points common to those theories and especially by their apparent explanatory power. These theories appeared to be able to explain practically everything that happened within the fields to which they referred. They study of any of them seemed to have the effect of an intellectual conversion or revelation, opening your eyes to a new truth hidden from those not yet initiated. Once your eyes were thus opened you saw confirming instances everywhere. The world was full of verifications of the theory. Whatever happened confirmed it. Thus, its truth remained manifest; and unbelievers were simply people who did not see the manifest truth, who refused to see it.[17]

We are also acutely aware of the famous preconceived schema idea of E.H. Gombrich. Gombrich argues that artists see things according to their specific cultural lenses and when rendering their art in foreign countries, they tend to see things not as they are but according to what they believe them to be. Gombrich inverts the famous "seeing is believing" to "believing is seeing" to stress that artists render not what they see but in accordance with preconceived ideas.[18] Even if we are aware of this type of easy confirmation or the tendency to see according to a preconceived theory, we can also say that the theory we are advocating is the exception to rule. But if we take that tact (as we will), we must do more than put it forward as the only candidate in a beauty contest. We must painstakingly address the primary candidates (the major law theories) and demonstrate how their intellectual principles can be understood according to values.

THE ALLEGORY OF THE CUBE ORGANIZER

Imagine a family has a person who is really mechanically inclined and can assemble beds, bikes, and toolsheds in a blink of an eye. Now imagine a family that has us to put together stuff. We are not mechanically disinclined, so we cling to the directions like a desperate person clings to the edge of a cliff. Thankfully, there are only four steps to assembling this thing called a "Cube Organizer":

(1) Insert two wood dowels into the first part D partition board. Insert four wood dowels into the second part D partition board.
(2) [See a confusing drawing]
(3) Align and attach the side panel on the structure. Note: Board C1 attach to Board B1 only!
(4) Tighten all screw bolts with attached alien key. Washers need to be used correctly as shown.

We might say the cube organizer has nothing to do with values. But we selected it on the basis of its economic, functional, and aesthetic values: it was affordable, useful for organization purposes, and nice-looking. We could only disingenuously lead ourselves to believe the cube organizer escapes value. We selected it on the basis of values. The cube organizer may just be fine and it may never be an issue for me after we assemble it. It may occupy space in a corner, and we may in time forget it is even there (like the floor under our feet) or just come to regard it as particleboard, an object among objects. Even then when we regard the cube organizer in a casual way, its value as a functioning thing protrudes (in the same way we value the spigot for emitting water). This is where values are at their dimmest. However, values become more obvious when things become dysfunctional. If the cube organizer has sharp edges that prove dangerous to infants, this may make us take another look on the value of the cube organizer, or if the paint starts peeling or one of the shelves collapses. And if damaged, we might reassess really what kind of bargain it actually was. In these cases, we come face-to-face with values again because the cube organizer becomes dysfunctional in some sense. It might cause cancer, for example. I might even say to myself:

why are these things even in existence—they're awful? It is those for whom the law is dysfunctional who actually point us back to the origination of those laws in value. It's usually when we get the short end of the stick that we begin to think deeply about the value of the stick, just as in the film *Planet of the Apes* an oppressed human being probes the values of the dominant simian culture.

Laws are formulated according to values, and those values are quite clear to the creators of laws, for example, how the protruding values of life, liberty, and pursuit of happiness resonated with the Founders. However, those resonant and protuberant values fade and become encrusted in formulaic law. Law takes on the appearance of an entity distinct from values, and after a time, many people only hear the echoes of values. Those values are smoothed into the creases of formulaic law and submerged in the din of dim. For those for whom the law creates dysfunction, the values of the law are more protuberant, just as one's mortality is more protuberant when a gun is put up to one's head. The true originalism is not this far-fetched idea of resurrecting the past, holding a séance if you will to bring back the voices of the dead through the mediums of the present. Ontological originalism—to purposely pervert the term—entails going straight to the values that are the basis of law and everything else for that matter.

This applies to ontological distinctions as much as it does for law. When, for example, essentialism is assailed, it is assailed by virtue of a value: "Essentialism in feminist theory has two characteristics that ensure that black women's voices will be ignored [our emphasis, and a disvalue]."[19] In other words, essentialism serves to exclude black women's voices, which are disvalued, while inclusion is the unstated or tacit value. The assessment of "white solipsism" consists of the ignorance of the weaving of many selves into a changing, shifting, yet integral whole conception of selfhood that is not either female or black, but "both-and."[20] But this is hardly a value-free observation, but value-vitalized:

> [The] insistence of that every self is deeply and primarily gendered, then, with its corollary that gender is more important to personal identity than race [and valued more highly], is finally another example of white solipsism. By suggesting that gender is more deeply embedded in self than race . . . [the] theory privileges [disvalue] the experience of white people over all others, and thus serves to reproduce relations of domination in the larger culture.[21]

The assertion that gender is primary to selfhood and is more important than race is rejected because it promotes two disvalues: privilege and dominance. It could be argued that the values result from continued exposure to the political and social reality of oppression, from experience. But at the very least, the experience is valued as oppressive and from that value insight, other value insights emerge, including how essentialism buttresses such oppression.

MEANING OPERATES THROUGH VALUE

The question is not whether value presupposes meaning, but how value functions within meaning. What something means is how it calls attention to itself. What draws us in or catches our attention is the same as how something draws us in or catches our attention. What catches my attention or calls attention to itself? Value. The gray morning sky. How does it catch my attention? Its bleakness is one way. Its solemnity may be another. Its calmness may be another. "7+5=12," one of the most famous simple math problems in the history of philosophy, apparently has nothing to do with value. However, it always does:

- "Boring" to the student learning addition by rote
- "Precise" to the cashier giving change
- "Useful" to the student intent on passing a test
- "Contempt" for the person correcting another's math
- "Schadenfreude" for the person counting another person's failures
- "Warning" to a person counseling a friend not to imbibe so much
- "Exciting" to the scholar counting up a long list of publications on a CV
- "Damning" to the forensic who finds bits of evidence at a crime scene
- "Crucial" to a person compiling a pros and cons list
- "Holistic" for the philosopher (Kant) intent on combining the rational and empirical

If we are not drawn in, if something does not catch our attention, or something does not call attention to itself, then meaning doesn't happen—plain and simple. Values are this drawing in, catching our attention, a point calling attention to itself, what protrudes. Values may at times be vaporous, but they are essential to meaning.

Values are not superadded to meaning, like salt and pepper and oregano are to soup. Each meaning, every meaning, reflects something we deem important or unimportant: significant or insignificant, far-fetched or pragmatic, interesting or uninteresting, stupid or smart, witty or inane, holy or unholy, revolutionary or redundant, courageous or cowardly, crucial or extraneous, serious or frivolous, good or evil, beautiful or ugly, perfect or imperfect, comfort or discomfort, clarity or ambiguity, generous or petty, diverse or monolithic, refined or crass, reducible or irreducible, closure or open-ended, stability or fluctuation, risk-taking or risk-averse, beautiful or ugly.

We are drawn to meanings, all meanings, even down to colors and sounds. The experience of meaning is the experience of value of being drawn in or repelled. It is like when we view a painting and are drawn to certain shapes and colors or ideas or repulsed by a song because of lyrics we find jejune or vulgar. "A" and "the" may be of value here to make our point." "A cup" values all cups the same. "The cup" refers to one valued over others. Preference and meaning are tied together. To prefer is to mean and to mean is to prefer. If everything is a language-game as Wittgenstein proclaims, everything is also value-preference. The language-games we play consist of valued meaning and which language-games we choose or decline to play are determined by values. For example, I might prefer language-games of religion to the language-games of science in the same way one may prefer Monopoly to Clue.

This is hardly a revelation to skilled actors. They understand that each word they speak has value, whether they doing a commercial for dog food or a soliloquy from *King Lear*.

We hope by now we have a made a credible case for value, as this underpins our axiological approach to jurisprudence. We see this leading to more self-reflection, which we see leading to more fairness, which we place among our zenith values. An articulation of values and disvalues, however, can be obtained by describing out a complex of interacting valuations. Valued and disvalued meanings converge and diverge in continua.

As much as this sounds like a free-for-all, we reject the idea that all matters are matters of ambiguity, if by ambiguity is meant words having no set meaning. By valuing a set meaning of language-games, we thereby understand language-games. In the same vein, to take a Rorschach test, we have to value a set meaning of a Rorschach test. Each time we understand a meaning, the meaning is set in a value. Values and disvalues protrude from and recede in set meanings and are set in and set up the act of comprehension.

A FINAL SAMPLE OF VALUE ANALYSIS

At the outset of the chapter, we began with examples of two films to introduce axiological analysis. Before moving on to our value analysis of the major theories of law and Supreme Court decisions, we will bookend the chapter with "Universal Declaration of Human Rights"[22] and black-light the rich array of values within:

> Whereas recognition of the inherent dignity [*value*] and of the equal and inalienable rights [*values*] of all members of the human family [*family valued over strangers or others*] is the foundation of freedom, justice and peace in the world [*values*].

All human beings are born free and equal in dignity and rights [*values*]. They are endowed with reason and conscience and should act towards one another in a spirit of brotherhood [*valued over the use value of others in some sort of selfish manner*].

Everyone has the right to freedom of thought, conscience and religion; this right includes freedom to change his religion or belief, and freedom, either alone or in community with others and in public or private, to manifest his religion or belief in teaching, practice, worship and observance [*all values*].

Education shall be directed to the full development of the human personality and to the strengthening of respect for human rights and fundamental freedoms *[education has nothing to do with getting a job; the value of education is encrusted in the full development of the human person rather than for narrow utilitarian purposes].* It shall promote understanding, tolerance and friendship [*values*] among all nations, racial or religious groups [*value of inclusion*], and shall further the activities of the United Nations for the maintenance of peace [*zenith value*].

NOTES

1. Michael Wilson, *Planet of the Apes*, SCREENPLAYS FOR YOU, https://sfy.ru/?script=poa_1968 (last visited November 23, 2018).
2. Max Scheler, *Selected Philosophical Essays*, trans. David Lacterman (Evanston, IL: Northwestern University Press, 1973), 98.
3. Ibid.
4. Ibid., 98–99.
5. Ibid., 99.
6. Ibid., 100.
7. Ibid., 101.
8. Ibid., 100.
9. Max Scheler, *Formalism in Ethics and Non-Formalism in Values*, trans. Manfred S. Frings and Roger L. Funk (Evanston, IL: Northwestern University Press, 1973), 89.
10. *Selected Philosophical Essays*, 120.
11. Ibid., 118, 119.
12. Ibid., 120, 117. (Scheler's complaint of "*the general slovenliness of in matters of feelings*" has been addressed with the pluralizing of intelligence in Howard Gardiner's multiple intelligences (interpersonal and intrapersonal), emotional IQ, and the popularity of the right brain-left brain ideology. However, we would suggest the slovenliness continues because the connection between emotion and values as an objective reality has not been made.)

13. Ibid., 123.

14. Ibid., 118.

15. Thomas Kuhn, "Objectivity, Value Judgment, and Theory Choice," http://shamiller.net/phi031/readings.d/kuhn.pdf (last visited January 7, 2019).

16. Howard Zinn, *A People's History of the United States*, libcom.org, https://libcom.org/files/A%20People's%20History%20of%20the%20Unite%20-%20Howard%20Zinn.pdf (April 22, 2021).

17. Karl Popper, "Conjectures and Refutations," in *Scientific Knowledge: Basic Issues in Philosophy of Science*, ed. Janet Kourany (Belmont, CA: Wadsworth, 1987), 140: "It was precisely this fact—that they always fitted, that they always confirmed—which in the eyes of their admirers constituted the strongest argument in favor of these theories."

18. E.H. Gombrich, *Art and Illusion*, 2nd ed. (Princeton, NJ: Princeton University Press, 1972), 210.

19. Angela R, Harris, "Race and Essentialism in Feminist Legal Theory," *Stanford Law Review* 42, 3 (February 1990): 581, 582.

20. Ibid., 604.

21. Ibid.

22. *Universal Declaration of Human Rights,* UNITED NATIONS http://www.un.org/en/universal-declaration-human-rights/ (last visited November 18, 2018).

Chapter 2

Theories of Law through the Lens of Value

Since our project is new and unique, it is incumbent upon us to justify it in a rigorous manner by applying it to the major movements in legal theory. Our objective is to demonstrate how value functions in each of the major law theories. It will be our job to show the axiological forensic evidence at the scene of each theory. We will opt for the most obvious evidence, namely, from the words of the various advocates. In the case of Positivism, which claims to be value-free, the analysis will be more intensive than in the case of Natural Law Theory, which is explicitly based on values (although we will argue these values are descriptive and not prescriptive). The most obvious charge against this approach will be the glossing over of differences within each movement. However, we need not go into every nook and cranny of a law theory to demonstrate that values are in play. In this exercise, our fundamental purpose consists of creating a value vignette for each theory.

NATURAL LAW THEORY

Natural Law Theory claims that universal laws guide human behavior. Universal laws come to our awareness in three distinct ways: we observe them in nature, God reveals them, or reason intuits them.[1] Going back to Plato's *Crito*, Socrates disvalues doing harm: "neither doing nor returning injustice is ever right, nor should one who is ill-treated defend himself by retaliation."[2] Human law, Aquinas declares, rests on two values: peace and happiness.[3] As a young lawyer, Thomas Jefferson used a natural law argument to defend a biracial man (Samuel Howell) who by Virginia statutes would remain in servitude until thirty-one years of age.[4] In *Samuel Howell v. Wade Netherland*, Jefferson argued that "'everyone comes into the world with a right to his own person and using it at his own will.'"[5] The value of "personal liberty," Jefferson maintained "'is given by the author of nature, because it is necessary for its sustenance.'"[6] Henry David Thoreau's disvaluing of government interference in the lives of private citizens grounds his critique of war[7] and Martin Luther King, Jr.'s critique of segregation folds into the value of a law degrading or uplifting human personality.[8] In the most prominent natural law treatise of the twentieth century, John Rawls values justice as fairness.[9]

In "Letter from Birmingham City Jail," more than the value of justice and disvalue of injustice protrude:

> Moreover, I am cognizant of the interrelatedness of all communities and states. I cannot sit idly by in Atlanta and not be concerned about what happens in Birmingham. Injustice anywhere is a threat to justice everywhere. We are caught in an inescapable network of mutuality, tied in a single garment of destiny. Whatever affects one directly, affects all indirectly. Never again can we afford to live with the narrow, provincial "outside agitator" idea. Anyone who lives inside the United States can never be considered an outsider anywhere within its bounds.[10]

King values a cosmopolitan view ("inescapable network of mutuality, tied in a single garment of destiny") over a provincial view on justice. The value of cosmopolitanism vitalizes the value of justice, encapsulated in the famous statement: "Injustice anywhere is a threat to justice everywhere."

Several other values protrude from "Letter from Birmingham City Jail," for example, the value of orderliness in the four-step process of the nonviolent campaign, the value of "creative nonviolent" tension, and extremism in the loving sense.

If skeptics argue that absolute values of Natural Law Theory lead to intolerance, they themselves fall into the trap of asserting one absolute value over another: tolerance over intolerance. Axiological Law Theory escapes the absolutist charge because although it establishes the primacy of a spectrum of values, it does not establish the primacy of any particular moral code. Moral Realism by arguing that "[o]nly if there is a moral reality can judges be enjoined to seek it when they decide cases,"[11] takes the unwarranted next step to knowable objective values. Natural Law Theory wrongly sees the reality of values as an invitation to assert a single moral reality. Interpreters do values in the same way a painter does paints. Axiological Law Theory points to values without imposing them. Even in the face of Aristotle's pronouncement that "there is a common principle of just and unjust that all people in some way divine"[12] and Cicero's proclamation that "true law is right reason in agreement with nature,"[13] it does not follow that law arises from objective universal truths shared by all people. Even if these truths did derive from a single source, there could be multiple interpretations of that source, just as there are multiple interpretations of the same event witnessed by different people or multiple interpretations of the same sacred texts by different religions.

POSITIVISM

Positivism rests on scientific verification, on what can be empirically verifiable, the observable and measurable. It values neutral objective knowledge and permanent truth. Regarding jurisprudence, the empirically verifiable consists of legal texts. We call the sensed text in contradistinction to the rationalized text and interpreted text, which lines up philosophically with empiricism, rationalism, and perspectivism. For Positivism, words are a means to understand social phenomena or facts, society, and its institutions.[14] The truth of legal matters entails the correspondence to the social fact of the law: either an action conforms or conflicts with the First Amendment or conforms or conflicts with a state law.[15] Positivism seeks to disjoin the law from morality, the "is" from the "ought" as expounded most famously by David Hume.[16] To grasp some of the contours of Positivism, we will e*valu*ate within the framework of the three varieties suggested by Robin West[17] because she offers some wrinkles on Positivism. In one case, this amounts to removal of the law from morality, as if removing the wheat from the chaff. Morality is removed, but its existence is not questioned (critical positivism). In contrast to critical positivism, skeptical positivism denies the existence of universal moral codes and deems them illusions. Like skeptical positivism, economic positivism sees universal moral codes as illusions. While for skeptical positivism, "value is a product of power," for economic positivism "value is the product of individual choice."[18] All three cases of positivism articulated by West are based in value.

To prepare the way for this assertion, we will take on the notion of skepticism, and turn this tool against Positivism by demonstrating the tool itself is value-laden. This will reveal degrees of skepticism that range from mild to extreme, but even in extreme skepticism values protrude. We will once again prove the inevitability of values in meaning and therefore jurisprudence in order to point out a Positivistic misapprehension.

Our examination of skepticism focuses on Section XII of David Hume's *Inquiry of Human Understanding*, which elaborates on different modes of skepticism and provides opportunities to point out inconsistent applications within Hume's thought as a paradigm for understanding how Positivism makes a similar misapprehension.

It takes no deep inquiry or fanciful inferences to see the values at work in Hume's examination. Universal Cartesian doubt, Hume insists, even if attainable, is not useful, failing to offer a "state of assurance" and "conviction."[19] Assurance and conviction emerge as positive in terms of being useful and extreme doubt by extension a negative value in terms of being useless. Hume values moderate skepticism: impartiality of judgments, clear and self-evident principles, and small steps toward consequences for the purpose of realizing the values stability and certainty in philosophical discourse.[20] He values the evidence of the senses over abstract reasoning, a reflection of his famous distinction between the easy and obvious and accurate and abstruse approaches to philosophy.[21] He sees reason rightly employed as a corrective to two evils: extreme doubt and wild speculation. Hume values a natural instinct that insists on a universe existing apart from our perception of it and that objects we perceive resemble objects that exist independently of our minds: "It seems evident that men are carried by a natural instinct or prepossession to repose faith in their senses, and that without any reasoning, or even before the use of reason, we always suppose an external universe which depends not on our perceptions of it but would exist though we and every sensible creature were absent or annihilated."[22] Hume disvalues reason, the purpose of which is to destroy argument and ratiocination, in the same way he disvalues unfettered speculative reason that posited the indivisibility of extended things. Of excessive or scorched earth skepticism, Hume judges no "durable good"[23] [a value] that could come from it. Hume also disvalues speculative reason, exemplified by the claim of infinite divisibility of finite quantities, calling

> this edifice so bold and prodigious that it is too weighty for any pretended demonstration because it shocks the clearest [valued] and most natural [valued] principles of human reason. But what renders the matter more extraordinary is that these seemingly absurd opinions are supported by a chain of reasoning the clearest and most natural [values], nor is it possible to admit the premises without admitting the consequences.[24]

Human action, Hume claims, subverts extreme skepticism.[25] Such extreme skepticism would render everyone lethargic and would not be beneficial for society.[26] To the contrary, illusions such as faith in an unverifiable being have motivated billions to act. In any case, Hume values action over inaction and counted common sense, reflection, focus on the common life, proper doubt, modesty, and "the strong power of the natural instinct" among positive values.[27] Value essentialism protrudes from Hume's brand of skepticism. Even scorched earth skepticism cannot avoid value essentialism.

Our second point illustrates inconsistent implementations of the diverse species of skepticism. In section XII, Hume espouses moderate skepticism and invites the external world and external objects into the fold. Denying the necessary connection between cause and effect (deeming their relationship loose and separate) as he does in sections IV and V respresents a far less inclusive type of skepticism than the moderate skepticism articulated in section XII. Belief in the necessary connection between cause and effect can be seen as natural as belief in an external world and external objects. Who but a skeptic, for example, denies the causal relationship between bread and nourishment?[28] While an extreme skeptic in sections IV and V, Hume softens his skepticism in section XII. The extreme skepticism denying the relationship between cause and effect could also be seen as incompatible with Hume's contention that impressions produce ideas.[29] This resembles a causal relationship and what warrants impressions cause ideas and not the other way around? And one could be equally wary of vivacity being a clear principle to distinguish between ideas and impressions and not prone to skeptical elision?

Like Hume, Positivism inconsistently employs skepticism, sticking it into the heart of morality and sparing the law. When we think about morality and law, we are talking about:

Moral-Immoral
Legal-Illegal

Skeptical positivism sees the moral-immoral as illusionary and law as objective. The moralist who says "murder is wrong" merely expresses a feeling or a custom of a society; the legalist who says "murder is illegal" states an objectivity. But consider the following: the illegality of chewing gum in Singapore and its legality in the United States. How can this be considered anything less than the expression of feeling any more than a moral statement is? Or simply different customs in different cultures? Singaporeans hypervalue order, which expresses some emotion or is a custom, but certainly nothing verifiable like gravity.

Positivism seeks either to bracket values from the law or eradicate them. In the case of critical positivism, its removal is only from the body of the law. In the cases of skeptical and economic positivism, eradication is the policy. No place for the values of peace and well-being of the community as found in Aquinas. No place for the values of humanitarian norms and consent rather than coercion as found in Grotius. No place for the values of equality and independence as found in Locke. No place for the value of fairness as found in Rawls. No place for the value of uplifting and degrading laws as found in King. No place for the value of non-retaliation as found in Plato and expressed by Socrates. No place for the value of noninterference as found in Thoreau.

Even a cursory axiological inspection reveals the value-aspects of Positivism. First and foremost, the bedrock of positivism: the value of neutral objective knowledge and permanent truths (in contradistinction to the disvalue of subjectivity and evanescent suppositions). Second, the value of obedience to the law: value in obeying commands. Economic positivism, according to West, is a "libertarian political philosophy that celebrates, relentlessly, choice, and denigrates, just as relentlessly, a morality of obligation, of duty, and of responsibility."[30] This "celebration" values individual choice and goes hand-in-hand with the devaluing of obligation, duty, and responsibility. Morality "unduly suppresses release of the real source of societal and individual value,"[31] that is, the individual. Suppressing individual choice protrudes as a disvalue while enabling it protrudes as a value.

Values represent more than subjective tastes or society's norms. Scheler makes a good case for values being as real as anything else in the human purview. We put it this way: meaning exhibits value-replete rather than value-free meaning environs. Values cannot be exiled as pretenders or illusions. Values emerge in the common preferring process. Each time we prefer one thing to another we value. To dismiss values is to dismiss preference. Thus, preference animates meaning. As we write, we prefer one word to another, on the basis of its appropriateness, lucidity, vividness, or some other value. As we think, we prefer one thought to another on the basis of whether it brings peace or turmoil to my mind. As we breathe, we prefer smooth inhales and exhales to gasping for air.

The Is-Ought distinction has done much to distort matters. In simple terms, *what is* can be verified and *what ought* cannot. But ought itself as obedience or fidelity is an example of a value. More precisely, the distinction may be rendered more accurately as an Is-Value predicament. Things that are can be verified, while values cannot if by verification we mean physical things. In every meaning situation, values protrude from meaning. Values are not seasonings to facts, such as salt, pepper, and oregano are to soup. If we say meaning concerns how facts cohere in a system, we nonetheless value coherence over incoherence and must evaluate what gains admittance to this coherence (based on the values of inclusivity and exclusivity). Furthermore, meaning remains inert unless animated by preferring and preferring is valuing. Finally, survival is predicated on preferring one value to another. Without such preferring, we can reach neither our short-term nor long-terms goals.

The Is-Ought Problem becomes the Is-Values Problem—but not really. As we have argued, values animate the human meaning enterprise and intertwine the "is." Thus, an axiological critique of jurisprudence describes how ineluctable values function in jurisprudence. At the bottom of even a positivistic approach, we find values, which "must be respected if we are to create anything that can be called law, even bad law."[32] The language below is Natural Law Theory, but can be easily amended to Axiological Law Theory:

> On the one hand, we have an amoral [allegedly value-free] datum called law, which has the peculiar quality of creating a moral duty [value of fidelity] to obey it. On the other hand, we have a moral duty to do what we think is right and decent [value of justice]. When we are confronted by a statute we believe to be thoroughly evil, we have to choose between those two duties [values].[33]

FORMALISM

For Positivism, the empirically verifiable law text serves as its prime matter; for Formalism, the coherent text serves in the same capacity. "What you see is what you get" (sense perception) versus "what you conceive is what you get" (rationality). Formalism anoints coherence or "immanent rationality" in the doctrines, institutions, and decisions of positive law.[34] Instead of the correspondence approach of Legal Positivism, Legal Formalism looks for the immanent rationality to "judicial arrangements and relationships" and what they intimate.[35] For Formalists, "[t]he function of the law is to express this immanent rationality in the doctrines, institutions, and decisions of positive law."[36] Often characterized as mechanical and lockstep, recent incarnations of Legal Formalism, for example, Originalism, explain formalistic legal reasoning as expansive and inclusive within a circle: "Coherence is inherently expansive: It resists compartmentalization and seeks to encompass as much as possible."[37] This does not mean manufacturing law, but discovering it.[38] Law excludes the political and cannot be externally assessed or be seen as a means to achieve wealth maximization, market deterrence, liberty, utility, and solidarity.[39] In the final analysis: "Jurisprudence, then, as an autonomous system of legal concepts, rules, and arguments, must be independent of ethics and of such positive sciences as economics or psychology."[40] Jurisprudence stands by itself in a rationally coherent self-enclosed universe.

Formalism values what laws intimate so long as this comes from immanent rationality. Yet which doctrines, institutions, and decisions come to be valued is determined by whether a broad view is taken on precedent or a narrow view on tradition is valued.[41]

The values of Formalism go beyond the net of ratiocination, so perhaps invoking "appropriateness" will solve the problem:

> The origin of these as legal principles lies not in a particular decision of some legislation or court, but in a sense of appropriateness developed in the

profession and the public over time. The continued power depends upon this sense of appropriateness.[42]

But what is this appropriateness other than values that have stood the test of time? Furthermore, to say that something stands the test of time entails preferring the sustained over the ephemeral. In the same vein, Ronald Dworkin's statements describing the integrity of value are value-laden:

> According to law as integrity, propositions of law are true as they figure in or follow from the principles [and values] of justice, fairness, and procedural due process.[43]

> Law as integrity deplores [disvalues] the mechanism of the older 'law is law" as well as the cynicism of the newer "realism."[44]

> Law as integrity, then requires a judge to test his interpretation of any part of the great network of political structures and decisions of his community by asking whether it can form part of a coherent theory [value, rather than the disvalue of situational law] justifying the network as a whole.[45]

> Law's attitude is constructive: it aims, in the interpretive spirit, to lay principle over practice to show the best route to a better future, keeping the right faith with the past [balance in judging, looking back to the past and toward the future].[46]

The sensed text of Positivism is purportedly value-free, but the rationalized text of Formalism is not. In the case of Originalism, rationalizing the original meaning of the constitutional text at the time consists of understanding dictionaries, grammar books, related legal documents, and legal and public debates that figured into the making of the law and seeing it through the eyes of a reasonable person[47] (what is reasonable, of course, is hotly contested and dependent upon to some extent to the degree to which law works for or against people—whether one is happily situated or not.)[48] Nineteenth-century Langdellian Formalism—based on formal connections arising from deductive and inductive reasoning and derived from a limited number foundational concepts and doctrines—nonetheless valued protection of private property and freedom of contract.[49] Langdellian Formalism offers a much more constrictive net than does Originalism. Originalism expands the value of reason beyond logic trees and abstraction and injects an imaginative element into reason—by imagining how reasonable people in the distant past viewed legal documents. It also extends reason beyond law books into documents and debates related to the formulation of American constitutional law. However, Originalism values imagination—and imagination and interpretation, while perhaps not blood brothers, are not distantly related. Let us look at the nature of discretion that is allowed into Positivism and compare it with the coherent ratiocination of Formalism. Positivism adopts discretion to prevent undesirable outcomes as witnessed, for example, in World War II, people following bad law and committing atrocities based on bad law. The Formalist does not believe in such "discretion." However, discretion is built into the form of adjudicating by expanding the realm of legal reasons. While the Positivist calls it discretion and appeals to the extralegal, the Formalist expands legal reasons to fit it into his malleable net of doctrines, institutions, and legal decisions,[50] the expansion and contraction of which is variable, as are all types of expansions and contractions. An employer can pronounce no bonuses for employees, but then add the same amount of income the bonuses would have yielded by means of paid time off, special projects, and gift cards. A teacher can say no extra credit, but then inflate grades. Thus, we can maintain that while the Second Amendment does not guarantee individuals gun rights, discretion can argue for it. Or we can just ratiocinate gun rights into the Second Amendment. Positivism offers a clearer and more honest approach than Formalism as it admits to extralegal discretion, whereas Formalism hides the discretion in its malleable ratiocinative net. The Formalist values discretion just as the prude values sex: both conceal it in their ratiocinations and protestations.

Originalism much prefers constrained decision-making to decidedly disvalued constitutional creativity. Constrained decision-making narrows and standardizes legal texts (although because of the variability of coherence, standardization is a slogan more than a reality). Behind ratiocination, stability protrudes as the leading value of Formalism. The pure fact of law (not mixed with anything else), its autonomy (not influenced with anything else, like social reality or ideas from other disciplines), and its dependence on immanent reasoning contribute to stable legal decision-making and a stable system of laws. Suggesting, then, Originalist Scalia fears "unconstrained judgment"[51] promotes a profound misunderstanding because this reduces his perspective to the *feeling* of fear instead of the larger context of the *protuberant value* of Formalism—stability. And what ensures stability? The determinate: the established, fixed, settled, specified. In the same vein, rather than rendering a psychological account of Justice Thomas's lack of empathy,[52] focus again on the value of stability inherent in coherence rooted in old, familiar categories. Whatever destabilizes becomes a disvalue for Formalists and eschewed. As Frederick Schauer comments:

> Because rule-bound decisionmaking is inherently stabilizing, it is inherently conservative, in the political sense of the word. By limiting the ability of decisionmakers to consider every factor relevant to an event, rules make it more

> difficult to adapt to a changing future. Rules force the future into the categories of the past.[53]

By this axiological reading, one values conservativism because one values stability and not the other way around.

Originalism has so many defects it is hard to know where to start. It is like a horrible essay written by a first-year student that is so logically flawed that one is brought to the verge of tears of what the first step should be (1) Any reputable scholar rejects that idea that a person can pristinely grasp "original texts." Original texts are warped by the historical, social, political, and value lens of those who read them. Originalism overvalues human intellect. (2) Any reputable scholar rejects the idea of "knowing" the intentions of other people. Simply put, epistemologically implausible except for mind-readers. We can't know the intentions of the Fedex driver who just dropped off a package at my front door any more than we can know the intentions of the Founding Fathers. From texts, we can gain a sense of the value embedded from the beliefs and make a case for a scholarly interpretation. Again, overvaluing the human intellect. (3) "The past" is not a single block, but is understood from single, superficial, and narrow human perspectives that continuously reinvent it. Originalism demands a full view of history, which is epistemologically implausible and unjustified. The past is not grasped as a whole, but piecemeal. It is an illusion to think that tying together different ideas makes the past accessible in toto. Again, overvaluing human intellect. (4) Even assuming there is only the original text, there is the matter of valuing each part of the text. Which principle or idea or sentence fragment gets more value and why? Assuming there is any sort of ambiguity, which is a near necessity in human language, then people are going to judge according to their own valuations. The issue: undervaluing ambiguity. (5) Originalism sets up a priestly caste of infallible judges who flawlessly adjudicate texts. This represents both arrogance and scholarly incompetence in the highest degree. Arrogance in this sense consists of the Originalists believing they possess divine powers. Incompetence in the sense consists of adjudicating unfairly, akin to doctors who used to bleed epileptics. Gross incompetence consists of delusions of grandeur by overvaluing the human intellect.

LEGAL REALISM

Legal Realism inverts the primary value of Formalism, stability. Whereas Langdellian Formalism embraces stability and the determinate, Legal Realism values flux and the indeterminate. Langdellian Formalism, the butt of Legal Realism's critique, preserves stability by encasing law in a hermetically sealed vacuum: "The claim that justice, efficiency, and indeed everything but the internal logic of the system were 'irrelevant' dramatized the Langdellian legal scientist's principled neglect of the facts of human nature and culture."[54] Or as Oliver Wendell Holmes puts it: "The fallacy to which I refer is the notion that the only force at work in the development of law is logic."[55] Legal Realism, on the other hand, embraces flux, sees both society and law as fluid. Rather than being understood as static, fully actualized, and infallible, law constitutes "a growing and self-correcting system."[56] Lockstep deductive thinking, going from the universal to the particular, the hallmark of traditional Langellian Formalism, ensures uniformity, predictability, and certainty for the sake of stability. Yet because of Langdellian Formalism, the legal system became "overburdened and unworkably complex."[57] In contrast, Legal Realism construes law "as fragile, contradictory, fragmentary, and disperse."[58] Rather than abstraction, Legal Realism prefers the tangible and concrete. Its concrete reasoning transcends legal texts and values holism, which encompasses multidisciplinary sources, including sociology, psychology, economics, and the sciences, and whatever was necessary to gather the relevant facts.[59] Instead of following the accepted or paper rules, Legal Realism focuses on the real rules, or what the courts would do in a given case,[60] and valued prediction or prophesy. The values of general welfare and human happiness protrude from Legal Realism. Law in a vacuum would hurt rather than help society: "To kill the patient in order to follow the rules of hygiene is no more absurd than to ruin a society for the sake of observing a supposed rule of justice."[61] The disconnection between law and society makes law inefficient and irresponsive to social problems and human needs. Legal Realism recognizes and values the subjective dimension of jurisprudence. Individual human beings inevitably influence law-making—not only the person's idiosyncrasies but also the social determinants affecting legal decision-making: "Observing particular, concrete facts of conduct and of expectation which suggests the presence of 'an interest,' one arrives at the value conclusion that something in those facts calls for protection at the ends of state officials."[62] In the same vein: "What is law depends not merely upon the facts of the past and of the present but also upon the will the will of those who prescribe and those who administer rules of conduct by the authority of the state."[63]

Fluidity, holism, subjectivity, prediction, and the common good are the leading values of Legal Realism. Legal Realism also values fluidity over stability, subjectivity over objectivity, holism over insularity, prediction of legal consequences over ratiocination of legal texts, and the common good over law for law's sake.

LAW AND ECONOMICS

Economic theory positively hyper-values efficiency to a sacred zenith value. Efficiency equals the maximization of interests and the minimization of costs[64] (to get the most out of the least) or E=MI/MC. According to the concept of economic rationality, people act in their own interests, their own interests being driven by efficiency. Despite the obvious protrusion of the value of efficiency, "value-free" economics mistakenly denies its existence:

> "Efficient" is a desirable property of law, just as "nutritious" is a desirable property of food. "Nutritious" is a term of praise for food because it implies predictions about the effect of food on health, which is one of food's most important values. That is why it would seem odd if a person said, "The food is nutritious but I am not making any value judgments." Similarly, "efficiency" commends and "inefficiency" condemns for law and economics. Law A's efficiency relative to Law B is a reason for policy makers to prefer the former over the latter.[65]

Even in a venue like economics where one value reigns supreme, other values emerge. A critique of Pareto efficiency, for example, that condemns materialism, ideology, and over-simplification[66] reveals materialism, ideology, and over-simplification (reductionism) as disvalues and their contraries, spiritualism, critical thinking, and holism, as values. On the contrary, prediction, central to economic theory, appears to escape valuation: "Predicting whether, say, the frequency of accidents will increase or decrease in response to a change in the liability law, much like estimating consumer demand curves, is free from value-judgment."[67] However, prediction rides in the same value boat as efficiency, materialism, ideology, and over-simplification. The values of clarity and control quickly come to the surface of prediction when understood in terms of efficiency. In contrast, for the yogi, only the present matters and "predictions" about the future unsettle peace of mind and obfuscate reality and are decidedly disvalued. For corporations, the future matters and accurate predictions about it serve to wealth-maximize. Clarity about the future means control over it and more efficiency.

Fundamental questions of value ripple through economic theory. How do we value poverty? As a necessary evil? An evil? Do we value private property over the commons? Do we value economies that create a permanent underclass over economies that offer upward mobility? Do we value corporate self-determination over government intervention? Do we value profit over person? Do we value economies that produce more things over economies that produce more happiness? Do we value economies that concentrate rather redistribute wealth? Do we value economies built on waging war? Do we value economies that harm segments of the population if they create a great economic output? Do we value economies that cause environmental damage, especially if irreparable? Do we value competition over cooperation? Do we value independence over interdependency? Values protrude in the conception, creation, and maintenance of economies.[68]

CRITICAL LEGAL STUDIES

In concurrence with Axiological Law Theory, Critical Legal Studies asserts: "Teachers teach nonsense when they persuade their students that legal reasoning is distinct as a method for reaching correct results from ethical and political discourse in general [and the values therein]."[69] Law does not exist in a gated community, untouched by values, since "legal reasoning is "indeterminate and contradictory,[70] manipulated by value-laden agendas designed to preserve hierarchies. By eliminating "'outworn vocabularies and attitudes'" and embracing intuitions and present customs, the law has the potential to edify.[71] Instead of using abstract reasoning, legal matters can be resolved by "experience, emotion, introspection, and conversation."[72] Thus, the broader spectrum of human understanding or cognition becomes valued. The trashing of law, pure negativity, serves as a means to develop a society in which people find meaningful work and meaningful relations.[73] Critical Legal Studies does not see legal doctrines, rules, and categories as necessary and unalterable and the law as the mechanical unfolding of inevitable decisions, but values disagreement and intuition as healthy in law-making.[74] Even sacrosanct "rights" come under the scrutiny of Critical Legal Studies:

> [I]t [rights discourse] is logically incoherent and manipulable, traditionally individualist, and willfully blind to the realities of substantive inequality, rights discourse is a trap. As long as one stays within it, one can produce good pieces of argument about the occasional case on the periphery where everyone recognizes value judgments have to be made. But one is without guidance in deciding what to do about fundamental questions.[75]

The recipient of rights becomes a passive spectator and at the mercy of the state manipulating those rights, slicing, and dicing them according to power interests. Rights become disvalues to the extent they perpetuate economic, racial, and class subjugation.

Egalitarianism emerges as the leading value of Critical Legal Studies and as such the diminishment and demise of oppression become disvalues. Critical Legal Studies rejects the notion that law is determinate not only because it isn't but also because the determinate law lends itself to oppression and the destruction of community (disvalues). Community, seen as interdependency,[76] protrudes as a leading value; alienation, especially in the form of atomized individualism, protrudes as a leading disvalue. Critical Legal Studies values laws that create meaningful experiences for all human beings. It wants to minimize misery, indifference, personal imposition, totalitarianism, and egoism[77] and foster mutual trust and love.[78] Both cruelty and misery are disvalued: "*We should prevent cruelty*"[79] and "*We should prevent misery.*"[80]

Critical Legal Studies values the "purity of its negativism," and it has been argued that its only purpose is trashing:

> The realists of the twenties and thirties were also intent on demystifying the law, and insisted that that the law's claim to determinacy and objectivity was a sham, but their critique was aimed at freeing law from the past to the particular (in particular, from its commitment to laissez-faire). Their critique was a prelude to having the law become an effective instrument o good "public policy." Today, there is a strain of feminism that also seeks to unmask the law—to show how the privileged position of men in the legal profession has tended to skew the law, and how neutral sounding concepts or principles have often served as a cloak for patriarchy. They, like the realists, are moved by an affirmative vision—if not liberty, then a true and substantive equality—and they appreciate how the law can be used to further that vision. But that is not critical legal scholarship. Critical legal studies scholars are distinguished (if at all) from feminists and from the legal realists of an earlier generation by the purity of negativism. When critical legal studies scholars insist that "law is politics," they mean something quite different and more nihilistic than either realists or feminists. Critical legal studies scholars want to unmask the law, but not to make law into an effective instrument of good public policy or equality. *The aim of their critique is critique* [our emphasis]. Critical legal studies scholars realize that any normative structure created to supplement law would be subject to the very same critique they used to attack the law.[81]

The same author who insists that pure negativism or "trashing" as the only value agenda in Critical Legal Studies also admits: "I share the egalitarianism that inspires much of the movement"[82]; "[d]isagreement is in fact an essential part of any collaborative moral enterprise within a changing society"[83]; and "It [law] requires only constrained judgement."[84] Egalitarianism, disagreement, and constrained judgment clearly stand out as values in addition to trashing.

In the final analysis, Critical Legal Theory does a great service by demystifying jurisprudence. Yet Critical Legal Studies exposes a narrow sphere of values that pertain to hierarchy and oppression. But when it comes to its own value scheme, it proves unreflective. Its "pure negativity" obscures a vast landscape of values. Its pure negativity narrows rather than expands the inquiry of values. While Axiological Law Theory cannot prove which values are best, it can attune us to a spectrum of values. Values can be shaded, emphasized, deemphasized, included or excluded in different ways by different participants toward different ends.

POSTMODERNISM

"If postmodernism means anything, it is that no single narrative can ever suffice: it is this dominance, in a sense, that is dead."[85] A preference of plurality to unity characterizes this description. One cannot apply foundational theory or transcendental methodology of interpretation and do postmodernism. Postmodernism disvalues the objective, subjective, real, and self and only language has value. With logocetrism (a disvalue) abandoned and anti-foundationalism embraced, hierarchy [a disvalue] topples and the following value-disvalue preferences preferred: the eternal over transitory, original over copy, the spoken over the written word.[86] Language constitutes our only habitat and language remains fluid. In this domain of anti-foundationalism and fluidity, multi-dimensionality and multi-directionality are esteemed.[87] Postmodernism esteems undecidability and leaves all questions open (eternal undecidability). For Wittgenstein, meaning cannot be separated from use (valued). The "edifying conversations" of pluralistic pragmatism rank higher than abstract reasoning and include an element of disorientation and surprise, both of which are esteemed.[88] What are these "promising directions within a complex society"[89] other than something pertaining to the value of a less-oppressive society? The success or failure of our conceptions must be judged . . . with respect to the degree in which problems are solved (or dissolved).[90] Thus, ideas have value according to their utility. "It is the particular particularities associated with legacies of power and oppression that we mean to highlight in the interest of context."[91] The highlighting of power and oppression, rather than highlighting other elements, implies their devaluation in terms of adversely affecting vulnerable people. Another postmodernist reveals the value of an experimental democracy to understand oppression and alleviate suffering:

> [P]ostmodernism challenges the bourgeois format of society. It aims to reorganize itself in line with the radical imperatives of an experimental democracy that recognizes the systemic and social character of oppression at the same time that it facilitates provisional, revisable, yet real responses to the alleviation of suffering.[92]

The deployment of the skeptical postmodern strategy aims to "destabilize power, displace domination and dismantle hierarchy"[93] in the political realm—power, domination, and hierarchy clearly being disvalues. In the following statement, how can the "normatively appealing" be anything but a value, the value of law being mutually agreed upon law rather than the capriciousness of individuals:

> We will still find it deeply normatively appealing to conceive of ourselves as a people governed by its law rather than by arbitrary individual power, because conceiving of ourselves in this way I take to be constitutive of ourselves as a political community.[94]

The distinction between Rorty's bad and good prophets rests on the value of pluralism.[95] The bad type of prophet monopolizes dialogue, while the good type of prophet desires to have her voice heard with others—here the value of inclusivity protrudes.[96] "False consciousness" implies a true consciousness (and the value therein), as true consciousness emancipates people and renovates society.[97] The temporary undecidability of leaving the text open is preferred to decidability or closure.[98] Deconstruction values undecidability as much as economic theory values efficiency. We find undecidability no less an imperative than the ten famous imperatives of Moses, all of which protruding with value. In the final analysis: "Without preexisting values, purposes, or commitments [purposes and commitments, I would argue, are value-based] deconstruction cannot begin. With them, it can never be other than logocentric."[99]

While meaning cannot be value-free, value can be ought-free. Valuing the beauty of a sunset, the nobility of an action, the harmony of a song, or the originality of a play is distinct from being obligated to realize those values. Of course, we can value obedience and even attach the value of obedience to other values, for example, feeling obligated to be original. The Is-Value Binary is no different from the Gender Binary or Race Binary. Two pure and mutually exclusive gender and race poles don't exist. Neither do two pure and mutually exclusive aspects of meaning—facts and values. Facts and values intermingle.

CRITICAL RACE THEORY

Racial justice protrudes as a vital value of critical race theory. To achieve that end, racial hierarchy and the systemic pervasiveness of racism must be exposed, and minority communities must have a voice by altering jurisprudential dialogue to include hearing divergent histories, narratives, and counter-mythologies. Critical race theory values alternative perspectives and modes of discourse to build racial justice. For instance, "The Space Traders" by Derrick Bell[100] is a fable that addresses the idea that systemic racism in the United States not only lead the white majority to sacrifice Blacks in the past during the times of slavery and Black Codes, but in fact persists to this day and allows for continuing sacrifice of Blacks. In the fable, the United States decides to exchange all its Blacks to aliens for a revitalized environment and economic wealth. This myth counters the idea that social situations improve incrementally for Blacks and exposes the ugly truth that the core of the American dream is about the perpetual servitude, in one way or another, of African Americans. Critical race theory values a systemic evaluation rather than an individual accounting of race. Like pollution, racism is omnipresent: we breathe it in the way we breathe in pollutants, without our even knowing it. Thus, "we are all racists" [because] "racism is so deeply engrained in our culture, it is likely to be transmitted to tacit understandings."[101] Critical race theory, like axiological law theory, recognizes that values rest at the core of decisions and that it is best to get those values on the table rather than subscribing to "the positivist approach [that] disguises value conflicts and legitimizes the status quo"[102]:

> In short, it would not be a bad thing for judges to base constitutional decisions on their own sense of what values best reflect our cultural tradition, so long as the conflicting perspectives competing to define those values are made explicit. The search to define those values could then serve as a clarifying rather than a mystifying role.[103]

This is precisely the endgame of axiological value theory: rather than conceal values, admit they are the basis of legal decisions. Axiological value theory provides the instrument to detect such values.

Critical race theory insists that we admit the reality of race-consciousness rather than color-blindness. One strategy of the racial realism postulated by Derrick Bell entails abandoning traditional civil rights strategies, placing self-interest ranks over integration and finding meaning in an authentic struggle:

> While implementing Racial Realism we must simultaneously acknowledge that our actions are not likely to lead to transcendent change and, despite our best efforts, may be of more help to the system we despise than to the victims of that system we are trying to help. Nevertheless, our realization, and the dedication based on that realization, can lead to policy positions and campaigns that are less likely to worsen conditions for those we are trying to help, and will be more likely to remind those in power that there are imaginative, unabashed risk-takers who refuse to be trammeled upon. Yet confrontation with our oppressors is not our sole reason for engaging in Racial Realism. Continued struggle can bring about unexpected benefits and gains that in themselves justify continued

> endeavor. The fight in itself has meaning and should give us hope for the future.[104]

Critical race theory demythologizes and disvalues the rule of law, for example, encouraging jury nullification.[105] Its objective consists in subverting the American "justice" system.[106] Resistance to oppression becomes a core value in exposing white privilege in all its manifestations. Not justice in the abstract but within the context of personhood protrudes as a leading value: "Justice requires that we see the whole person in her or his social context."[107] Loaded with -isms's that reinforce racial binaries,[108] language reinforces the devaluation of the personhood of people of color. In contrast to racial binaries, intersectionality depicts the plurality of oppressions and how they harbor themselves in uniquely situated persons. Ultimately, the value of personhood protrudes as the leading value in critical race theory. In the 1960s, Black people carried posters that stated "I AM A MAN." Although we take exception for the lack of inclusiveness of the statement, the idea is the same: you have not treated me with the dignity I deserve as a person.

QUEER LAW

Since 2003, there have been major legislative, legal, and cultural triumphs for LGBT people:

- The legalization of sodomy—*Lawrence v. Texas*, 539 U.S. 558 (2003)
- Openly serving in the military—The Don't Ask, Don't Tell Repeal Act of 2010 (H.R. 2965, S 4023)
- Defense of Marriage Act Revision: *United States v. Windsor*, 570 U.S. 744 (2013)
- Marriage equality—*Obergefell v. Hodges*, 576 U.S.__ (2015)
- LGBT presence in a standard bearer for conservative and traditional values—inclusion of gay youth (2014), gay people in leadership roles (2015), and inclusion of transgender persons in the Boy Scouts of America (2017)

At the same time storm clouds have been gathering: states have enacted Religious Restoration or Liberty Acts allowing businesses not to serve LGBT people on the basis of their religious beliefs[109]; the President of the United States signed off on a memorandum to ban some transgender people from the military (his early blanket having been overruled)[110]; and transgender people have been denied the bathroom facility of their choice.[111] In the mid-twentieth century, anti-sodomy laws and the fear of disclosure ushered gay people into bathrooms (and bars and bathhouses) to conduct their sexual business. Today, the same forces of bigotry excommunicate transgender people from those same bathrooms. While these developments can be construed as the tail end of bigotry against LGBTQI people, the last shouts from a sinking ship, and of course the argument that the older generation of bigots is dying off, more than remnants of bigotry abide in "the unauthorized, unofficial disciplinary power of private actors and the authorized, official police power of state institutions," targeting "the behavior of those to whom its edicts are directed."[112]

Queer Law challenges the law's traditional neat categorization and misalignment of sex, gender, and sexual orientation and works to overturn hierarchies and constraints that bear on the unfair treatment of members of the LGBTQ community.[113] Gay legal narratives are valued because "the individual stories reveal the substantial social costs of the exclusionary policy, and also put a human face on the policy's victims."[114] Gay legal narratives, like the narratives of all minorities, challenge the conventional and alleged neutral values embedded in the law and serving dominant classes:

> The stories told in traditional scholarship focus on issues important to legal elites and are told from their point of view, which is often presented as the consensus or neutral perspective. Since these elites have been overwhelmingly white, male, affluent and ostensibly heterosexual, one might wonder whether their stories really reflect social consensus or neutral values.[115]

The law isn't the law, as if the law is neutral, but an expression of heteronormativity. Even if the law is now serving the L and the G and the B (especially with the inclusion of gay-friendly language), its heteronormatively is adversely affecting the T. The gender binary still exerts its pull, and the old plays in the old playbook of marginalization—they're sick, they're predators, they're bad role models and will adversely affect young children—are being employed.

FEMINIST LEGAL THEORIES

Like critical race theory, feminist legal theories decode and unmask oppressive forces in the law (patriarchy). It concentrates on "looking between the images of legalism"[116] and defining social reality in the "socially lived-out concrete,"[117] for example, how workplace pregnancy should not be seen as a special need but as a typical basic need.[118] By valuing the concrete rather than the abstract and engaging in consciousness-raising, women gain their self-identities and recognize their dehumanization "as valueless, as objects, as children, or as invisible."[119] Patriarchy not only bleeds into the word of law, but also into the narrow rational administration of the law, excluding integrative knowledge that views women in concrete situations and opens up legal decision-making to a wide range of intellectual gifts, including women's narrative, critical eye, ways of knowing, and hearts.[120] Not only must the law be revaluated but also the way people think about and do law. Feminist legal theories devalue the leading values of patriarchal law—autonomy, individuality, justice, and right—valuing instead nurture, community, and intimacy. By rejecting abstract idealism, transcendence, foundationalism, and atemporal universality,[121] feminist legal theories resituate law into particular social realities from the perspective of the narratives of differently situated women. Rather than the view from above, as in abstract idealism or atemporal universality, narratives originating from women who are historically embedded in particular contexts are valued.[122] Women must not be thought of as a monolithic whole, but as diversely positional. Hence, the preference for multivocal theories over univocal theories.[123]

Esteeming diversity, feminist legal theories embrace anti-essentialism. Like critical race theory, legal realism, and queer law studies, the goal becomes a reorientation of jurisprudence, diversifying it and making it accountable to people who are not served by it. Each of these theories prefers concrete experience to abstract theories. For each of these theories, the goal is to break law out of a prison of orthodoxy, rigidity, unfairness, abstraction, and concentration of power into a wider world where a wider variety of people can partner to create, adjudicate, and administer it. Law, as an instrument of torture, must be disassembled. Each unwittingly employs values and partakes of value essentialism.

LITERATURE IN LAW

Feminist theory, critical race theory, and queer law prefer contextualization to abstraction. Through contextualization, narratives from the marginalized and oppressed can be included in law and legal hegemony challenged. In Literature in Law, opening the minds and hearts of legal professionals to universal struggles and ethical dimensions assumes a zenith value.[124] Literature as law focuses on the discussion of whether legal texts have stable or indeterminate meanings.[125] Law as story-telling functions to share concerns and to counteract the official stories serving as the backdrop to traditional doctrines, to put a human face on legal principles and regulations, and to promote empathy through imaginative literary devices.[126] In each of these areas, the opening up proves to the common value: opening up the minds and hearts of legal professionals; opening up legal texts to multiple interpretations; opening up the law to different voices so that concerns can be shared to build solidarity and as a countermeasure to the official stories embedded in law.[127]

Literature can realize the values of building community, challenging received wisdom, opening up new vistas of reality, stirring the imagination, and engaging conscience[128]; it can connect law and the humanities and perhaps unify diverse intellectual endeavors[129] (thus valuing holism). Storytelling can also foster a different type of lawyer-client relationship, especially in the case of lawyers who, because of their often-elite social stature, cannot fathom their clients' perspectives. Traditional practices silence the voices of the marginalized and thus devalue them: "Lawyer storytelling falsifies client story when lawyer narratives silence and displace client narratives."[130] The voices of the dispossessed can be heard by introducing "new methods of interviewing, counseling, investigation, negotiation, and litigation capable of empowering client narratives in lawyer storytelling."[131]

Telling stories invests narratives with feeling, gives voice to those who were taught to hide emotions. Hearing stories invites hearers to participate by challenging their assumptions, jarring their complacency, lifting their spirits, and lowering their defenses:

> Stories are useful tools for the underdog because they invite the listener to suspend judgment, listen for the story's point, and test it against his or her own version of reality. This process is essential in a pluralist society like ours, and it is a practical necessity for underdogs: All movements for change must gain the support, or at least understanding, of the dominant group, which is white.[132]

For whom do these narratives matter? For whom does this have value? For those who want the law to be stable, whether they value stability in itself or view stability as a means of maintaining the status quo? Or for those for whom the stability perpetuates oppression? For those who are not privileged enough to write or adjudicate the law, whose interests never become codified? Those who value inclusion and social justice over value stability find value in pursuing literary dimensions of law. Concerns about what books should be read, what canon should be adopted, whether literature provides moral uplift, or whether literature should be used at all when a plentitude of "emotions, values, and general human messiness can be found"[133] overlook a central point. The protuberant value of literature law consists of providing a venue for previously silenced voices and unearthing forgotten narratives. Furthermore, by adding a literary component to jurisprudence, the artistic dimension of jurisprudence appreciates and has its place beside the strictly rationalistic aspect of rulemaking. Rather than the narrow faculty of reasoning, a broader use of the human intellect is appreciated.

NOTES

1. *Jurisprudence Contemporary and Classical*, 2nd ed., eds. Robert L. Hayman, Jr., Nancy Leavit, Richard Delgado (St. Paul, MN: West Group 2002), 1–2. This text has nurtured our value analysis by pointing us to the central texts.

2. Plato, *Crito*, in *Political Philosophy*, 3rd ed., ed. Steven M. Cahn (New York and Oxford: Oxford University Press, 2015), 27.

3. Thomas Aquinas, *Summa Theologica* http://www.documentacatholicaomnia.eu/03d/1225-1274,_Thomas_Aquinas,_Summa_Theologiae_%5B1%5D,_EN.pdf (last visited November 23, 2018).

4. Jon Meacham, *Thomas Jefferson: The Art of Power* (New York: Random House, 2012), 49.

5. Ibid.

6. Ibid.

7. Henry David Thoreau, *Civil Disobedience*, http://xroads.virginia.edu/~hyper2/thoreau/civil.html (last visited November 10, 2018).

8. Martin Luther King, Jr., "Letter from Birmingham City Jail," Project Gutenberg, http://self.gutenberg.org/articles/eng/letter_from_birmingham_jail (last visited April 30, 2021)

> (Any law that uplifts human personality is just. Any law that degrades human personality is unjust. All segregation statutes are unjust because segregation distorts the soul and damages the personality. It gives the segregator a false sense of superiority and the segregated a false sense of inferiority. Segregation, to use the terminology of the Jewish philosopher Martin Buber, substitutes an "I–it" relationship for an "I–thou" relationship and ends up relegating persons to the status of things. Hence segregation is not only politically, economically and sociologically unsound, it is morally wrong and sinful.)

9. John Rawls, *A Theory of Justice* (Cambridge, MA: The Belknap Press of Harvard University Press, 1971), 14–15.

10. King, "Letter from Birmingham City Jail."

11. Michael Moore, "Moral Reality," *Wisconsin Law Review* 6 (1982): 1154. Values may only be descriptive rather than normative, but they cannot be gotten around like a car swerving around a puddle. There is no way of going around them. Each value is imbued with varying degrees of oughtness to the extent it approaches the status of an absolute value.

12. Aristotle, *Rhetoric*, PROJECT GUTTENBERG, http://self.gutenberg.org/articles/Art_of_Rhetoric (last visited April 30, 2021).

13. Marcus Tullius Cicero, *The Republic of Cicero*, PROJECT GUTENBERG https://www.gutenberg.org/files/54161/54161-h/54161-h.htm (last visited November 30, 2021).

14. Brian Lieter, *Positivism, Formalism, Realism, Colorado Law Review* 99 (1999): 1140.

15. Ibid., 1143.

16. David Hume, *A Treatise of Human Nature*, PROJECT GUTENBERG, https://www.gutenberg.org/files/4705/4705-h/4705-h.htm (last visited May 2, 2021):

> [M]orality consists not in any relations that are the objects of science; but if examined, will prove with equal certainty not any *matter of fact*, which can be discovered by the understanding. . . . I am surprised, that instead of the usual copulations of propositions, *is* and *is not*, I meet with no proposition that is not connected with an *ought* and an *ought not*. This change is imperceptible; but is, however, of the last consequence. For as this *ought*, or *ought not*, expresses some new relation or affirmation, it is necessary that it should be observed and explained, and at the same time that a reason should be given, for what seems altogether inconceivable.

17. Robin West, *Three Positivisms, Boston University Law Review* 78 (1998): 791.
18. Ibid., 800.
19. David Hume, *Enquiry Concerning Human Understanding*, https://www.gutenberg.org/files/9662/9662-h/9662-h.htm (last visited May 2, 2021).
20. Ibid.
21. Ibid.
22. Ibid.
23. Ibid.
24. Ibid.
25. Ibid.
26. Ibid.
27. Ibid.
28. Ibid.
29. Ibid.
30. West, "Three Positivisms," 797.
31. Ibid., 799.
32. Lon Fuller, "Positivism and Fidelity to the Law—A Reply to Professor Hart," *Harvard Law Review* 71 (1958): 645.
33. Ibid., 656.
34. Ernest J. Weinrib, "Legal Formalism: "On the Immanent Rationality of Law," *Yale Law.Journal* 97 (1988): 957.
35. Ibid., 956.
36. Ibid., 957.
37. Ibid., 972.
38. Ibid., 956.
39. Ibid., 955.
40. Felix S. Cohen, "Transcendental Nonsense and the Functional Approach," *Columbia Law Review* 35 (1935): 821.
41. Jack M. Balkin, *Tradition, Betrayal, and the Politics of Deconstruction*, Faculty Scholarship Series. Paper 283, http://digitalcommons.law. yale.edu/fss_papers/283.
42. Ronald Dworkin, "The Model of Rules," *University of. Chicago Law Review* 35 (1967): 41.
43. Ronald Dworkin, Law's Empir 225 (1986), http://www.filosoficas.unam.mx/~cruzparc/empire.pdf (last visited November 23, 2018).
44. Ibid., 228.
45. Ibid., 245.

46. Ibid., 413.

47. Steve G. Calabresi, On Originalism in Constitutional Interpretation," HYPERLINK "https://constitutioncenter.org/interactive-constitution/white-pages/on-originalism-in-constitutional-interpretation" https://constitutioncenter.org/interactive-constitution/white-pages/on-originalism-in-constitutional-interpretation (last visited November 13, 2018).

48. John Stuart Mill, *On Liberty*, Project Guttenberg, http://www.gutenberg.org/files/34901/34901-h/34901-h.htm (last visited March 15, 2021). Mill explains that the "happily situated man" has implicit trust in the infallibility of the society. The happily situated

> place the same unbounded reliance only on such of their opinions as are shared by all who surround them, or to whom they habitually defer; for in proposition to man's want of confidence in his own solitary judgment does he usually repose, with implicit trust, on the infallibility of "the world" in general.

There is also an implicit trust in the infallibility of reasoning of "the world."

49. Thomas C. Grey, "Modern American Legal Thought," *Yale Law Journal* 106 (1996). Available at: http:// digitalcommons.law.yale.edu/ylj/vol106/iss2/6.

50. Weinrib, "Legal Formalism: On the Immanent Rationality of Law," 59.

51. Brian Leiter, *Rethinking Legal realism: Toward a Naturalized Jurisprudence, Texas Legal Review* 76 (1997): 314.

52. Ibid.

53. Frederick Schauer, "Formalism," *Yale Law Journal* 97 (1988): 542.

54. Thomas C. Grey, "Modern American Legal Thought," *Yale Law Journal* 106 (1996): 496.

55. Oliver Wendell Holmes, "The Path of the Law," *Harvard Law Review* 10 (1897): 997.

56. Morris R. Cohen, "On Absolutism in Legal Thought," *University Pennsylvania Law Review* 84 (1936): 691–692.

57. Grant Gilmore, "Legal Realism: Its Cause and Cure," *Yale Law Journal* 70 (1961): 1047.

58. David M. Trubek, "Back to the Future: Happy Life of the Law and Society Movement," *Florida State University Law Review* 18 (1990): 42.

59. Cohen, "On Absolutism in Legal Thought," 844.

60. Karl N. Llewellyn, "A Realistic Jurisprudence—The Next Step," *Columbia Law Review* 30 (1930): 447–448.

61. Cohen, "On Absolutism in Legal Thought," 713.

62. Llewellyn, "A Realistic Jurisprudence—The Next Step," 449.

63. Roscoe Pound, "The Scope and Purpose of Sociological Jurisprudence," *Harvard Law Review* 24 (1911): 598.

64. *Jurisprudence Classical and Contemporary*, 300.

65. Robert D. Cooter, "The Best Right Value Foundations of the Economic Analysis of the Law," *Notre Dame Law Review* 64 (1989): 830.

66. Ibid., 817.

67. Ibid., 830.

68. We stick to verbs like "protrude" and "ripple" and adjectives like "protuberant" and "protrusive" to underscore that values rest on the surface of meaning.

69. Duncan Kennedy, "Legal Education and the Reproduction of Hierarchy," *Journal of Legal Education* 32 (1982): 598.

70. Joseph William Singer, "The Player and the Cards: Nihilism and Legal Theory," *Yale Law Journal* 94 (1984): 6.

71. Ibid., 8.

72. Ibid., 56.

73. Jay Fineman, "Critical Approaches to Contract Law," *UCLA Law Review* 30 (1983): 856.

74. Owen M. Fiss, "The Death of the Law," *Cornell Law Review* 72 (1986): 11.

75. Kennedy, "Legal Education and the Reproduction of Hierarchy," 598.

76. Richard Delgado, "The Ethereal Scholar: Does Critical Legal Studies Have What Minorities Need?," *Harvard Civil Rights-Civil Liberties Law Review* 22 (1987): 301, 304.

77. Singer, "Legal Education and the Reproduction of Hierarchy," 52.

78. Alan Freeman and Elizabeth Mensch, "The Public-Private Distinction in American Law and Life," *Buffalo Law Review* 36 (1987): 237, 256.

79. Singer, "Legal Education and the Reproduction of Hierarchy," 67.

80. Ibid., 68.

81. Fiss, "The Death of the Law," 9–10.

82. Ibid., 1.

83. Ibid., 11.

84. Ibid., 13.

85. *Jurisprudence Classical and Contemporary*, 752.

86. Ibid., 756.

87. Ibid., 762.

88. Joan C. Williams, "*Culture and Certainty:* Legal History and the Reconstructive Project," *Virginia Law Review* 76 (1990): 735.

89. Ibid.

90. Dennis M. Patterson, "Law's Pragmatism and Practice and Narrative," *Virginia Law Review* 76, 5 (1990): 996

91. Martha Minnow and Elizabeth Spelman, *Southern California Law Review* 63 (1990): 1601. The pluralism ad nauseam carried out by Deconstructionists culminates in the evanescence of meaning, which Plato sees clearly. See Plato, *Plato's Parmenides,* trans. R.E. Allen, (Minneapolis, MN: University of Minnesota Press, 1983), 54. (Then each is other each other as multitudes: they cannot be other than each other as one, since unity is not. But each of them, as it seems, is a mass unlimited in multitude, and should someone take what seems to be the smallest, then, in an instant, as in a dream, in place of what seemed one there appears many, and in place of what seemed smallest something enormous appears relative to the little pieces into which it is split up. Meaning can neither be pluralized nor unified, but is attracted and repulsed from the poles of unification and pluralization, tending toward but never reaching either pole. Meaning cannot be left completely open

or be completely closed. It can trend toward unity as much as it can trend toward plurality.)

92. Alan C. Hutchinson, "Identity Crisis: The Politics of Interpretation," *New England Law Review* 26, 4 (1992): 1185. To see the utter inutility of Deconstruction, see J.M. Balkin, Jack M. Balkin, *Tradition, Betrayal, and the Politics of Deconstruction*, Faculty Scholarship Series. Paper 283, http://digitalcommons.law.yale.edu/fss_papers/283: "What can deconstruction possibly tell us about our choice of values if all texts are deconstructible, and there is nothing outside the text? . . . Deconstruction, in and of itself, has nothing particular to tell us about justice, or ethics, or any questions of values."

93. Ibid.

94. Margaret Jane Radin, "Reconsidering the Rule of Law," *Boston University Law Review* 69 (1989): 813.

95. Richard Rorty, "What You Can Expect from Anti-Foundationalist Philosophers: A Reply to Lynn Baker," *Virginia Law Review* 78 (1992): 719.

96. Ibid., 720.

97. Hutchinson, "Identity Crisis: The Politics of Interpretation," 1196–1197.

98. Ibid., 1185.

99. Jack M. Balkin, *Tradition, Betrayal, and the Politics of Deconstruction*, Faculty Scholarship Series. Paper 283, http://digitalcommons.law. yale.edu/fss_papers/283.

100. Derrick Bell, *Faces at the Bottom of the Well* https://www.archive.org/stream/facesatbottomofw00bellrich/facesatbottomofw00bellrich_djvu.txt (last visited November 18, 2018).

101. Charles R. Lawrence III, "The Id, the Ego, and Equal Protection: Reckoning with Unconscious Racism," *Stanford Law Review* 39 (1987): 322, 323.

102. Ibid., 386.

103. Ibid.

104. Derrick Bell, "Racial Realism," *Connecticut Law Review* 27 (1992): 378.

105. See Paul Butler, "Racially Based Jury Nullification: Black Power in the Criminal Social System," *Yale Law Journal* 105 (1995): 677–679.

106. Ibid., 680.

107. Stephanie M. Wildman and Adrienne D. Davis, "Language and Silence: Making Systems of Privilege Visible," *Santa Clara Law Review* 35 (1995): 900.

108. Ibid., 888.

109. State progenies of the federal The Religious Freedom Restoration Act of 1993, Pub. L. No. 103-141, 107 Stat. 1488 (November 16, 1993), codified at 42 U.S.C. § 2000bb through 42 U.S.C. § 2000bb-4 (also known as RFRA), which protects the interests in religious freedom.

110. The President's agenda regarding transgender persons goes beyond the military: "The Trump administration is considering narrowly defining gender as a biological, immutable condition determined by genitalia at birth, the most drastic move yet in a governmentwide effort to roll back recognition and protections of transgender people under federal civil rights law." *'Transgender' Could Be Defined Out of Existence Under Trump Administration* https://www.nytimes.com/2018/10/21/us/politics/transgender-trump-administration-sex-definition.html.

111. *3 Myths That Shape the Transgender Bathroom Debate*, https://www.cnn.com/2017/03/07/health/transgender-bathroom-law-facts-myths/index.html.
112. Kendall Thomas, "Beyond the Privacy Principle," *Columbia Law Review* 92 (1992): 1441.
113. https://cyber.harvard.edu/bridge/CriticalTheory/critical5.htm.
114. William N. Eskridge, Jr., "Gaylegal Narratives," *Stanford Law Review* 46 (1994): 614.
115. Ibid., at 607–608.
116. Robin West, "Jurisprudence and Gender," *Chicago Law Review* 55 (1988): 67.
117. Catherine MacKinnon, "Points Against Postmodernism," *Chicago Kent Law Review* 75 (2000): 688.
118. Wendy Williams, "Equality's Riddle: Pregnancy and the Equal Treatment/Special Treatment Debate," *Review Law and Social Change* 13 (1984–1985): 327.
119. West, *supra* note 141, at 67.
120. Ibid., 18.
121. Ibid., 28.
122. Margaret J. Radin, "The Pragmatist and the Feminist," *California Law Review* 63 (1990): 1707.
123. Angela P. Harris, "Race and Essentialism in Feminist Legal Theory," *Stanford Law Review* 42 (1990): 587–588.
124. *Jurisprudence Classical and Contemporary*, 462.
125. Ibid., 463.
126. Ibid., 464.
127. Richard Delgado, "Story-Telling for Oppositionists and Others: A Plea for Narrative," *Michigan Law Review* 87 (1989): 2412.
128. Ibid., 2415–2416.
129. Owen M. Fiss, "Objectivity and Interpretation," *Stanford Law Review* 34 (1982): 740.
130. Anthony V. Alfieri, "Reconstructive Poverty Law Practice: Learning Lessons in Client Narrative," *Yale Law Journal* 100 (1991): 2111.
131. Ibid., 2147.
132. Delgado, "Story-Telling for Oppositionists and Others: A Plea for Narrative," 2440.
133. Jane Baron, "Law, Literature, and the Problems of Interdisciplinarity," *Yale Law Journal* 108 (1999): 1059, 1067, 1066, 1079.

Part II

SUPREME COURT CASES

Chapter 3

Self-Determination v. Efficiency

Buck v. Bell

NARRATIVE IN A NUTSHELL

What happened to Carrie Buck?

She was sterilized.

Why?

Because she was mentally challenged (in the 1920s, Americans used the terms like "feeble-minded" and "mental defectives."

Was her mother mentally challenged?

Yes, her mother was mentally challenged. So was Carrie's daughter.

What was the majority opinion's assessment of this lineage?

"Three generations of imbeciles are enough," Oliver Wendell Holmes infamously wrote.

In this case, what institution did the sterilizations?

The Virginia facility in which Carrie Buck was institutionalized.

Who made these decisions?

The superintendent of the facility in consultation with the board of directors.

And this was legal?

Yes. A 1924 Virginia Act legalized vasectomies and hysterectomies on the mentally challenged and mentally ill.

And the justification for this was?

It was better for the health of the patient and better for the welfare of the society that these individuals not reproduce. Also, without the burden of children, some mentally challenged and mentally ill people could function outside the institution, be self-supporting, and become productive members of society.

Wasn't the Fourteenth Amendment an obstacle?

No, the Supreme Court sidestepped it.

VALUE-INFUSED SCHOLARSHIP

Moral outrage and more than a heaping tablespoon of sanctimoniousness characterize the drift of scholarship in this case. Framing the verdict as a "tragic opinion" that is "evil" derives from the notion that "the factual exegesis" was "full of disdain for the Constitution and humanity itself" and represented the nadir disvalue of a "natural aristocracy."[1] In Justice Holmes, we encounter "a person who was utterly devoid of compassion and respect for another human being."[2] Highly or hyper-valuing compassion and respect is the basis for condemning the decision as bereft of both. What "recovers equal protection's important role in eugenic sterilization litigation before *Buck v. Bell*" actually maximizes the value of equality, which is the basis for the following powerful judgment: Holmes's decision "demeaned not only Carrie Buck but also all the judges and lawyers during the decade and a half of litigation over eugenic sterilization who had accepted similar arguments or taken them seriously enough to formulate extended responses."[3] In speaking about Carrie Buck: "Real persons suffer when there is an obeisance to an inadequate science that begets a distended and deterministic form of moral reasoning" calls attention to the disvalue of rubber-stamping sketchy science and lockstep moral reasoning as a means of degrading the dignity of human beings.[4] Zenith-valuing personhood leads one to understand its depreciation to a nadir value:

> The Court's opinion in *Buck* could hardly be clearer in its disparagement of citizens with mental retardation. Its tone is grudging in acknowledging the possibility that they were entitled to anything from society at all, much less any claim to equal citizenship. The Court in *Buck* viewed people with mental retardation in the most negative light imaginable.[5]

For Justice Holmes, the subhuman Carrie Buck did not qualify for equal protection:

> Holmes's cavalier treatment of Carrie Buck's equal protection argument has masked the fact that, in the state and lower federal court decisions that preceded *Buck v. Bell*, equal protection had proven to be the strongest constitutional claim for defendants seeking to prevent their involuntary sterilization.[6]

In contrast to commentators who hold Justice Holmes and eugenicist-minded colleagues in contempt, as reviled and repugnant, having no compassion for the differently abled people, another value orientation casts the characters in a more sympathetic light. Legislators did the best they could with the science they had at the time and legislators deferred to majoritarian lawmaking.[7] This view values human fallibility. Taking this path, we do not pelt with denunciation but mediate with mercy. In the value-hue of mercy, our perspective shifts, and we can see other alternatives. For example, to see that there is usually a lag between the new knowledge and its acceptance by the general public. There are also varying degrees of acceptance and walls of resistance in the wake of conflicting traditions. It takes time to become accustomed or more precisely until the new idea becomes customary and not an alien presence. Our science, for example, proves there is no such thing as race, but that truth has not resonated for many people, even those to whom the word "educated" is assigned. Furthermore, in that time period, there was not even an emerging awareness of the rights of the mentally and physically challenged.

Axiological analysis presents possibilities other than moral outrage and sanctimoniousness and a eugenics-centered approach. We focus on the protuberant value of efficiency as of greater value in contrast to the diminished value of self-determination.

MAJORITY OPINION BY JUSTICE OLIVER WENDELL HOLMES

Justice Holmes justified the sterilization of Carrie Buck on the back of the following statute:

> An Act of Virginia, approved March 20, 1924, recites that the health of the patient and the welfare of society may be promoted in certain cases by the sterilization of mental defectives, under careful safeguard, &c.; that the sterilization may be effected in males by vasectomy and in females by salpingectomy, without serious pain or substantial danger to life; that the Commonwealth is supporting in various institutions many defective persons who, if now discharged, would become a menace, but, if incapable of procreating, might be discharged with safety and become self-supporting with benefit to themselves and to society, and that experience has shown that heredity plays an important part in the transmission of insanity, imbecility, &c. The statute then enacts that, whenever the superintendent of certain institutions, including the above-named State Colony, shall be of opinion that it is for the best interests of the patients and of society that an inmate under his care should be sexually sterilized, he may have the operation performed upon any patient afflicted with hereditary forms

> of insanity, imbecility, &c., on complying with the very careful provisions by which the act protects the patients from possible abuse.[8]

Sterilization was justified by two leading values: the health of the patient and the welfare of society. "Mental defectives" with the capacity to procreate would be menaces to themselves and to society. Their sterilization would benefit both themselves and society: the sterilized mental defective could be self-supporting and society would not be burdened by an institutionalized person draining the coffers or by additional mentally defective offspring. The removal of one or both fallopian tubes and the cutting, tying, or sealing of the vasa deferentia would be safe and not painful or life-threatening to "mental defectives."

While it might appear that the health of the patient mattered to Justice Holmes, that notion was quickly belied. The value of efficiency took center stage and all other values to wings:

> We have seen more than once that the public welfare may call upon the best citizens for their lives. It would be strange if it could not call upon those who already sap the strength of the State for these lesser sacrifices, often not felt to be such by those concerned, in order to prevent our being swamped with incompetence. It is better for all the world if, instead of waiting to execute degenerate offspring for crime or to let them starve for their imbecility, society can prevent those who are manifestly unfit from continuing their kind. The principle that sustains compulsory vaccination is broad enough to cover cutting the Fallopian tubes.[9]

Public welfare called for sacrifices, and in this case, the sacrifice was the procreative capacities of a "feeble-minded" person. The value of sacrifice was also considered in light of the particular type of person who made it. The "best citizens" were presumably those who made positive or productive contributions to the state. Lesser citizens, presumably the mentally challenged in this case, burdened the state and made its operations inefficient. If the best citizens could make greater sacrifices, why couldn't lesser citizens make smaller sacrifices? Rather than burden society with potential criminals or allow mental defectives to starve from their incompetence, sterilization was preferred. It was in the end more effective, preventing the problem from occurring in the first place. The value of efficiency closely connected with the value of competence. Allowing "mental defectives" to reproduce entailed "being swamped with incompetence." Incompetence interfered with the efficient functioning of society. Concern for "degenerate offspring" (endearingly put) could only be seen as a throwaway value. "Degenerate offspring" evidenced disvalues in two ways. "Degenerate" meant having lost the physical, mental, or moral qualities considered normal and desirable. In other words, undesirable and abnormal. "Offspring" might appear as a neutral word, but it evinced laboratory-like coldness to it disassociated from the word "child" or "children." "Degenerate offspring" referred to abnormal and undesirable entities and hardly persons or anything tied to parental affection (children).

If "mental defects" could be sterilized, why couldn't other people as well? Justice Holmes's response could not have been more evasive or sphinxlike. "[T]he law does all that is needed when it does all that it can," he contended, explaining that the law drew lines around the "similarly situated" (in this case "mental defectives") toward which expedient action can be taken. This did not speak to the issue of whether this Supreme Court decision could justify sterilization of other groups deemed unproductive to society.

> But, it is said, however it might be if this reasoning were applied generally, it fails when it is confined to the small number who are in the institutions named and is not applied to the multitudes outside. It is the usual last resort of constitutional arguments to point out shortcomings of this sort. But the answer is that the law does all that is needed when it does all that it can, indicates a policy, applies it to all within the lines, and seeks to bring within the lines all similarly situated so far and so fast as its means allow. Of course, so far as the operations enable those who otherwise must be kept confined to be returned to the world, and thus open the asylum to others, the equality aimed at will be more nearly reached.[10]

The appeal to equality was certainly more than a reach. What kind of equality was this? Not equality between persons in the political or social sense, but equality serving efficiency. Justice Holmes justified sterilization by stating that once sterilized feeble-minded people left asylums and functioned in society, more spaces could become available in the institution. Society gained another functioning citizen (+1) and another degenerate gets assistance from the society (–1).

A LONELY AND UNPERSUASIVE PRECEDENT

To justify the sterilization of mentally challenged and mentally ill people, Justice Holmes adduced a single precedent: *Jacobson v. Massachusetts*, 197 U.S. 11 (1905). In this ruling, the Supreme Court upheld a Massachusetts law making it legal to make smallpox vaccinations compulsory for all adults in order to prevent smallpox and to protect public health. Yet the spread of a disease that could infect millions of people and threaten the economic and political structures of a society was far more impacting than birthing mentally challenged and mentally ill people, which may be a nuisance but hardly an epidemic capable of wiping out major segments of the population. "The principle that sustains compulsory vaccination is broad enough to cover cutting the Fallopian tubes,"[11] Justice Holmes averred. Whereas all people over twenty-one had to be inoculated, the Virginia Act singled out a single group for sterilization. This was another reason why the principle of compulsory inoculation could not cover the compulsory sterilization. The majority opinion in *Jacobson* stated compulsory vaccinations that benefited the community did not violate the rights of people under the Fourteenth Amendment. Justice Holmes saw the propagation of mentally challenged and mentally ill people as just as much a threat to the efficient functioning of society as he did the spread of smallpox. The disease and diseased had to be stopped. In the same way a disease was not covered by the Fourteenth Amendment, neither could the diseased. They were bad peas in the same pod, a threat to efficiency.

RECKONING OF THE ROGUE JUSTICES

Can society forbear people like Carrie Buck or are they such a drain on society that the likes of them should be stopped from reproducing? The first question: who exactly are the drains on society? What are the criteria for this? For some people, the poor are a drain on society, giving society much less than they give. For others, the idle rich or royalty are drains on society. For some, teachers are the drains. For others, undocumented workers are drains on society. For wealthy nations, poor nations are drains on the world. There are drains galore. Yet who decides who are the drains of society? Second, who drains off more than others? Does John with a recurrent substance abuse issue going in and out of rehab a bigger drain than Carrie Buck and her "feeble-minded" children? Is the person who goes into bankruptcy more of a drain than Carrie Buck? Does the person who overeats and has health challenges pose a bigger drain on society than Carrie Buck? Third, it could be argued that that well-off, technologically advanced societies can flourish even with a minority of "feeble-minded" people. This might prove a different story in threadbare societies lacking the resources to care for people with extra needs. In the case of Carrie Buck, she was living in a society that could endure her and her offspring without damaging its fundamental well-being. No case has been made that even an army of Carrie Bucks would endanger the great and prosperous United States of America. Also, efficiency could be understood not merely in terms of material production, but in terms of increasing compassion for each other, which could serve to unite rather than divide us, which could make society more efficient. Furthermore, there is a clear difference between choosing to give up one's life for the greater good and having that choice made for you, as in the case of Carrie Buck. Justice Holmes took that decision from her on the basis of overall societal efficiency and to a lesser extent what was best for Carrie Buck, in any case depriving her of self-determination. The emphasis on efficiency prevented Justice Holmes from seeing Carrie Buck as a human being, who could love and could find fulfillment in having children. This was only secondarily a case about eugenics. Eugenics provided yet another way to justify exploitation through efficiency. The recurring value struggle in human history is between the dignity of a human being and the self-determination that constitutes that dignity and how useful that human being was considered—efficiency being the index to evaluate that usefulness. This is recurring value scenario addressed by Kant, Buber, Heidegger, and Sartre in their different ways. The larger issue concerns how any individual's self-determination was less valued than efficiency, whether that be through crude utilitarianism, lifeboat ethics, or any version of hierarchy featuring an underappreciated underclass disvalued as inefficient. Many have been mistreated in name of efficiency: seniors relegated to nursing homes or to the wilds, systematic female infanticide, minors working in sweatshops, slaves working in cotton fields, a whole class of poor people required to support the lifestyle of the elite, and nations whose resources and geography are extracted for the greater geopolitical good (efficiency). Wars, corporate downsizing, economic and environmental policy, and allocation of health resources have been guided by the value of efficiency. In the end, why wasn't the Fourteenth Amendment applied to Carrie Buck and other mentally challenged or mentally ill individuals? Justice Holmes held a Sacred Cow-Scapegoat value scheme in which efficiency was held as a sacred zenith value and inefficiency was held in contempt as nadir profane disvalue. In this case, the umbrella of the Fourteenth Amendment could not cover contemptibly inefficient feeble-minded people, who were viewed as remote others.

NOTES

1. Victoria Nourse, "*Buck v. Bell*: A Constitutional Tragedy from a Lost World," *Pepperdine Law Review* 39, 1 (2013): 101, 102.

2. Roberta M. Berry, "From Involuntary Sterilization to Genetic Enhancement: The Unsettled Legacy of *Buck v. Bell*," *Notre Dame Journal Law Ethics and Public Policy* 12, 2 (1998): 447.

3. Stephen A. Siegel, "Justice Holmes, *Buck V. Bell*, and the History of Equal Protection," *Minnesota Law Review* 90 (2005): 136.

4. Phillip Thompson, "Silent Protest: A Catholic Justice Dissents in *Buck v. Bell*," *The Catholic Lawyer* 43, 1 (Spring 2004): 147.

5. James W. Ellis, "Disability Advocacy and Atkins," *DePaul Law Review* 57 (2008): 657.

6. Siegel, "Justice Holmes, *Buck V. Bell*, and the History of Equal Protection," 108.

7. Edward J. Larson "Putting *Buck v. Bell* in Scientific and Historical Context: A Response to Victoria Nourse," *Pepperdine Law Review* 39, 1 (2013): 120.
8. *Buck v. Bell*, 274 U.S. 200, 205–206 (1927).
9. Ibid., 207.
10. Ibid., 208.
11. Ibid., 207.

Chapter 4

Human Being v. Degraded Being

Yick Wo v. Hopkins

NARRATIVE IN A NUTSHELL

> If Chinese laborers, or Chinese of any other class, now either permanently or temporarily residing in the territory of the United States, meet with ill treatment at the hands of any other persons, the Government of the United States will exert all its powers to devise measures for their protection, and to secure to them the same rights, privileges, immunities and exemptions as may be enjoyed by the citizens or subjects of the most favored nation, and to which they are entitled by treaty. (Treaty between the Government and China, concluded November 17, 1880, 22 Stat. 827)[1]

> Nor shall any state deprive any person of life, liberty, or property without due process of law; nor deny to any person within its jurisdiction the equal protection of the laws. (Fourteenth Amendment)

With the Fourteenth Amendment and a Treaty between the United States and China standing in front of its legal path like a roadblock, how any could court not see the most obvious racism again the Chinese people when it occurred, as it did in San Francisco in the 1880s? A funny thing happened on the way to the courthouse. . . .

Lee Yick owned and operated Yick Wo, a laundry facility in California. Although he had been in business for over two decades, the San Francisco board of supervisors ruled that he could not operate his business in a wooden building. When he continued to run his operation, he was fined ten dollars. He refused to pay and was imprisoned.

VALUE-INFUSED SCHOLARSHIP

Protecting minority interests from fear-infected legislation aimed at the other elevates the value of *Yo Wick* to a sacred judicial landmark.[2] One of the reasons for this sanctified position concerns the sacred zenith value of property rights and the profane nadir disvalue of tyrannically depriving people of them: "Property rights have, from time immemorial, been regarded as among the most sacred, basic and fundamental rights men can enjoy, by reason solely of the fact that they are human beings."[3] Equal protection decisions are not simply based on reading the law, but in dissolving the other by exercising values based on the "the family of ideas encompassing notions such as community, solidarity, fellow-feeling, extended sympathy, and fraternity, all expanded to encompass at least the members of the relevant geographical unit."[4] *Yo Wick* retains its star value, but haters have disvalued it as "mundane" because it simply held that "states must comply with valid and applicable treaties, hardly a controversial principle."[5] Seeing this through a libertarian value scheme frames the case in terms of its relationship to a pro-*Lochner* reading, valuing the free market over governmental intervention.[6] Scholarship falls short of understanding this case because in the final analysis, this decision rested valuing Chinese launderers as "everymen" instead of aliens to whom the Fourteenth Amendment did not apply.

THE OPEN SECRET

It was an open secret what was actually happening to the Chinese in San Francisco, as mentioned in the syllabus to the case:

> If this means prohibition of the occupation and destruction of the business and property of the Chinese laundrymen in San Francisco—and it seems to us this must be the effect of executing the ordinance—and not merely the proper regulation of the business, then there is discrimination and a violation of other highly important rights secured by the Fourteenth Amendment and the treaty. That it does mean prohibition as to the Chinese it seems to us must be apparent to every citizen of San Francisco who has been here long enough to be familiar with the cause of an active and aggressive branch of public opinion and of public notorious events. *Can a court be blind to what must be necessarily known to every intelligent person in the State?* (Our emphasis)[7]

Why were the California courts so blind to the obvious discrimination of Chinese people? This turned on a question of value. To return to the narrative: Lee Wick was a native of China (and still a subject of the Emperor of China) who settled California in 1861 and operated a laundry business at the same site and in the same building for twenty-two years and received a license to operate (1884). In 1884, a board of fire wardens signed off on a license for Yick Wo's laundry:

> [U]pon such inspection said board found all proper arrangements for carrying on the business; that the stoves, washing and drying apparatus, and the appliances for heating smoothing irons are in good condition, and that their use is not dangerous to the surrounding property from fire, and that all proper precautions have been taken to comply with the provisions of order No. 1617, defining "the fire limits of the city and county of San Francisco and making regulations concerning the erection and use of buildings in said city and county," and of order No. 1670, "prohibiting the kindling, maintenance, and use of open fires in houses"; that he had a certificate from the health officer that the same premises had been inspected by him, and that he found that they were properly and sufficiently drained, and that all proper arrangements for carrying on the business of a laundry, without injury to the sanitary condition of the neighborhood, had been complied with.[8]

But Lee Wick was refused a license in 1885 because of a new ordinance requiring the laundry facilities to be built of stone or brick-made laundry facilities built of wood operated by Chinese to be illegal. Operating their wooden laundry businesses without permits and refusing to pay the $10.00 fine for violated this ordinance, Lee Wick was incarcerated. Before 1885, there was nothing wrong with laundry mats constructed of wood, but in 1885, it became an issue. Of the 320 laundry mats in San Francisco, Chinese people ran 240 of them.[9] Chinese launderers invested $200,000 in capital and paid at least $180,000 in rent, license, taxes, gas, and water.[10] Lee Wick and 150 other similarly situated Chinese launderers were arrested for doing business without a permit.[11] The board of supervisors denied permits to Lee Wick and 200 other similarly situated launderers.[12] The board of supervisors granted all but one of the petitions of non-Chinese people.[13] The presumptive fair and impartial law was administered in an evil and unequal way:

> Though the law itself be fair on its face and impartial in appearance, yet, if it is applied and administered by public authority with an evil eye and an unequal hand, so as practically to make unjust and illegal discriminations between persons in similar circumstances, material to their rights, the denial of equal justice is still within the prohibition of the Constitution.[14]

To Circuit Judge Lorenzo Sawyer, quoted copiously in the syllabus of this case, the San Francisco ordinance would shut down many existing Chinese laundries and force their owners to reconstruct the facilities with brick and stone (which they likely could not afford) or force them to adjoining counties where for lack of customers they would go out of business. In effect, the small Chinese launderers would have their properties confiscated by large Caucasian institutions:

> The effect of the execution of this ordinance in the manner indicated in the record would seem to be necessarily to close up the many Chinese laundries now existing, or compel their owners to pull down their present buildings and reconstruct of brick or stone, or to drive them outside the city and county of San Francisco to the adjoining counties, beyond the convenient reach of customers, either of which results would be little short of absolute confiscation of the large amount of property shown to be now, and to have been for a long time, invested in these occupations. If this would not be depriving such parties of their property without due process of law, it would be difficult to say what would effect that prohibited result. The necessary tendency, if not the specific purpose, of this ordinance, and of enforcing it in the manner indicated in the record, is to drive out of business all the numerous small laundries, especially those owned by Chinese, and give a monopoly of the business to the large institutions established and carried on by means of large associated Caucasian capital.[15]

This was intolerable for the people who valued the Chinese as persons. From the other side, why should these nonhumans be protected by the Fourteenth Amendment or any such treaty? As the California Supreme Court stated:

> "The order No. 1569 and section 68 of order No. 1587 are not in contravention of *common right or unjust, unequal, partial, or oppressive in such sense* (our emphasis) as authorizes us in this proceeding to pronounce them invalid." . . .
>
> "We have not deemed it necessary to discuss the question in the light of supposed infringement of petitioner's rights under the Constitution of the United States."[16]

The California Supreme Court found nothing wrong in this law:

> "SEC. 1. It shall be unlawful, from and after the passage of this order, for any person or persons to establish, maintain, or carry on a laundry within the corporate limits of the city and county of San Francisco without having first obtained the consent of the board of supervisors, except the same be located in a building constructed either of brick or stone."
>
> "SEC. 2. It shall be unlawful for any person to erect, build, or maintain, or cause to be erected, built, or maintained, over or upon the roof of any building now erected or which may hereafter be erected within the limits of said city and

county, any scaffolding without first obtaining the written permission of the board of supervisors, which permit shall state fully for what purpose said scaffolding is to be erected and used, and such scaffolding shall not be used for any other purpose than that designated in such permit."

"SEC. 3. Any person who shall violate any of the provisions of this order shall be deemed guilty of a misdemeanor, and upon conviction thereof shall be punished by a fine of not more than one thousand dollars, or by imprisonment in the county jail not more than six months, or by both such fine and imprisonment. . . ."

"SEC. 68. It shall be unlawful, from and after the passage of this order, for any person or persons to establish, maintain, or carry on a laundry within the corporate limits of the city and county of San Francisco without having first obtained the consent of the board of supervisors, except the same be located in a building constructed either of brick or stone."[17]

MAJORITY OPINION BY JUSTICE T. STANLEY MATTHEWS

Misapplied Authorities

Justice Matthews called out the California Supreme Court for using the following two cases as precedential justification: *Barbier v. Connolly*, 113 U.S. 27 (1885) and *Soon Hing v. Crowley*, 113 U.S. 703 (1885). In these cases, the ordinance in question prohibited washing and ironing in San Francisco city and county warehouses and washhouses from 10 P.M. until 6 A.M. This ordinance was applied to all businesses in the same way and could not be considered invidious discrimination. The law applied to the similarly situated in the same way. Order No. 156 was different. It applied to launderers with wooden buildings, which were mainly owned by Chinese people. It did not apply at all to those with brick buildings, which were operated by Caucasians. These wooden buildings, which had been in use for some time, were deemed illegal operations.

OPERATIVE VALUES

The Value of Freedom and Disvalue of Arbitrary and Personal Power

The majority opinion esteemed the value of freedom, which was explained in contradistinction to slavery:

> For the very idea that one man may be compelled to hold his life, or the means of living, or any material right essential to the enjoyment of life at the mere will of another seems to be intolerable in any country where freedom prevails, as being the essence of slavery itself.[18]

> [I]t divides the owners or occupiers into two classes, not having respect to their personal character and qualifications for the business, nor the situation and nature and adaptation of the buildings themselves, but merely by an arbitrary line, on one side of which are those who are permitted to pursue their industry by the mere will and consent of the supervisors, and on the other those from whom *that consent is withheld at their mere will and pleasure* [or emphasis]. And both classes are alike only in this, that they are tenants at will, under the supervisors, of their means of living.[19]

To underscore the value of freedom and the disvalue of arbitrary and personal power, Justice Matthews cited *City of Baltimore v. Radecke*, 49 Maryland 217 (1878). Radecke, a carpenter and box-maker, assembled and used a steam engine in Baltimore, which he could only do with a permit from the mayor and the city council. That permit had the following condition: the mayor could bypass the city council. Radecke received notice from the mayor after the six months were up, but refused to conform to it. The City of Baltimore filed a suit to recover the penalty provided by the ordinance. Seeing this statute as "clearly unreasonable, so arbitrary, oppressive, or partial" grant of power, the Court of Appeals recognized that absolute value wielded in the single hand of the mayor over all steam engines and overturned the law:

> But it commits to the unrestrained will of a single public officer the power to notify every person who now employs a steam engine in the prosecution of any business in the city of Baltimore to cease to do so, and, by providing compulsory fines for every day's disobedience of such notice and order of removal, renders his power over the use of steam in that city practically absolute, so that he may prohibit its use altogether.[20]

Like the San Francisco ordinance, this ordinance arose from enmity, prejudice, partisan zeal, and concentrated power (in Baltimore with the mayor, in San Francisco with a small group of commissioners):

> It is clear that giving and enforcing these notices may, and quite likely will, bring ruin to the business of those against whom they are directed, while others, from whom they are withheld, may be actually benefited by what is thus done to their neighbors; and, when we remember that this action or nonaction may proceed from enmity or prejudice, from partisan zeal or animosity, from favoritism

> and other improper influences and motives easy of concealment and difficult to be detected and exposed, it becomes unnecessary to suggest or to comment upon the injustice capable of being brought under cover of such a power, for that becomes apparent to everyone who gives to the subject a moment's consideration. In fact, an ordinance which clothes a single individual with such power hardly falls within the *domain of law,* and we are constrained to pronounce it inoperative and void.[21]

The Values of Harmlessness, Usefulness, and Particular Personhood

One line in the majority ruling was revealing and the catalyst value in this case: "No reason whatever, except the will of the supervisors, is assigned why they should not be permitted to carry on, in the accustomed manner, their harmless and useful occupation, on which they depend for a livelihood."[22] The Chinese launderers weren't harming else, provided a useful service to the community, and required the occupation to survive. Three positive values were packed together: the harmlessness and usefulness of their occupation and more subtly personhood out of concern for them to make a living. It was the equivalent of saying: "These Chinese launderers aren't hurting you and are actually useful to you because of the services they provide, and these persons need this occupation to live. Leave them alone and let them live their lives." But these values would not resonate for those who don't already value the Chinese as persons.

RECKONING OF THE ROGUE JUSTICES

This case came down to Justice Matthews's recognition of Lee Wick and his fellow Chinese launderers as fellow human beings, not as remote others or even near others. This was the very same Fourteenth Amendment that did not compel the California Supreme Court to find the laws unconstitutional. The difference between the California Supreme Court and Supreme Court's ruling had nothing to do with the letter of the law. It had to do with valuing or disvaluing the Chinese people. Through valuing or disvaluing, the Fourteenth Amendment either obtruded or receded. It obtruded for Justice Matthews in the majority opinion. Judge Matthews wrote,

> For the very idea that one man may be compelled to hold his life, or the means of living, or any material right essential to the enjoyment of life at the mere will of another seems to be intolerable in any country where freedom prevails, as being the essence of slavery itself.[23]

The sacred zenith value of freedom was buttressed by a specific value conglomerate grounding Chinese launderers as both productive members of the community and breadwinners for their families, as particular persons. The Fourteenth Amendment resonated for Justice Matthews only because he could value Lee Wick and his similarly situated Chinese launderers as fellow human beings, as everymen, as persons.

NOTES

1. *Yick Wo v. Hopkins*, 118 U.S. 356, 368–369 (1886).
2. Marie A. Failinger, "*Yick Wo* at 125: Four Simple Lessons for the Contemporary Supreme Court," *Michigan Journal of Race and Law* 17 (2012): 268.
3. Fintan M. Flanagan, George Lorinczi, and Frank Schlax, "Constitutional Problems Under the Alien Land Laws," *Marquette Law Review* 36, 3 (1953): 277, 278.
4. R. G. Wright, "Equal Protection and the Idea of Equality," *Law and Inequality* 34, 1 (June 2016): 5.
5. Gabriel Chin, "Unexplainable on Grounds of Race: Doubts about *Yo Wick*," *University Illinois Law Review* (2008): 1364.
6. David E. Bernstein, "*Lochner*, Parity, and the Chinese Laundry Cases," *William and Mary Law Review* 41, 1 (1999): 216.
7. *Yo Wick v Hopkins*, 364.
8. Ibid., 358.
9. Ibid., 358–359.
10. Ibid., 359.
11. Ibid.
12. Ibid.
13. Ibid.
14. Ibid., 374.
15. Ibid., 362.
16. Ibid., 360.
17. Ibid., 367–368.
18. Ibid., 370.
19. Ibid., 368.
20. Ibid., 372.
21. Ibid., 373.
22. Ibid., 374.
23. Ibid., 370.

Chapter 5

Security of Free Speech v. Wartime National Security

Abrams v. United States

NARRATIVE IN A NUTSHELL

This Abrams person . . .

John Abrams.

Was an immigrant from Russia . . .

Yes.

And he and three of his colleagues, also Russian immigrants, wrote two leaflets and threw thousands of them out of a Manhattan window.

Their grievances were . . .

That the United States government was involved in a war against their country and their political party, the Bolsheviks.

One pamphlet criticized the United States government for sending American troops to Russia, and the other condemned the war and the production of weapons to be used against Soviet Russia.

The problem was . . .

The problem was . . . America had just entered World War I and in times of war civil liberties often shrink.

How much did they shrink in 1918 America?

The Espionage Act of Congress made it a crime to say or write abusive things about the government. This was seen as interfering with the war effort.

And Abrams and Co. were convicted . . .

They were and for their trouble sentenced to twenty years in prison.

VALUE-INFUSED SCHOLARSHIP

"No matter how rapidly we utter the phrase 'clear and present danger,' or how closely we hyphenate the words, they are not a substitute for the weighing of values."[1] In this ruling, the value of a marketplace of ideas and the value of a clear and present danger wrestle for supremacy.[2] The more we value safety, the less concerned we are going to be about speech. An institutionally aware First Amendment entails fitting speech within institutions.[3] In other words, valuing institutional control over free speech. An aspect of this institutional control would "would require courts to consider the identity of a speaker, and perhaps the content of its speech, in determining what level of protection that speaker should receive."[4] Justice Holmes's dissent values intellectual humility over intellectual arrogance, which could contribute to better dialogue in today's polarized political environment:

> This interpretation enlists Holmes as an advocate for more charitable discourse across deep differences. In today's pluralistic society, acknowledging our lack of certainty can help us move toward better dialogue with one another. At a time when we too often sacralize our own views and condemn our opponents, epistemic humility could help our society avoid escalating from weaponized words to actual weapons.[5]

In addition to protuberant valuations, there are more recessed valuations that impact a decision that sometimes are overlooked because they don't seem significant. In this case, such recessive values include Justice Holmes's affirmation of life as experimentation and his assessment of the defendants as non-threatening. They were near others: dumb but non-threatening.

THE ESPIONAGE ACT—JUNE 15, 1917

> Whoever, when the United States is at war, shall wilfully make or convey false reports or false statements with intent to interfere with the operation or success of the military or naval forces of the United States, or to promote the success of its enemies, or shall wilfully make or convey false reports, or false statements, or say or do anything except by way of bona fide and not disloyal advice to an investor . . . with intent to obstruct the sale by the United States of bonds . . . or the making of loans by or to the United States, or whoever, when the United States is at war, shall wilfully cause . . . or incite . . . insubordination, disloyalty, mutiny, or refusal of duty, in the military or naval forces of the United States, or shall wilfully obstruct . . . the recruiting or enlistment service of the United States, and whoever, when the United States is at war, shall wilfully utter, print, write, or publish any disloyal, profane, scurrilous, or abusive language about the form of government of the United States, or the Constitution of the United States, or the military or naval forces of the United States, or the flag . . . or the uniform of the Army or Navy of the United States, or any language intended to

> bring the form of government . . . or the Constitution . . . or the military or naval forces . . . or the flag . . . of the United States into contempt, scorn, contumely, or disrepute . . . or shall wilfully display the flag of any foreign enemy, or shall wilfully . . . urge, incite, or advocate any curtailment of production in this country of any thing or things . . . necessary or essential to the prosecution of the war . . . and whoever shall wilfully advocate, teach, defend, or suggest the doing of any of the acts or things in this section enumerated and whoever shall by word or act support or favor the cause of any country with which the United States is at war or by word or act oppose the cause of the United States therein, shall be punished by a fine of not more than $10,000 or imprisonment for not more than twenty years, or both. . . .[6]

MAJORITY OPINION BY JUSTICE JOHN CLARKE

Legal Wrapping Paper

It was clear to Justice Clarke that the language of the defendants in their pamphlets met the criteria of the Espionage Act:

> Each of the first three counts charged the defendants with conspiring, when the United States was at war with the Imperial Government of Germany, to unlawfully utter, print, write and publish: in the first count, "disloyal, scurrilous and abusive language about the form of Government of the United States"; in the second count, language "intended to bring the form of Government of the United States into contempt, scorn, contumely and disrepute"; and in the third count, language "intended to incite, provoke and encourage resistance to the United States in said war." The charge in the fourth count was that the defendants conspired. [Regarding the fourth count, the defendants used language intended to stop the manufacture of arms.][7]

The contents of these leaflets were not considered "candid discussion to bring about a change of administration," but aimed at taking down the United States war effort:

> This is not an attempt to bring about a change of administration by candid discussion, for, no matter what may have incited the outbreak on the part of the defendant anarchists, the manifest purpose of such a publication was to create an attempt to defeat the war plans of the Government of the United States by bringing upon the country the paralysis of a general strike, thereby arresting the production of all munitions and other things essential to the conduct of the war.[8]

The location of the pamphlet drop was of vital importance. Had 5,000 pamphlets fallen from a silo in Topeka, Kansas, it would not have been a problem, but the fact they were circulated where servicemen could read them and great supplies of arms were going to sea (which could incite people in the area to sabotage them) was the issue:

> That the interpretation we have put upon these articles, circulated in the greatest port of our land, from which great numbers of soldiers were at the time taking ship daily, and in which great quantities of war supplies of every kind were at the time being manufactured for transportation overseas, is not only the fair interpretation of them but that it is the meaning which their authors consciously intended should be conveyed by them to others is further shown by the additional writings found in the meeting place of the defendant group and on the person of one of them. One of these circulars is headed: "Revolutionists! Unite for Action!"[9]

Justice Clarke saw the pamphlets as a direct threat to the war effort and rejected the idea that the rationale behind the pamphlets was to aid the Russian Revolution rather than sabotage the war with Germany:

> It will not do to say, as is now argued, that the only intent of these defendants was to prevent injury to the Russian cause. *Men must be held to have intended, and to be accountable for, the effects which their acts were likely to produce [our emphasis].* Even if their primary purpose and intent were to aid the cause of the Russian Revolution, the plan of action which they adopted necessarily involved, before it could be realized, defeat of the war program of the United States, for the obvious effect of this appeal, if it should become effective, as they hoped it might, would be to persuade persons of character such as those whom they regarded themselves as addressing, not to aid government loans, and not to work in ammunition factories where their work would produce "bullets, bayonets, cannon" and other munitions of war the use of which would cause the "murder" of Germans and Russians.[10]

QUICK CHRONOLOGY OF AUTHORITIES

Espionage Act of Congress (§ 3, Title I, of Act approved June 15, 1917, as amended May 16, 1918, 40 Stat. 553).

1919, *Schenck v. United States*, 249 U.S. 47 (1919) *Baer v. United States,* 249 U. S. 47—Mailing printed circulars to obstruct the recruiting and enlistment service considered a clear and present danger and contrary to the Espionage Act of June 15, 1917.

1919 *Frohwerk v. United States*, 249 U. S. 204. A conspiracy to obstruct recruiting in violation of the Espionage Act deemed criminal.

OPERATIVE VALUES

Devalued as Remote Others

The defendants were devalued as remote others or aliens, not only in terms of their citizenship, but also in terms of their ideology. The remote other is seen as threatening. This was the hidden swing value in the majority opinion. Abrams & Co. were threats because they were "alien anarchists":

> All of the five defendants were born in Russia. They were intelligent, had considerable schooling, and, at the time they were arrested, they had lived in the United States terms varying from five to ten years, but none of them had applied for naturalization. Four of them testified as witnesses in their own behalf, and, of these, three frankly avowed that they were "rebels," "revolutionists," "anarchists," that they did not believe in government in any form, and they declared that they had no interest whatever in the Government of the United States. The fourth defendant testified that he was a "socialist," and believed in "a proper kind of government, not capitalistic," but, in his classification, the Government of the United States was "capitalistic."[11]

Value of Candid Discussion versus the Disvalue of the Revolutionary Language

What constituted candid discussion? This was up to debate. Language more amenable to sustaining the status quo and working within the system rather than against it? Also, candid discussions were likely quartered and private instead of ubiquitous and public. It was the equivalent of asking people to lower one's voice and come to a private place to have a conversation rather than shouting from the rooftops.

Value of Intent

Intent was valued for its broadness and flexibility. It could easily be molded to show the malice of the alien anarchists.

Value of Direct Threats

"Aliens" who refuse to abide by the language of accommodation were valued as direct threats. The direct threat assignation would not be conferred on United States' citizens who advocated similar actions, as Justice Holmes pointed out:

> A patriot might think that we were wasting money on aeroplanes, or making more cannon of a certain kind than we needed, and might advocate curtailment with success, yet, even if it turned out that the curtailment hindered and was thought by other minds to have been obviously likely to hinder the United States in the prosecution of the war, no one would hold such conduct a crime.[12]

SUMMARY OF VALUE CONGREGATION

This opinion ostensibly pivoted on the value of the statute. After further axiological review, we see it pivoted on the disvalued defendants, thought to be alien in birth and alien in ideology, which expanded the swath of intent to guarantee their guilt. Their devaluation as remote others or aliens constituted the swing value of the decision that transformed their hair-brained ideas into espionage.

DISSENT BY JUSTICE OLIVER WENDELL HOLMES

Legal Wrapping Paper

Exceptions to the first amendment can be justified only by speech being "immediately dangerous":

> Only the emergency that makes it immediately dangerous to leave the correction of evil counsels to time warrants making any exception to the sweeping command, "Congress shall make no law . . . abridging the freedom of speech."[13]

But, as against dangers peculiar to war, as against others, the principle of the right to free speech is always the same. It is only the present danger of immediate evil or an intent to bring it about that warrants Congress in setting a limit to the expression of opinion where private rights are not concerned.[14]

The First Amendment called for a marketplace of ideas where through competition the best ideas would win out:

> But when men have realized that time has upset many fighting faiths, they may come to believe even more than they believe the very foundations of their own conduct that the ultimate good desired is better reached by free trade in ideas—that the best test of truth is the power of the thought to get itself accepted in the competition of the market, and that truth is the only ground upon which their wishes safely can be carried out.[15]

For Justice Holmes, it could not be proven that ideas in leaflets crippled the war effort:

> But to make the conduct criminal, that statute requires that it should be "with intent by such curtailment to cripple or hinder the United States in the prosecution of the war." It seems to me that no such intent is proved.[16]

> It is necessary where the success of the attempt depends upon others because, if that intent is not present, the actor's aim may be accomplished without bringing about the evils sought to be checked. An intent to prevent interference with the revolution in Russia might have been satisfied without any hindrance to carrying on the war in which we were engaged.[17]

> I think the intent must be the specific intent that I have described, and, for the reasons that I have given, I think that no such intent was proved or existed in fact.[18]

Holmes pointed to the specific intent spelled rather than the more general intent attributed to the defendants by Justice Clarke. He concluded that not only that intent was absent from the leaflet, but also the potency to do any damage to the war effort.

> Now nobody can suppose that the surreptitious publishing of a silly leaflet by an unknown man, without more, would present any immediate danger that its opinions would hinder the success of the government arms or have any appreciable tendency to do so.[19]

CHRONOLOGY OF AUTHORITIES

1791 First Amendment
1798 Sedition Act—introduced to demonstrate the shortcomings of similar laws under similar wartime situations
1905 *Swift & Co. v. United States*, 196 U. S. 375, 196 U. S. 396: The thing done and intended to be done must be perfectly definite
1919 Schenck, Frohwerk and Debs, 249 U. S. 249 U.S. 47, 249 U. S. 204, 249 U. S. 211—cases in which clear and present danger justified curtailing freedom of speech

OPERATIVE VALUES

Value of Human Fallibility, Experimentation, and Process

> That, at any rate, is the theory of our Constitution. It is an experiment, as all life is an experiment. Every year, if not every day, we have to wager our salvation upon some prophecy based upon imperfect knowledge.[20]

Freedom of speech was a protuberant value in this dissent, but so were experimentation and human fallibility. The erring ways of human beings can only be corrected by experimentation and such experimentation is speech or the expression of opinions generally. The marketplace of ideas was a kind of laboratory in which different hypotheses were put forth and only by experimenting with them can truth emerge. Speech was valued as means to guard against human fallibility, which could only be countered by experimentation. The fallibility of human beings was underscored with religious nomenclature like "fighting faiths," "salvation," and "prophecy." The parameters of human understanding were greatly narrowed and thus human understanding was depreciated and epistemic humility embraced.

Value of Marketplace of Ideas

With this greatly depreciated intellectual capacity both in terms of power and value, the value of working out ideas in a marketplace of ideas was greatly appreciated:

> But when men have realized that time has upset many fighting faiths, they may come to believe even more than they believe the very foundations of their own conduct that the ultimate good desired is better reached by free trade in ideas—that the best test of truth is the power of the thought to get itself accepted in the competition of the market, and that truth is the only ground upon which their wishes safely can be carried out.[21]

Values of Tolerance and Empathy

While the values of tolerance and empathy were absent from the majority opinion, they pervaded the dissent as "the defendants are to be made to suffer not for what the indictment alleges, but for the creed that they avow."[22] The value of tolerance opened up a vista of understanding for the defendants, while intolerance closed it down. It allowed Holmes to see the defendants were being punished not for the crimes but for their beliefs.

Value of Intent

Intent was valued for its specificity and definiteness. It marked the difference between saying "I want to go on a vacation" and actually booking flights, hotels, and transportation or "I'd like to kill my husband" and actually buying weapons to do so or hiring a hitman.

Defendants Valued as Non-Threats, The Nebish Factor

The defendants were valued as non-threats to the American government: powerless, immature, ignorant, unimportant people who secretly wrote an idiotic pamphlet:

> Now nobody can suppose that the surreptitious publishing of a silly leaflet by an unknown man, without more, would present any immediate danger that its opinions would hinder the success of the government arms or have any appreciable tendency to do so.[23]

> "[T]hese poor and puny anonymities."[24]

> "[I]gnorance and immaturity."[25]

In essence, know-nothing nobodies represented no threat to the war effort of the United States of America. If they were four gnats on the windshield of a speeding car, that would be saying too much about them. They were negatively valued as objects of pity and ridicule, but not considered threatening far others.

SUMMARY OF VALUE CONGREGATION

Human fallibility, experimentation, and process were valued as intrinsic to the human condition. In our every-day lives, mistake-prone humans go through a process of experimentation to discover the truth. The idea of eliminating other ideas goes against what is best for human beings. In law, freedom of speech guarantees that this truth-bearing process continues. The value confluence or congregation of the values of human fallibility, experimentation, and process in the service of truth-bearing gird the value of freedom of speech. The other operative value concerns the status of the defendants. They were not disvalued as aliens or wild-eyed radicals with the power to disturb the plans of the United States military with their potent pamphlets, but pathetic losers with no power to change the outcome of the war. The values of empathy and tolerance were also encrypted in the dissent. To realize that American patriots just as much as anarchists could criticize the war effort without undermining it presupposed a value of tolerance. Tolerance tethers judgment long enough for us to see that people in glass houses should not throw stones.

RECKONING OF THE ROGUE JUSTICES

Legal Wrapping Paper

The First Amendment overarched the legality of this case and is cast in absolute language: "Congress shall make no law respecting an establishment of religion, or prohibiting the free exercise thereof; or abridging the freedom of speech." The Espionage Act patently contradicted the First Amendment, which has been attacked by the Alien and Sedition Acts of 1798 and the Espionage Act of 1917 and 1918 as well as *Schenck*, *Frohwerk*, and *Debs* in 1919.

CHRONOLOGY OF AUTHORITIES

1791 First Amendment
1798 Alien and Sedition Acts—a mistake not be repeated
1905 Swift & Co. v. United States, 196 U. S. 375, 196 U. S. 396: The thing done and intended to be done must be perfectly definite

SUMMARY OF VALUE CONGREGATION

In this case, it came down to how the defendants were seen. Were they dangerous foreigners or fellow experimenters in free speech? Without epistemic humility and tolerance, the defendants would remain remote others and they would strangled by the law.

NOTES

1. Paul Freund, *On Understanding the Supreme Court* (1949), 27, as quoted by Leslie Kendrick, "On 'Clear and Present Danger,'" *Notre Dame Law Review* 94 (2019): 1669.
2. Leslie Kendrick, "On 'Clear and Present Danger,'" *Notre Dame Law Review* 94 (2019): 1669.
3. Joseph Blocher, "Institutions in the Marketplace of Ideas," *Duke Law Journal* 57, 4 (February 2008): 888.
4. Ibid., 849.

5. John Inazu, "Holmes, Humility, and How Not to Kill Each Other," *Notre Dame Law Review* 94, 4 (2019): 1632.

6. The Espionage Act—June 15, 1917 http://academic.brooklyn.cuny.edu/history/johnson/espionageact.htm#:~:text=Whoever%2C%20when%20the%20United%20States%20is%20at%20war%2C%20shall%20wilfully,convey%20false%20reports%2C%20or%20false.

7. *Abrams v. United States*, 250 U.S. 616, 617 (1919).

8. Ibid., 622.

9. Ibid.

10. Ibid., 621.

11. Ibid., 617–618.

12. Ibid., 627.

13. Ibid., 630–631.

14. Ibid., 628.

15. Ibid., 630.

16. Ibid., 626.

17. Ibid., 628.

18. Ibid., 629.

19. Ibid., 628.

20. Ibid., 630.

21. Ibid.

22. Ibid., 629.

23. Ibid., 628.

24. Ibid., 629.

25. Ibid.

Chapter 6

Personhood v. Property

Dred Scott v. Sandford

NARRATIVE IN A NUTSHELL

Where was Dred Scott born into slavery?

In Virginia around 1799.

Did he move around?

Peter Blow, his original owner, took Scott to Alabama and then St. Louis.

When Blow died?

When Blow died, Dr. John Emerson, an army surgeon, purchased Scott.

How did Scott get to Illinois and Wisconsin?

When Emerson served in the free state of Illinois and later the free Wisconsin Territory, he took Scott with him.

Where slavery was illegal and Scott should have been freed.

Yes.

That's wasn't the end of Emerson's travels?

No. Transferred by the army to Louisiana, Emerson met and married Eliza Irene Sanford and eventually, they settled in Saint Louis.

And then Emerson died?

Yes.

And Sanford's widow refused to allow Scott to buy his freedom?

Yes. Which prompted Scott to litigate.

Who was John Sanford?

Sanford was Eliza's brother and Scott had been transferred to him.

SCHOLARLY INFUSED SCHOLARSHIP

Anti-canonical verdicts like *Dred Scott* possess an instrumental value: they "may serve to cleanse the Constitution of its inequities, smooth the rough edges of historical social conflict, bolster the argument for originalist modes of interpretation, or shed light on constitutional dissensus."[1] Such verdicts remain dormant until they are used, for instance, in theory or political and legal decisions.[2] *Dred Scott* can be disvalued as anti-canon or valued positively as the fodder for the Civil War, the emancipation of Blacks, and a break from a Constitution enshrining white supremacy.[3] By understanding the decision as a powerful weapon for the small minority of fanatical Abolitionists,[4] the nadir value assigned to the case dissipates. To the question "What does a judge or any other person obligated to interpret the Constitution do when their preferred theory of constitutional interpretation yields an evil result?"[5] the answer is always the same: reorient it according to one's values. Chief Justice Taney valued the views of the southern founders of the Constitution, who never could have imagined Blacks as citizens.[6] Often, only one side of the constitutional compromise has been valued (the one that grudgingly accepts slavery in southern states and desires its abolition) rather than the other (the one that grudgingly accepts the liberation of blacks in northern states and desires the universality of slavery). The mixed message of the compromise is overlooked. Axiological inquiry will demonstrate that *Scott* was anti-canonical not only for its decision but also on the basis of a congregation of valuations that buttressed white supremacy.

MAJORITY OPINION BY CHIEF JUSTICE ROGER TANEY

Legal Wrapping Paper

Stripped down, in its bare bones, the legal narrative was, could "Negroes" become U.S. citizens? Or said differently and more bluntly: could slaves become U.S. citizens? Or put even more bluntly: could beings considered as property become U.S. citizens?

> The question is simply this: can a negro whose ancestors were imported into this country and sold as slaves become a member of the political community formed and brought into existence by the Constitution of the United States, and as such become entitled to all the rights, and privileges, and immunities, guarantied by that instrument to the citizen, one of which rights is the privilege of suing in a court of the United States in the cases specified in the Constitution?[7]

> The question then arises, whether the provisions of the Constitution, in relation to the personal rights and privileges to which the citizen of a state should be entitled, embraced the negro African race, at that time in this country or who

> might afterward be imported, who had then or should afterward be made free in any state, and to put it in the power of a single state to make him a citizen of the United States and endue him with the full rights of citizenship in every other state without their consent? Does the Constitution of the United States act upon him whenever he shall be made free under the laws of a state, and raised there to the rank of a citizen, and immediately clothe him with all the privileges of a citizen in every other state, and in its own courts?[8]

> In the opinion of the court, the legislation and histories of the times, and the language used in the Declaration of Independence, show that neither the class of persons who had been imported as slaves nor their descendants, whether they had become free or not, were then acknowledged as a part of the people, nor intended to be included in the general words used in that memorable instrument.[9]

Once a slave, always a slave, the narrative continued, no matter where the Negro resided, the Negro was property.

As Scott was a slave when taken into the State of Illinois by his owner and was there held as such, and brought back in that character, his status as free or slave depended on the laws of Missouri, and not of Illinois.[10]

This is on the same lines as taking a laptop from Missouri to Illinois. The laptop is your property, no matter the state you're in, and so were slaves (sentient property).

CHRONOLOGY OF AUTHORITIES

Chief Justice Taney herded his authorities to demonstrate that even in free states, people of African heritage were always considered inferior and slaves:

1705 Massachusetts law ch. 6 provides any Negro or mulatto striking a Christian will be severely whipped

1717 Province of Maryland law ch. 13, s. 5, declared children of miscegenation slaves

1774 Connecticut act forbade the importation of slaves because of harmful effects on poor whites

1776 Declaration of Independence: "All men are created equal" interpreted to exclude black men

1781 Articles of Confederation, "free inhabitants" excluded those from the African race

1784 Connecticut statute freeing slaves to assist white people and Negroes being returned to masters

1786 Massachusetts passed a law forbidding the marriage of any white person with any negro, Indian, or mulatto

1787 Constitution
Article I, Section 9, Clause 1—beginning in 1808 imporation of persons was not allowed
Article IV, Section 2—slaves escaping to free states must be returned to their masters
1816 New Hampshire—law stipulated only free white citizens allowed in militia
1822 Rhode Island, fined for intermarriages, which were declared null and void
1829 *Le Grand v. Darnall*, 27 U.S. 664 (1829)—ostensibly a descendant of a slave could sue as a citizen in a court of the United States, but the question did not arise and could not have arisen in the case
1833 Connecticut law made it illegal to set up schools for Negroes
1836 Massachusetts revised marriage code to include imprisonment for mixed marriages
1844, Rhode Island marriage laws of 1822 reenacted
1851 *Strader v. Graham*, 51 U.S. (10 How.) 82 (1851)—slaves who traveled to free states once returned to slave states remain slaves

OPERATING VALUES

White Supremacy (Catalyst or Lead Value)

Before addressing the "Negro" issue, the value of white superiority was introduced with respect to "Indians." According to the white supremacist perspective, "Indians" also constituted an inferior people who needed the superior white race to guide them, presumably so they could be improved and also so they wouldn't become an impediment or nuisance:

> It is true that the course of events has brought the Indian tribes within the limits of the United States under subjection to the white race, and it has been found necessary, for their sake as well as our own, to regard them as in a state of pupilage, and to legislate to a certain extent over them and the territory they occupy.[11]

At the time of the writing of the Constitution "Negroes" were considered "subordinate," "inferior," "dominated by the white race," "merchandise," and a means to make "profit." They were the remotest of others, mere objects or property and not citizenship material:

> The words "people of the United States" and "citizens" are synonymous terms, and mean the same thing. They both describe the political body who, according to our republican institutions, form the sovereignty and who hold the power and conduct the Government through their representatives. They are what we familiarly call the "sovereign people," and every citizen is one of this people, and a constituent member of this sovereignty. The question before us is whether the class of persons described in the plea in abatement compose a portion of this people, and are constituent members of this sovereignty? We think they are not, and that they are not included, and were not intended to be included, under the word "citizens" in the Constitution, and can therefore claim none of the rights and privileges which that instrument provides for and secures to citizens of the United States. On the contrary, they were at that time considered as a *subordinate and inferior class of beings who had been subjugated by the dominant race*, [our emphasis] and, whether emancipated or not, yet remained subject to their authority, and had no rights or privileges but such as those who held the power and the Government might choose to grant them.[12]

> They had for more than a century before been regarded as beings of an inferior order, and altogether unfit to associate with the white race either in social or political relations, and so far inferior that they had no rights which the white man was bound to respect, and that the negro might justly and lawfully be reduced to slavery for his benefit. *He was bought and sold, and treated as an ordinary article of merchandise and traffic whenever a profit could be made by it.*[13]

> They [state laws] show that a perpetual and impassable barrier was intended to be erected between the white race and the one which they had reduced to slavery, and governed as subjects with absolute and despotic power, and which they then looked upon as so far below them in the scale of created beings.[14]

Past Practices and Past Morals (Buttressing Value)

Past practices and past morals were valued to justify white superiority. Because the British practiced slavery, that justified Americans practicing slavery:

> And in no nation was this opinion more firmly fixed or more uniformly acted upon than by the English Government and English people. They not only seized them on the coast of Africa and sold them or held them in slavery for their own use, but they took them as ordinary articles of merchandise to every country where they could make a profit on them, and were far more extensively engaged in this commerce than any other nation in the world.

> The opinion thus entertained and acted upon in England was naturally impressed upon the colonies they founded on this side of the Atlantic. And, accordingly, a negro of the African race was regarded by them as an article of property, and held, and bought and sold as such, in every one of the thirteen colonies which united in the Declaration of Independence and afterwards formed the Constitution of the United States. The slaves were more or less numerous in the different colonies as slave labor was found more or less profitable. But no one seems to have doubted the correctness of the prevailing opinion of the time.[15]

In their morality and politics as well their every-day habitual actions in both the private and public spheres, "[t]he civilized portion of the white race" regarded the inferiority of Negroes as fixed, universal, axiomatic, and indisputable.

> *This opinion was at that time fixed and universal in the civilized portion of the white race* [our emphasis]. It was regarded as an axiom in morals as well as in politics which no one thought of disputing or supposed to be open to dispute, and men in every grade and position in society daily and habitually acted upon it in their private pursuits, as well as in matters of public concern, without doubting for a moment the correctness of this opinion.[16]

Justice as a Past Deed (Buttressing Value)

For Justice Taney, justice was valued as a past deed rather than a present construction:

> It is not the province of the court to decide upon the justice or injustice, the policy or impolicy, of these laws. The decision of that question belonged to the political or lawmaking power, to those who formed the sovereignty and framed the Constitution. The duty of the court is to interpret the instrument they have framed with the best lights we can obtain on the subject, and to administer it as we find it, according to its true intent and meaning when it was adopted.[17]

Infallibility of Ancestors (Buttressing Value)

The Founders were valued as infallible (perfectly understanding the language they used) and as their words and ideas are irreproachable, unimpeachable, and cannot be challenged:

> Yet the men who framed this declaration were great men—high in literary acquirements, high in their sense of honor, and incapable of asserting principles

inconsistent with those on which they were acting. They perfectly understood the meaning of the language they used, and how it would be understood by others, and they knew that it would not in any part of the civilized world be supposed to embrace the negro race, which, by common consent, had been excluded from civilized Governments and the family of nations, and doomed to slavery. They spoke and acted according to the then established doctrines and principles, and in the ordinary language of the day, and no one misunderstood them.[18]

Inevitability of Negro Inferiority (Buttressing Value)

The "unhappy black race" was fated to servitude. Valuing this narrative justified stigmatizing and degrading them:

> The unhappy black race were separated from the white by indelible marks, and laws long before established, and were never thought of or spoken of except as property, and when the claims of the owner or the profit of the trader were supposed to need protection.[19]

> [A] class of beings whom they had thus stigmatized, whom, as we are bound out of respect to the State sovereignties to assume they had deemed it just and necessary thus to stigmatize, and upon whom they had impressed such deep and enduring marks of inferiority and degradation.[20]

Safety (Buttressing Value)

Were Negroes considered equal to Whites, this could only serve to disturb the social order and become a safety issue.

> And all of this would be done in the face of the subject race of the same color, both free and slaves, and inevitably producing discontent and insubordination among them, and endangering the peace and safety of the state.
>
> It is impossible, it would seem, to believe that the great men of the slaveholding states, who took so large a share in framing the Constitution of the United States and exercised so much influence in procuring its adoption, could have been so forgetful or regardless of their own safety and the safety of those who trusted and confided in them.[21]

New Knowledge and Awareness (Buttressing Disvalue)

New ideas about the emancipation of Negroes were disvalued, seen as changes in public opinion and feeling rather than enlightenment:

> No one, we presume, supposes that any change in public opinion or feeling, in relation to this unfortunate race, in the civilized nations of Europe or in this country, should induce the court to give to the words of the Constitution a more liberal construction in their favor than they were intended to bear when the instrument was framed and adopted. Such an argument would be altogether inadmissible in any tribunal called on to interpret it. If any of its provisions are deemed unjust, there is a mode prescribed in the instrument itself by which it may be amended; but while it remains unaltered, it must be construed now as it was understood at the time of its adoption. It is not only the same in words, but the same in meaning, and delegates the same powers to the Government, and reserves and secures the same rights and privileges to the citizen; and as long as it continues to exist in its present form, it speaks not only in the same words, but with the same meaning and intent with which it spoke when it came from the hands of its framers and was voted on and adopted by the people of the United States. Any other rule of construction would abrogate the judicial character of this court, and make it the mere reflex of the popular opinion or passion of the day. This court was not created by the Constitution for such purposes. Higher and graver trusts have been confided to it, and it must not falter in the path of duty.[22]

VALUE VIGNETTE

The leading value of white supremacy was buttressed by the values of infallible ancestors, infallible texts, carte blanche acceptance of past practices and morality, justice as a past deed instead of a present construction, the inevitability of black inferiority, and safety concerns, and the disvalue of new knowledge and awareness. This represented a textbook example of a congregation of values and disvalues to enforce oppression. First, value a group of people as property. Devalue any type of new knowledge or awareness that might challenge that view while hyper-valuing past practices and morality that support it; deify ancestors and hyper-value their ideas and written works to the irreproachable gospel; value justice as a past act instead of a present construction; value fate over responsibility (as if it was cruel fate that Negroes ended up as slaves); and value safety concerns and fear of "free" Negroes.

DISSENT BY JUSTICE JOHN MCLEAN

Legal Wrapping Paper

The case spilled over into the following six areas:

1. The locality of slavery, as settled by this court and the courts of the states.
2. The relation that the federal government bears to slavery in the states.
3. The power of Congress to establish Territorial Governments and to prohibit the introduction of slavery therein.
4. The effect of taking slaves into a new state or territory, and so holding them, where slavery is prohibited.
5. Whether the return of a slave under the control of his master, after being entitled to his freedom, reduces him to his former condition.
6. Whether the laws of Missouri are binding on the Supreme Court.[23]

CHRONOLOGY OF AUTHORITIES

The authorities set forth by McLean affirmed the value of Negroes as persons and not merchandise. A plethora of precedents pointed to a single point: slaves gained their freedom once entering states, territories, and countries that have abolished slavery. These precedents included laws from the ancient western tradition, European practices, and U.S. statutes.

Ancient Roman law—slaves taken outside of Rome were emancipated.

Civil Law in Contemporary Europe—slavery could only exist in territory where established and slaves who travel beyond such territories cannot be reclaimed.

1772 *Somerset v. Steuart*, slavery a municipal issue.

1787 free slaves within the jurisdiction of Northwest Territory could claim freedom in courts of Mississippi.

1787 Constitution of the United States, while government not "especially" created for "colored people,"[24] the rights of suffrage would improve their condition.

1796 The Act of Maryland 2 Maxcy's Laws 351 declared that anyone who shall bring any negro, mulatto, or other slave into Maryland was to be set free.

United States Territories Practices—in U.S. territories (Louisiana, Florida, Texas), people of different social classes, combinations, and color were admitted as citizens.

1820 Rankin v. Lydia, if law was the ultimate justification, then laws that allowed slavery in one state are equal to laws that prohibit it in another.

1820 Missouri Compromise, prohibited slavery with exception of Missouri north of the 36°30′ parallel.

18?? *Smith v. Smith*, 13 Louisiana Rep. 441, *Thomas v. Generis*, Louisiana Rep. 483, *Harry et al. v. Decker and Hopkins*, Walker's Mississippi Rep. 36—O.

18?? *Griffith v. Fanny*, 1 Virginia Rep. 143—Constitution of Ohio freed Negro held in servitude in Ohio by a deed executed in Virginia.

1824 *Winny v. Whitesides*, 1 Missouri Rep. 473, at October term—a slave who gained freedom in Illinois cannot be enslaved by reentering a slave state.

1820 *Julia v. McKinney*, 3 Missouri Rep. 279, a slave working in Illinois if only for a limited amount of time became free.

1833 *Jacob v. Sharp*, Court held when doubt entered into the construction of will regarding the emancipation of a slave; freedom takes precedence over doubt.

1835 *Marie-Louise v. Marot*, No. 2748, 8 La. 475. Slaves taken to foreign countries where slavery had been abolished could not subsequently be returned to the state of slavery.

1835 *Wilson v. Melvin*, 4 Mo., Court instructed the jury that slaveholder who left Tennessee for Illinois with his slaves was an Illinois sojourner.

1842 *Prigg v. Pennsylvania*—no nation need accept slavery even if other countries support it

1846 *Josephine v. Poultney*, 1 La. Ann. 329—slaves taken by masters take them to free state and whose masters reside there are free and that freedom abided even with their return to Louisiana.

1851 South Carolina Court of Appeals contended that a slave taken to a free state became free.

OPERATIVE VALUES

Disvalue of Slavery (Leading or Catalyzing Value)

Slavery was absolutely wrong:

> But if we are to turn our attention to the dark ages of the world, why confine our view to colored slavery? On the same principles, white men were made slaves. All slavery has its origin in power, and is against right.[25]

Why was slavery wrong? Slaves were not property. Slaves were children of God, responsible for obeying divine and human law, and like all other people have a soul that exists after this life: "A slave is not a mere chattel. He bears the impress of his Maker, and is amenable to the laws of God and man, and he is destined to an endless existence."[26] Slavery was also wrong because it was "piracy" and unchristian.[27]

Fallible Ancestors and Fallible Texts and Value of New Knowledge and Awareness (Buttressing Values)

Instead of viewing laws as set in stone and ancestors as the immaculate stone-setters, critique was valued. McLean embraced the following articulated by Judge Grier in *Pease v. Peck*, 59 U.S. 595 (1855):

> Accordingly, our reports furnish many cases of exceptions to it. In all cases where there is a settled construction of the laws of the a [*sic*] State by its highest judicature established by admitted precedent, it is the practice of the courts of the United States to receive and adopt it without criticism or further inquiry. When the decisions of the State court are not consistent, we do not feel bound to follow the last if it is contrary to our own convictions, and much more is this the case where, after a long course of consistent decisions, some new light suddenly springs up, or an excited public opinion has elicited new doctrines subversive of former safe precedent.[28]

Value of Occasional, Pigeon-Holed, and Conditional Personhood

The attraction to European practices was that slavery could only exist in territories where it was established and thus fugitive slaves could not be returned to their masters in slave states:

> There is no nation in Europe which considers itself bound to return to his master a fugitive slave under the civil law or the law of nations. On the contrary, the slave is held to be free where there is no treaty obligation, or compact in some other form, to return him to his master.[29]

There were, then, spaces on the planet where slavery was prohibited.

Disvalue of Past Practices and Morality in Favor of Ideals (Buttressing Value)

> I prefer the lights of Madison, Hamilton, and Jay as a means of construing the Constitution in all its bearings, rather than to look behind that period into a traffic which is now declared to be piracy, and punished with death by Christian nations. I do not like to draw the sources of our domestic relations from so dark a ground.[30]

The Inevitability of Negro Inferiority (Buttressing Value)

Whereas Chief Justice Taney described the plight of "Negroes" to some kind of inevitability, McClean recognized that Negroes ended up slaves not because of fate, but because of slave trafficking introduced by white people.

> We need not refer to the mercenary spirit which introduced the infamous traffic in slaves to show the degradation of negro slavery in our country. This system was imposed upon our colonial settlements by the mother country, and it is due to truth to say that the commercial colonies and States were chiefly engaged in the traffic.[31]

Value of Safety (Buttressing Value)

"Colored citizens" fit into society and their exclusion was merely a matter of taste:

> In the argument, it was said that a colored citizen would not be an agreeable member of society. This is more a matter of taste than of law. Several of the States have admitted persons of color to the right of suffrage, and, in this view, have recognised them as citizens, and this has been done in the slave as well as the free States.[32]

VALUE VIGNETTE

The leading value was not white supremacy, but personhood in two senses: one absolute, the other conditional, with the conditional one taking precedence. Yet once Negroes were valued as persons in any sense, then new knowledge and awareness could be readily accepted regarding oppressive past practices and moral codes devalued. This carried over to finding original texts like the Constitution open to interpretation and seeing the oppression of Negroes as socially constructed instead of divinely ordained and Negroes as members of society. The value of personhood in both senses animated the buttressing values.

RECKONING OF THE ROGUE JUSTICES

The reduction of human beings to property is an invitation for wholesale oppression. This is the crux of the issue.

LEGAL WRAPPING PAPER

The opening paragraph of the Constitution envisioned a great nation aspiring toward ideals not yet realized but always on the horizon:

> We the People of the United States, in Order to form a more perfect Union, establish Justice, insure domestic Tranquility, provide for the common defence, promote the general Welfare, and secure the Blessings of Liberty to ourselves and our Posterity, do ordain and establish this Constitution for the United States of America.

"Slavery" was never part of an ideal (especially justice) but an evil that has no place in the vision of a great nation. "Slavery" was part of the compromise between the anti-slavery Founders and pro-slavery Founders.

Numerous precedents set forth by Justice McLean in his dissent showed that slavery existed because of law. In nations and territories where slavery was law, there could be slaves. In nations and territories where slavery was abolished, there would not be slaves. Moreover, once a slave entered nations, territories, or states in which slavery was abolished, that slave was no longer a slave, but a free person.

CHRONOLOGY OF PRECEDENTS

Declaration of Independence—"All men are created equal" as an ideal of increasing inclusion indicative of Enlightenment philosophy trending toward equality and republican governments and away from inequality and stratified cultures

Constitution of United States—a document that never used the word "slave" and stated beginning in 1808 the importation of persons could not occur (the use of the term "persons" indicates that Negroes were persons all along)

Authorities adduced by Justice McLean—offer a partial but not full protection of personhood (occasional and pigeon-holed personhood), operative in certain spaces

OPERATIVE VALUES

Value of Pervasive Personhood (Leading Value)

All human beings are persons. Persons are not property. They own themselves and no one owns them because each has a unique subjective view of the world. They are aware of their own freedom and thus have a right to self-determination.

Value of Incompleteness of Texts (Buttressing Value)

The original texts of the United States were conceived and written by brilliant but historically pigeonholed individuals. The Constitution was written in the folds of history and its true message could only be unfolded and brought to fruition by people who come after and begin to see its full scope, both strong and weak.

Value of New Knowledge of Awareness (Buttressing Value)

Law enables habit, and habit enables law. It is a hard cycle to break. Its repetition transforms law and practices emanating from law into seeming certainties. Chief Justice Taney could point to many laws forbidding intermarriage and educating Negroes. Codified and concretized, these statutes were ossified. New knowledge and awareness challenge the seeming certainties and when valued counters ignorance and carte blanche acceptance of morality and common practices. It's not just the decision that makes Scott anti-canonical. It's how the decision was made in terms of its values and disvalues.

NOTES

1. Jamal Greene, "The Anticanon," *Harvard Law Review* 125 (2011): 385.
2. Ibid., 384–385.
3. Ibid., 412.
4. Wallace Mendelson, "Dred Scott's Case—Reconsidered," *Minnesota Law Review* (1953): 24.
5. Mark A. Graber, "Desperately Ducking Slavery: Dred Scott and Contemporary Constitutional Theory," *Constitutional Commentary* (1997): 318, https://scholarship.law.umn.edu/concomm/686.
6. Paul Finkelman, "Slavery in the United States: Persons or Property?," in *The Legal Understanding of Slavery: From the Historical to the Contemporary*, ed. Jean Allain (2012): 116, https://scholarship.law.duke.edu/cgi/viewcontent.cgi?article=5386&context=faculty_scholarship.
7. *Dred Scott v. Sandford*, 60 U.S. 393, 403 (1856).

8. Ibid.
9. Ibid., 407.
10. Ibid., 452.
11. Ibid., 404.
12. Ibid., 404–405.
13. Ibid., 407.
14. Ibid.
15. Ibid., 407–408.
16. Ibid., 407.
17. Ibid., 405.
18. Ibid., 410.
19. Ibid.
20. Ibid., 416.
21. Ibid., 417.
22. Ibid., 426.
23. Ibid., 533–534.
24. Ibid., 537.
25. Ibid., 538.
26. Ibid., 550.
27. Ibid., 537.
28. Ibid., 563.
29. Ibid., 534.
30. Ibid., 537.
31. Ibid.
32. Ibid., 533.

Chapter 7

Integration as a Means of Securing Personal Liberty for All and Preserving the Union v. Segregation as a Means of Limiting Personal Liberty and Permanently Securing White Supremacy

Plessy v. Ferguson

NARRATIVE IN A NUTSHELL

Who was Homère Adolphe Plessy?

A French-speaking Creole, who in 1892 took a vacant seat in a coach designated for whites only on a train departing from New Orleans and headed for Covington, Louisiana.

Could Plessy pass?

Yes. According to court documents, he was calculated to be seven-eighths white.

When Plessy refused to leave the all-white coach, I guess there was a commotion.

You could say that. Plessy was forcibly removed and imprisoned. He committed a crime by refusing to obey the color-coded seating arrangement spawned from white supremacy.

VALUE-INFUSED SCHOLARSHIP

Scholarship on *Plessy* navigates through many value-laden waters, including racial purity, Judge Harlan's interpretation of the civil war amendments, and reassessments around the notions color-blindness and color-consciousness.

> The logic of white supremacy interested them not at all: it is hard to justify white supremacy, the superiority of "white blood," when one defines as a Negro anyone with one-sixteenth, one-eighth, or one-quarter "Negro blood"; indeed, this is logically a patent admission of the supremacy of "Negro blood," one part of which could apparently overwhelm an infinite number of contributions made by white ancestors.[1]

Yet the logic of white supremacy can be understood in terms of value. Supremacy can be valued in terms of strength. In a tug of war, for example, the team that pulls the other team to its side is stronger and thus supreme. Supremacy can also be valued in terms of purity. As an absolute value, it must be seen as having no relationship with any other value, having absolutely nothing to do with it. Once into a relationship, it loses its absolute purity. The misbegotten notion that a woman is made "impure" by even a single premarital sexual relationship goes along the same lines. Valuing "propositions that are in some sense deeply connected to the Constitution, proximate to it, that have been ratified in some profound way, formally or informally, by the American people in the same manner that the Constitution has come to abide in our hearts and minds" (for example, The Declaration of Independence, Federalist Papers, The Gettysburg Address, Martin Luther King Jr.'s "I Have a Dream" speech, *Brown v. Board of Education*, and the Northwest Ordinance) leads to the conclusion that Justice Harlan's vision included yet transcended equality and liberty to integration and fraternity.[2] On the flip side, Americans who once felt the sting of oppression as immigrants have turned their backs on *Plessy*:

> Perhaps the most egregious slip into this amoral morass is the fact that the Plessy core rationale—that those deemed by society as inferior can constitutionally be treated as such—has later been embraced by the very same groups that previously cried foul when they were the target of oppression.[3]

Justice must be color-conscious as much as it is color-blind if it is "to remedy the evils of past discrimination based on color or to prevent *new evils of discrimination* based on color."[4] Justice Harlan's color-blindness was not enough to bring about a greater value. If Justice John Marshall Harlan "viewed the Reconstruction amendments as infusing the entire Constitution with new meaning and purpose,"[5] he regarded those Amendments as the Constitution's lead or overarching values.

LEGAL LANDSCAPE VIA VALUES

The majority decision by Justice Henry Billings Brown amounted to an end-run around the Thirteenth and Fourteenth Amendments. At base, it promoted segregation. This value (for him) could not be trumpeted and announced in a full-throated fashion under the watchful eyes of the Thirteenth and Fourteenth Amendments. On the other hand, the dissent by Justice John Marshall Harlan gave full breadth to and breathed life into the Thirteenth and Fourteenth Amendments and in them he found absolute liberty and freedom. At base, the dissent promoted integration ("co-mingling") as a means to secure individual liberty. Without such integration, Blacks would be denied access to certain spaces. Also, the dissent espoused the value of social harmony by stating in so many words without integration that the United States of America could only look forward to continued hostilities and an absence of peace, which would be bad for both Blacks and Whites and the nation as a whole.

In the majority opinion, great lengths were gone to justify segregation. The word was never used in the majority opinion but hovered like a dark cloud over every idea. In the hands of segregationists, the Thirteenth and Fourteenth Amendments were defanged and declawed and deviously delimited. The spawn of slavery was arguably not as powerful as its progenitor but had as its mission to deprive Blacks of liberties and thereby diminish them. This control had to be with where Blacks could and couldn't be, what spaces they could be in and which they couldn't. When Blacks were denied spaces on a train coach on the basis of their skin color, their liberties were being denied.

No, Monsieur Plessy was not being enchained on a plantation and forced to pick cotton sixteen hours a day for the rest of his short, miserable life. Such was the degrading life of the slave as a laborer. But Monsieur Plessy was being treated as inferior by not being able to comingle with white people on a train coach, as were Black people who were legally prevented from comingling with whites in schools or theaters or in marriage. These carryovers from slavery were badges of inferiority denying Black people their full personal liberty. For Justice Brown in the majority opinion, separate and equal was a step up from slavery and justifiable. For Justice Harlan in his dissent, equal and separate was a step down from the ideal of "universal" or absolute freedom in the Thirteenth and Fourteenth Amendments. Justice Brown thought this feeling of inferiority due to segregation as a phantom in the head of Black people:

> We consider the underlying fallacy of the plaintiff's argument to consist in the assumption that the enforced separation of the two races stamps the colored race with a badge of inferiority. If this be so, it is not by reason of anything found in the act, but solely because the colored race chooses to put that construction upon it.[6]

Justice Harlan saw the badge of inferiority stemming from segregation as anything but a mind mirage, but as a concrete political reality: "The arbitrary separation of citizens on the basis of race while they are on a public highway is a badge of servitude wholly inconsistent with the civil freedom and the equality before the law established by the Constitution."[7]

It doesn't take much imagination to see where this was going and how this statute could justify pervasive segregation:

> If a State can prescribe, as a rule of civil conduct, that whites and blacks shall not travel as passengers in the same railroad coach, why may it not so regulate the use of the streets of its cities and towns as to compel white citizens to keep on one side of a street and black citizens to keep on the other? Why may it not, upon like grounds, punish whites and blacks who ride together in streetcars or in open vehicles on a public road or street? Why may it not require sheriffs to assign whites to one side of a courtroom and blacks to the other? And why may it not also prohibit the commingling of the two races in the galleries of legislative halls or in public assemblages convened for the consideration of the political questions of the day? Further, if this statute of Louisiana is consistent with the personal liberty of citizens, why may not the State require the separation in railroad coaches of native and naturalized citizens of the United States, or of Protestants and Roman Catholics?[8]

Justice Brown could not envision this future world of pervasive integration, invested as he was in the value of segregation and belabored with the mistaken belief that police born and bred into segregation would exercise the law in good faith:

> In this connection, it is also suggested by the learned counsel for the plaintiff in error that the same argument that will justify the state legislature in requiring railways to provide separate accommodations for the two races will also authorize them to require separate cars to be provided for people whose hair is of a certain color, or who are aliens, or who belong to certain nationalities, or to enact laws requiring colored people to walk upon one side of the street and white people upon the other, or requiring white men's houses to be painted white and colored men's black, or their vehicles or business signs to be of different colors, upon the theory that one side of the street is as good as the other, or that a house or vehicle of one color is as good as one of another color. The reply to all this is that every exercise of the police power must be reasonable, and extend only to such laws as are enacted in good faith for the promotion for the public good, and not for the annoyance or oppression of a particular class.[9]

Value Difference in Equal but Separate and Separate but Equal

The Louisiana statute read:

> that all railway companies carrying passengers in their coaches in this State shall provide equal but separate accommodations for the white and colored races by providing two or more passenger coaches for each passenger train, or by dividing the passenger coaches by a partition so as to secure separate accommodations: *Provided,* That this section shall not be construed to apply to street railroads. No person or persons, shall be admitted to occupy seats in coaches other than the ones assigned to them on account of the race they belong to.[10]

"Equal but separate"? Did it make a difference in this legal fray? Justice Brown explained that the value equality more than compensated for the value of separateness:

> Upon the other hand, where a statute of Louisiana required those engaged in the transportation of passengers among the States to give to all persons traveling within that State, upon vessels employed in that business, equal rights and privileges in all parts of the vessel, without distinction on account of race or color, and subjected to an action for damages the owner of such a vessel, who excluded colored passengers on account of their color from the cabin set aside by him for the use of whites, it was held to be, so far as it applied to interstate commerce, unconstitutional and void. Hall v. De Cuir, 95 U. S. 48. The court in this case, however, expressly disclaimed that it had anything whatever to do with the statute as a regulation of internal commerce, or affecting anything else than commerce among the States.[11]

Through the lens of absolute liberty (liberty as a sacred zenith value), Justice Harlan could hardly agree:

> If evils will result from the commingling of the two races upon public highways established for the benefit of all, they will be infinitely less than those that will surely come from state legislation regulating the enjoyment of civil rights upon the basis of race. We boast of the freedom enjoyed by our people above all other peoples. But it is difficult to reconcile that boast with a state of the law which, practically, puts the brand of servitude and degradation upon a large class of our fellow citizens, our equals before the law. The thin disguise of "equal" accommodations for passengers in railroad coaches will not mislead anyone, nor atone for the wrong this day done.[12]

In the majority opinion, equal was valued over separate. Since the accommodations were equal, that took precedence over the fact that they were separate. As long as they were equal, what did it matter if they were separate? In the dissent, separate took precedence over equal. The separateness was seen as a negative value, creating spaces in which some people were denied access. Equality then became much less valued when understood as the result of such denial. Justice Harlan emphasized the exclusion aspect of the phrase. One group of people was being legally excluded from comingling with another group. The value of equality recedes. The fact that each had an equal portion was diminished because of exclusion.

Valuing the "equal" aspect of the phrase enhanced the "separate" aspect of the phrase. First and foremost, the policy was fair because each group is getting an equal share. The law in question called it "equal and separate" for that reason.

Value of Past Practices and Precedents

Judge Brown embraced past precedents that separated whites and blacks in "public conveyances":

> In determining the question of reasonableness, it is at liberty to act with reference to the established usages, customs, and traditions of the people, and with a view to the promotion of their comfort and the preservation of the public peace and good order. Gauged by this standard, we cannot say that a law which authorizes or even requires the separation of the two races in public conveyances is unreasonable, or more obnoxious to the Fourteenth Amendment than the acts of Congress requiring separate schools for colored children in the District of Columbia, the constitutionality of which does not seem to have been questioned, or the corresponding acts of state legislatures.[13]

And why not throw in as more support, anti-miscegenation laws, which were "universally recognized":

> Laws forbidding the intermarriage of the two races may be said in a technical sense to interfere with the freedom of contract, and yet have been universally recognized as within the police power of the State.[14]

As long as these laws were reasonable, it was justifiable:

> The reply to all this is that every exercise of the police power must be reasonable, and extend only to such laws as are enacted in good faith for the promotion for the public good, and not for the annoyance or oppression of a particular class.[15]

So far, then, as a conflict with the Fourteenth Amendment was concerned, the case reduced itself to the question of whether the statute of Louisiana was a reasonable regulation, and, with respect to this, there must necessarily be a large discretion on the part of the legislature. In determining the question of reasonableness, it was liberty to act with reference to the established usages, customs, and traditions of the people, and with a view to the promotion of their comfort and the preservation of the public peace and good order.[16]

Justice Harlan took the other side of the issue. He recognized and respected the significance of precedents, "But however construed, the intent of the legislature is to be respected, if the particular statute in question is valid, although the courts, looking at the public interests, may conceive the statute to be both unreasonable and impolitic."[17]

Yet he also understood some laws had been made prior to the adoption of the Thirteenth and Fourteenth Amendments and others had been enacted in places where the dominance of racial prejudice and the institution of slavery would not have allowed for pushback:

> I do not deem it necessary to review the decisions of state courts to which reference was made in argument. Some, and the most important, of them are wholly inapplicable because rendered prior to the adoption of the last amendments of the Constitution, when colored people had very few rights which the dominant race felt obliged to respect. Others were made at a time when public opinion in many localities was dominated by the institution of slavery, when it would not have been safe to do justice to the black man, and when, so far as the rights of blacks were concerned, race prejudice was, practically, the supreme law of the land. Those decisions cannot be guides in the era introduced by the recent amendments of the supreme law, which established universal civil freedom, gave citizenship to all born or naturalized in the United States and residing here, obliterated the race line from our systems of governments, National and State, and placed our free institutions upon the broad and sure foundation of the equality of all men before the law.[18]

Value of Social Harmony

Separate but equal laws endangered the social harmony of the United States by using law to implant the seeds of hate and mistrust. Justice Harlan recognized the interconnectedness of the Blacks and Whites and thought it in their best interests to seek a common government:

> The present decision, it may well be apprehended, will not only stimulate aggressions, more or less brutal and irritating, upon the admitted rights of colored citizens, but will encourage the belief that it is possible, by means of state enactments, to defeat the beneficent purposes which the people of the United States had in view when they adopted the recent amendments of the Constitution, by one of which the blacks of this country were made citizens of

the United States and of the States in which they respectively reside, and whose privileges and immunities, as citizens, the States are forbidden to abridge. Sixty millions of whites are in no danger from the presence here of eight millions of blacks. The destinies of the two races in this country are indissolubly linked together, and the interests of both require that the common government of all shall not permit the seeds of race hate to be planted under the sanction of law. What can more certainly arouse race hate, what more certainly create and perpetuate a feeling of distrust between these races, than state enactments which, in fact, proceed on the ground that colored citizens are so inferior and degraded that they cannot be allowed to sit in public coaches occupied by white citizens. That, as all will admit, is the real meaning of such legislation as was enacted in Louisiana.

The sure guarantee of the peace and security of each race is the clear, distinct, unconditional recognition by our governments, National and State, of every right that inheres in civil freedom, and of the equality before the law of all citizens of the United States, without regard to race.[19]

Justice Brown, too, valued social harmony, but thought it best actualized through segregation:

In determining the question of reasonableness, it is at liberty to act with reference to the established usages, customs, and traditions of the people, and with a view to the promotion of their comfort and the preservation of the public peace and good order.[20]

Clash of Values: Segregation and Liberty

While the word "segregation" never appeared in the majority opinion, it was the proverbial elephant in the room. As Justice Harlan declared: "Everyone knows that the statute in question had its origin in the purpose not so much to exclude white persons from railroad cars occupied by blacks as to exclude colored people from coaches occupied by or assigned to white persons."[21] Most obviously, citing legal precedents affirming the segregation of the races in schools and theaters and anti-miscegenation laws sent a loud segregationist message. As did the desire to abide by "the established usages, customs, and traditions of the people," "the people" being white people and those usages, customs, and traditions being segregationist in nature. Segregation could also be justified on the basis of the inferiority of a group of people:

Legislation is powerless to eradicate racial instincts or to abolish distinctions based upon physical differences, and the attempt to do so can only result in

> accentuating the difficulties of the present situation. If the civil and political rights of both races be equal, one cannot be inferior to the other civilly or politically. If one race be inferior to the other socially, the Constitution of the United States cannot put them upon the same plane.[22]

Justice Harlan rejected "the imposition of any burdens or disabilities that constituted badges of inferiority or servitude"[23]; supported "universal civil freedom in this country,"[24] approvingly quoted personal freedom as "'the power of locomotion, of changing situation, or removing one's person to whatsoever places one's own inclination may direct, without imprisonment or restraint unless by due course of law'"[25]; recognized "in view of the Constitution, in the eye of the law, there is in this country no superior, dominant, ruling class of citizens"[26]; and declared "the statute of Louisiana is inconsistent with the personal liberty of citizens, white and black, in that State, and hostile to both the spirit and letter of the Constitution of the United States."[27]

HOW DIFFERENT VALUES ANIMATED THE CIVIL WAR AMENDMENTS

Viewed side by side, it becomes clear how value animated the Civil War Amendments in different ways for each justice. For Justice Brown, slavery was seen as the image of a person in bondage or as property or a person controlling the labor and services of another person such that person was legally deprived of his person, property, and services. Yet for Justice Brown, denying Black Americans to comingle with Whites in train coaches, classrooms, and theaters would not inviolate liberty. Liberty was not valued absolutely (as a sacred zenith value), but distilled for segregationist purposes. For Justice Harlan, liberty was valued as a sacred zenith value. Any restriction preventing Blacks from occupying public space was considered a badge of slavery and servitude. This was where the value action takes place. The dissent valued liberty as an absolute while the majority opinion though not disvaluing it restricted it. Such restrictions of liberty hearkened back to slave days and were considered badges of inferiority, of slavery or servitude. In other words, a group of people was singled out and identified as not having the power to occupy certain spaces. While for Justice Brown this did not constitute a badge of inferiority, for Justice Harlan it certainly did. The badges of inferiority branded black people as inferior to whites by restricting them from comingling with whites.

When humans were valued one-dimensionally rather than multidimensionally, the full spectrum of their humanity was ignored, and they could not be seen as free beings deserving of universal freedom. A standalone Fourteenth Amendment could be bent to the will of the state and thereby depreciated.

Table 7.1 Defusing or Infusing the Civil War Amendments

Majority Opinion by Judge Brown	*Dissent by Justice Harlan*
One-Dimensional Value of the Thirteenth Amendment	*Multi-Dimensional Value of the Thirteenth Amendment*
"*Slavery implies involuntary servitude* [our emphasis]—a state of bondage; the ownership of mankind as a chattel, or at least the control of the labor and services of one man for the benefit of another, and the absence of a legal right to the disposal of his own person, property and services."[1]	"It [Thirteenth Amendment] not only struck down the institution of slavery as previously existing in the United States, but *it prevents the imposition of any burdens or disabilities that constitute badges of slavery or servitude* [our emphasis]. It decreed *universal civil freedom* [our emphasis] in this country."[2]
Devaluation of Fourteenth Amendment	*Fortification of Thirteenth Amendment with Fourteenth and Fifteenth Amendment*
"Positive rights and privileges are undoubtedly secured by the Fourteenth Amendment, but they are secured by way of prohibition against state laws and state proceedings affecting those rights and privileges, and by power given to Congress to legislate for the purpose of carrying such prohibition into effect, and such legislation must necessarily be predicated upon such supposed state laws or state proceedings, and be directed to the correction of their operation and effect."[3]	"These two amendments, if enforced according to their true intent and meaning, will protect all the civil rights that pertain to freedom and citizenship. Finally, and to the end that no citizen should be denied, on account of his race, the privilege of participating in the political control of his country, it as declared by the Fifteenth Amendment that [all citizens can vote]."[4]
Separating Political and Social Equality	*Integrating Social and Political Equality*
"The object of the amendment was undoubtedly to enforce the absolute equality of the two races before the law, but, in the nature of things, it could not have been intended to abolish distinctions based upon color, or to enforce social, as distinguished from political, equality, or a commingling of the two races upon terms unsatisfactory to either [*social inequalities are valued over political equality*]."[5]	"[T]he statute of Louisiana is inconsistent with the personal liberty of citizens, white and black, in that State, and hostile to both *the spirit and letter of the Constitution of the United States* [our emphasis]. . . . Slavery, as an institution tolerated by law would, it is true, have disappeared from our country, but there would remain a power in the States, by sinister legislation, to interfere with the full enjoyment of the blessings of freedom to regulate civil rights [*absolute value*]."[6]

Source: *Plessy v. Ferguson*, 163 U.S. 537 (1896).
[1]Ibid., 542.
[2]Ibid., 555.
[3]Ibid., 547.
[4]Ibid., 555.
[5]Ibid., 544.
[6]Ibid., 563–564.

However, a Fourteenth Amendment buttressed by both the Thirteenth and Fifteenth Amendments became a sacred zenith value. Those who valued freedom preferred to see social freedom as an extension of political freedom, while the depreciators of freedom make the two loose and separate.

RECKONING OF ROGUE THE JUSTICES

Justice Brown claimed: "If the two races are to meet upon terms of social equality, it must be the result of natural affinities, a mutual appreciation of each other's merits, and a voluntary consent of individuals." But how can this happen without comingling? How can we have natural affinities with people we can never meet? How can we appreciate their merits if we don't know what their merits because they are alien to us due to their remoteness? Without knowing the merits of other people or being in spaces where natural affinities can develop, voluntary consent is skewed toward the continuance of segregation. The other two conditions make a mockery of voluntary consent inasmuch as the scope of choices is limited to knowledge of only one culture.

Holding liberty to its fullest in both its theoretical and practical aspects and recognizing that personal liberty is secured by comingling were the leading values in the rogue view of this case. A free country is freedom for people to move through and occupy public spaces. Exclusionary laws, tactics, and stratagems fully express the disvalue of segregation and promote social parallelism in which whites choose contact with blacks only to exploit them. Both individual liberty and the social good of the United States of America depend upon comingling of the races. Criminalizing presence in public spaces is tantamount to saying that the offender is trespassing, as if on someone's private property. Justice Harlan read into the Thirteenth and Fourteenth Amendments the idea that vestiges of slavery were tantamount to slavery itself. The value of universal liberty (as a sacred zenith value) paved the way for his interpretation. The accession of the value of segregation in the majority opinion paved the way for reading the Thirteenth and Fourteenth Amendments to diminish the liberty of Blacks. The Constitution is not simply filled with ideas that have no connection with the social world. In fact, the Constitution is the beacon of light toward which social practices aim. Therefore, to disconnect political equality from social equality amounts to ignoring ideals, even disdaining them. It would be a bit like saying the Ten Commandments were great in theory, but not living in light of them. Segregation laws and practices are not living light of the Thirteenth and Fourteenth Amendments of the Constitution. They are looking up at that shining city on the hill and then running in the opposite direction.

NOTES

1. John P. Roche, "*Plessy v. Ferguson: Requiescat in Pace*," *University of Pennsylvania Law Review* 103 (1954): 45.
2. Akhil Reed Amar, "*Plessy v. Ferguson* and the Anti-Canon," *Pepperdine Law Review* 39, 1 (2013): 76.
3. Maureen Johnson, "*Separate But (Un)Equal:* Why Institutionalized Anti-Racism is the Answer to the Never-Ending Cycle of *Plessy v. Ferguson*," *University of Richmond Law Review* 52 (2018): 328.
4. Hon. John Minor Wisdom, "*Plessy v. Ferguson*—100 Years Later," *Washington and Lee Law Review* 9 (1996): 20.
5. John A. Powell, "The Law and Significance of *Plessy*." *The Russell Sage Foundation Journal of the Social Sciences* 7, 1 (February 2021): 27.
6. Plessy v. Ferguson, 163, U.S., 537, 551.
7. Ibid., 562.
8. Ibid., 557–558.
9. Ibid., 549–550.
10. Ibid., 540.
11. Ibid., 546.
12. Ibid., 562.
13. Ibid., 550–551.
14. Ibid., 550.
15. Ibid.
16. Ibid., 550.
17. Ibid., 559.
18. Ibid., 563.
19. Ibid., 560.
20. Ibid., 550.
21. Ibid., 557.
22. Ibid., 551–552.
23. Ibid., 555.
24. Ibid., 563.
25. Ibid., 557.
26. Ibid., 559.
27. Ibid., 563.

Chapter 8

Economic Liberty over Paternalism v. Judicious State Intervention over Exploitative Liberty v. Malleable Constitution v. Dubious Liberty

Lochner v. New York

NARRATIVE IN A NUTSHELL

It's 1905 and since 1895 the state of New York had a law that bakers weren't allowed to work more than 10 hours a day and 60 hours a week.

And?

There were people who argued that this law interfered with the liberty of the employer-employee contractual process, for example, Joseph Lochner, owner of Lochner's Home Bakery in Utica.

And what was purpose of limiting the number of hours bakers could work?

Health concerns. Spending that length of time exposed to heat and chemicals could harm bakers.

And bakers, having little or no leverage with their bosses, had to look elsewhere for help. . . .

Thus, enter the state.

AXIOLOGICAL ANALYSIS OF VALUE-INFUSED SCHOLARSHIP

Lochner scholarship gravitates toward two distinct camps: one libertarian, the other progressive. Those heavily invested in such libertarian values as individuality, freedom, and limited government see the decision as justified. Their narrative plays up laissez-faire constitutionalism and attributes the liberal misinterpretation of *Lochner* (as pro-big business and anti-poor) to allowing "prejudice to infect their broader constitutional jurisprudence."[1] Yet this viewpoint "fits nicely into the libertarian vision," expressing their lead values.[2] In particular, "Conservatives can now have their cake and eat it, too: they can support judicial intervention to invalidate government regulation of the marketplace while pledging interpretive fidelity to the Constitution's original meaning."[3] Each side may call the other prejudiced or blind (a common ploy), but actually both are simply coming at it from and seeing it from different value vantage points. Language like "he Court continued to ruthlessly apply the doctrine at this time period" and that right of contract superseded essential state services (public health and well-being)[4] reveal a sacred cow-scapegoat value scheme (compassion over ruthlessness) and in association with such a valuation, public health, and well-being preferred to the right of contract. One critique of adjudication points the majority not grasping the high value that was at stake: "The justices' failure was in a sense a lack of humility: an inability, or refusal, to understand that although they were vindicating an important value, matters were more complicated than they thought."[5] From a conservative perspective, government intervention represents an "alien, statist ideology."[6] The utilization of values in a supporting role, not directly applied to the decision, abound. For instance, for conservatives, the "exercise restraint and humility" regarding constitutional matters is a value and conversely the hubris of protecting unenumerated rights[7] is a disvalue. One who contends that "[i]t is axiomatic that a small adjustment in policy is more easily adopted than a major overhaul"[8] reveals a preference for conforming or accommodating to a system rather than making deep changes to or replacing it. When rights are conceived as lessons or cautionary tales, they are valued as educational tools.[9] Axiological analysis affords a different perspective to *Lochner*, introducing three distinct perspectives.

AT LEGAL LOGGERHEADS

Lochner collapsed into a conflict between the Fourteenth Amendment and the New York law and as axiological analysis will demonstrate, each is animated by values.

Fourteenth Amendment

No state shall make or enforce any law which shall abridge the privileges or immunities of citizens of the United States; nor shall any State deprive any person of life, liberty, or property, without due process of law; nor deny to any person within its jurisdiction the equal protection of the laws.

New York Law

§ 110. *Hours of labor in bakeries and confectionery establishments.*—No employee shall be required or permitted to work in a biscuit, bread or cake bakery or confectionery establishment more than sixty hours in any one week, or more than ten hours in any one day, unless for the purpose of making a shorter work day on the last day of the week; nor more hours in any one week than will make an average of ten hours per day for the number of days during such week in which such employee shall work.[10]

A BAKER'S LIFE: A DISPARITY OF PERSPECTIVES

In the majority opinion, the life of a baker was considered safe and not unhealthy. In the dissent by Justice Harlan, the life of the baker was described as an unhealthy and unsafe profession.

Justice Rufus W. Peckham

> We think there can be no fair doubt the trade of the baker, in and of itself, is not an unhealthy one.[11]

> [T]he trade of a baker does not appear to be as healthy as some other trades, and is also vastly more healthy than still others.[12]

> To the common understanding, the trade of a baker has never been regarded as an unhealthy one.[13]

Justice John Marshall Harlan

> The labor of the bakers is among the hardest and most laborious imaginable, because it has to be performed under conditions injurious to the health of those engaged in it.[14]

> It is hard, very hard work, not only because it requires a great deal of physical exertion in an overheated workshop and during unreasonably long hours, but more so because of the erratic demands of the public.[15]

> Continuous inhalation of flour dust causes inflames the lungs and the bronchial tubes and runny running eyes; from constant standing rheumatism, cramps and swollen legs occur; their power of resistance against disease is greatly diminished; they succumb easily to epidemics; and most bakers barely live to fifty.[16]

EXPLAINING THE DISPARITY

The disparity of perspectives on the baker's life boiled down to values. The sacred zenith value of liberty catalyzed Justice Peckham's majority opinion. Economic liberty was more than a preferred value. Liberty ascended to a sacred cow status and the state assumed the scapegoated profane nadir value. The language was clear. The profane nadir status of the state could be detected by the description of the New York statute: as "necessarily" and meddlesomely interfering with and "seriously" limiting "the right of contract between the employer and employees."[17] The statute was further depreciated by calling it a product of "[V]aguely termed police powers and of state that acted like a *pater familias* to its citizens instead of treating them like mature people and interfered "with their independence of judgment and of action."[18] If paternalism was the nadir disvalue, independence of thinking was the zenith value. Driven by the zenith value of health, Justice Harlan saw the statute protecting "the physical well-being" of bakers and confectioners.[19] This decision, Harlan prognosticated, would "seriously cripple" the state from caring for "the health and safety of the people."[20] The protection and care of health pointed to its zenith status in Justice Harlan's value scheme. Yet Justice Harlan did not take economic liberty as a profane nadir value, but as a nonpreferred one in some circumstances: "I take it to be firmly established that what is called the liberty of contract may, within certain limits, be subjected to regulations designed and calculated to promote the general welfare or to guard the public health, the public morals or the public safety."[21]

APPROPRIATION OF AUTHORITIES: SOME SIGNALS

Justice Peckham appropriated authorities in line with the hyper-valuing of economic liberty. Only in extreme and rare circumstances could government interference be justified. *Holden v. Hardy*, 169 U.S. 366, which prohibited miners from working in mines for more than eight hours per day, was one of those extreme and rare circumstances.[22] *Jacobson v. Massachusetts*, 197 U.S. 11 (1905), which compelled a healthy person to be inoculated so as to not endanger the community during a pandemic, was another example of an extreme and rare circumstance.[23] Additionally, it had nothing to do with economic liberty.[24] For Justice Harlan, *Jacobson* represented a justification of state intervention, as there were many reasons for constraining individuals for the common good.[25] *Yick Wo v. Hopkins*, 118 U.S. 356 was cited as a reminder of the distinction between legislation that is "oppressive and unjust" and legislation that enhanced and public health, safety or morals, or decreased public nuisances.[26] For Justice Harlan, oppressive and unjust legislation also represented a rationale for abridging the Fourteenth Amendment. Many other statutes—related to public health, safety or morals, and public nuisances and presumably not oppressive and unjust—could abridge the Fourteenth Amendment. The much-heralded dissent by Oliver Wendell Holmes does much to cast the case as a polarization of economic liberty and state intervention. However, Justice Holmes and Justice Peckham were at the extremes and Justice Harlan in the middle. The flashpoint statement "The Fourteenth Amendment does not enact Mr. Herbert Spencer's Social Statics"[27] blinds us from seeing more subtle features of the case.

COMPARATIVE VALUE SCHEMES

It was clear from the ruling that Justice Peckham embraced the value of economic liberty and devalued state intervention as paternalism, while Justice Harlan valued judicious state intervention and devalued liberty.

Affirmation of Value of Liberty (Justice Peckham)

The effectiveness of the Fourteenth Amendment would be diminished by unbounded state power:

> It must, of course, be conceded that there is a limit to the valid exercise of the police power by the State. There is no dispute concerning this general proposition. Otherwise the Fourteenth Amendment would have no efficacy, and the legislatures of the States would have unbounded power, and it would be enough to say that any piece of legislation was enacted to conserve the morals, the health or the safety of the people; such legislation would be valid no matter how absolutely without foundation the claim might be. The claim of the police power would be a mere pretext—become another and delusive name for the supreme sovereignty of the State to be exercised free from constitutional restraint.[28]

Liberty of contract took precedence:

> Of course, the liberty of contract relating to labor includes both parties to it. The one has as much right to purchase as the other to sell labor.[29]

Only in border or extreme cases could the liberty to contract be limited:

> This court has recognized the existence and upheld the exercise of the police powers of the States in many cases which might fairly be considered as *border* ones, and it has, in the course of its determination of questions regarding the

> asserted invalidity of such statutes on the ground of their violation of the rights secured by the Federal Constitution, been guided by rules of a very liberal nature, the application of which has resulted, in numerous instances, in upholding the validity of state statutes thus assailed.[30]

The real agenda of the legislature was not the health of the employees, but to control the number of hours employees work:

> It is impossible for us to shut our eyes to the fact that many of the laws of this character, while passed under what is claimed to be the police power for the purpose of protecting the public health or welfare, are, in reality, passed from other motives. We are justified in saying so when, from the character of the law and the subject upon which it legislates, it is apparent that the public health or welfare bears but the most remote relation to the law.[31]

Affirmation of Social Welfare via Government (Justice Harlan)

Justice Harlan quoted from *Barbier v. Connolly* 113 U.S. 27 (1885) to affirm state intervention to promote health, peace, morals, education, and order:

> But neither the [14th] Amendment—broad and comprehensive as it is—nor any other Amendment was designed to interfere with the power of the State, sometimes termed its police power, to prescribe regulations to promote the health, peace, morals, education, and good order of the people.[32]

From *Lawton v. Steele*, 152 U.S. 133 (1894), he noted that the legislature was vested "to determine not only what the interests of the public require, but what measures are necessary for the protection of such interests." *Gundling v. Chicago*, 177 U.S. 183 (1900) pointed to the frequency of state intervention in business:

> Regulations respecting the pursuit of a lawful trade or business are of very frequent occurrence in the various cities of the country, and what such regulations shall be and to what particular trade, business or occupation they shall apply are questions for the State to determine, and their determination comes within the proper exercise of the police power by the State, and unless the regulations are so utterly unreasonable and extravagant in their nature and purpose that the property and personal rights of the citizen are unnecessarily, and in a manner wholly arbitrary, interfered with or destroyed without due process of law, they do not extend beyond the power of the State to pass, and they form no subject for Federal interference.[33]

Unless state power was excessive, federal court intervention could not be justified.

> Upon this point there is no room for dispute, for the rule is universal that a legislative enactment, Federal or state, is never to be disregarded or held invalid unless it be, beyond question, plainly and palpably in excess of legislative power.[34]

Furthermore, if doubts arose about the validity of the statute, the court must side with the legislature. This leaning toward the legislature resulted from a value inclination toward state intervention:

> If there be doubt as to the validity of the statute, that doubt must therefore be resolved in favor of its validity, and the courts must keep their hands off, leaving the legislature to meet the responsibility for unwise legislation.[35]

Disvalue of Paternalism (Justice Peckham)

Values usually congregate and appear in constellations. In the case of the majority opinion, the zenith value of liberty was closely correlated with the disvalue of paternalism. If liberty was esteemed, it makes sense that taking away that liberty as in the case of the state intervention, which was conceived negatively as paternalism:

> The question whether this act is valid as a labor law, pure and simple, may be dismissed in a few words. There is no reasonable ground for interfering with the liberty of person or the right of free contract by determining the hours of labor in the occupation of a baker. There is no contention that bakers as a class are not equal in intelligence and capacity to men in other trades or manual occupations, or that they are not able to assert their rights and care for themselves without the protecting arm of the State, interfering with their independence of judgment and of action. They are in no sense *wards of the State* [our emphasis]. Viewed in the light of a purely labor law, with no reference whatever to the question of health, we think that a law like the one before us involves neither the safety, the morals, nor the welfare of the public, and that the interest of the public is not in the slightest degree affected by such an act.[36]

The nadir disvalue of paternalism animated the fear that unchecked paternalism would corrupt American culture, as this slippery slope forecast portended:

> There must be more than the mere fact of the possible existence of some small amount of unhealthiness to warrant legislative interference with liberty. It is

> unfortunately true that labor, even in any department, may possibly carry with it the seeds of unhealthiness. But are we all, on that account, at the mercy of legislative majorities? A printer, a tinsmith, a locksmith, a carpenter, a cabinetmaker, a dry goods clerk, a bank's, a lawyer's or a physician's clerk, or a clerk in almost any kind of business, would all come under the power of the legislature on this assumption. No trade, no occupation, no mode of earning one's living could escape this all-pervading power, and the acts of the legislature in limiting the hours of labor in all employments would be valid although such limitation might seriously cripple the ability of the laborer to support himself and his family. In our large cities there are many buildings into which the sun penetrates for but a short time in each day, and these buildings are occupied by people carrying on the business of bankers, brokers, lawyers, real estate, and many other kinds of business, aided by many clerks, messengers, and other employs. Upon the assumption of the validity of this act under review, it is not possible to say that an act prohibiting lawyers' or bank clerks, or others from contracting to labor for their employers more than eight hours a day would be invalid. It might be said that it is unhealthy to work more than that number of hours in an apartment lighted by artificial light during the working hours of the day; that the occupation of the bank clerk, the lawyer's clerk, the real estate clerk, or the broker's clerk in such offices is therefore unhealthy, and the legislature, in its paternal wisdom, must therefore have the right to legislate on the subject of, and to limit the hours for, such labor, and, if it exercises that power and its validity be questioned, it is sufficient to say it has reference to the public health; it has reference to the health of the employees condemned to labor day after day in buildings where the sun never shines; it is a health law, and therefore it is valid, and cannot be questioned by the courts.[37]

Value of Judicious State Intervention (Justice Harlan)

The state could judiciously intervene, taking a middle ground between overprotection and underprotection of its citizens:

> We judicially know that the question of the number of hours during which a workman should continuously labor has been, for a long period, and is yet, a subject of serious consideration among civilized peoples and by those having special knowledge of the laws of health. Suppose the statute prohibited labor in bakery and confectionery establishments in excess of eighteen hours each day. No one, I take it, could dispute the power of the State to enact such a statute. But the statute before us does not embrace extreme or exceptional cases. It may be said to occupy a middle ground in respect of the hours of labor. What is the true ground for the State to take between legitimate protection, by legislation, of the public health and liberty of contract is not a question easily solved, nor one in

respect of which there is or can be absolute certainty. There are very few, if any, questions in political economy about which entire certainty may be predicated.[38]

Unless the state "beyond all question" violated the Federal Constitution, the state's role was to protect its people:

> Let the State alone in the management of its purely domestic affairs so long as it does not appear beyond all question that it has violated the Federal Constitution. This view necessarily results from the principle that the health and safety of the people of a State are primarily for the State to guard and protect.[39]

The Diminution of Liberty in General and Economic Liberty in Particular (Justice Oliver Wendell Holmes)

"Perverted" was what Holmes calls "the word liberty in the Fourteenth Amendment"[40] when it interfered with majority rule. Holmes valued majority rule unless it infringed upon fundamental principles. Protecting the health of citizens was not such an infringement. "Shibboleth" was what Holmes termed the belief that individual liberty extended up to the point of harming another person.[41] There were much lower standards than harm that routinely abridge personal liberty: compulsory school attendance laws, the Post Office (presumably in regulating the mail), and any state or municipal institution that takes our money for things of no value.[42] Liberty took two negative hits. Majority rule was more valuable than liberty except when fundamental principles were jeopardized. Second, liberty lost more of its luster as an outdated idea, as evidenced by its abridgment in numerous cases having nothing to do with the no harm principle. Another protuberant value concerned how Justice Holmes viewed the Constitution. For him, the Constitution was made to adapt to different views and not have an allegiance to either laissez-faire capitalism or paternalistic communitarianism. This Constitutional flexibility allowed for novel or even shocking views, including, we think, wholly new relationships between the state and the individual.

RECKONING OF THE ROGUE JUSTICES

At the end of the day, Justice Holmes and Justice Peckham were at the extremes of the economic liberty-state intervention. Justice Peckham saw economic liberty and independence of thought as zenith value congregation and the disvalue of state intervention and its buttressing disvalue of paternalism as a nadir disvalue congregation. Justice Holmes devalued liberty in general, which carried over into economic liberty specifically, by stating there could be many circumstances to abridge the Fourteenth Amendment. Only when fundamental principles were violated could the Fourteenth Amendment be justified. Justice Peckham held state intervention in contempt as much as Justice Holmes held liberty in contempt, in opposition to the zenith values of majority rule and of actual implementation (compared to past implementation). On the other hand, Justice Harlan took a middle course that leaned toward state intervention but maintained the tension between the two extremes. He came down on the side of judicious state intervention.

NOTES

1. David E. Bernstein, "*Lochner v. New York*: A Centennial Retrospective," *Washington University Law Quarterly* 83, 5 (2005): 1471.
2. Paul Kens, "*Lochner v. New York*: Tradition or Change in Constitutional Law," *NYU Journal of Law and Liberty* 1, 1 (2005): 415.
3. Thomas Colby and Peter J. Smith, "The Return of *Lochner*," *Cornell Law Review* 100 (2015): 601.
4. Abhishek Hariharan, "Implications of *Lochner v. New York*," *Columbia University Undergraduate Law Review* (January 4, 2019): https://www.culawreview.org/journal/implications-of-lochner-v-new-york https://www.culawreview.org/journal/implications-of-lochner-v-new-york.
5. David A. Strauss, "Why Was *Lochner* Wrong?" *University of Chicago Law Review* 70, 1 (2003): 386.
6. Ellen Frankel Paul, "Freedom of Contract and the 'Political Economy' of *Lochner v. New York*," *NYU Journal of Law and Liberty* 1, 1 (2005): 569.
7. Colby and Smith, "The Return of *Lochner*," 531.
8. D. G. Stephenson Jr., "The Supreme Court and Constitutional Change: *Lochner v. New York* Revisited," *Villanova Law Review* 21, 2 (1976): 238.
9. Victoria Nourse, "A Tale of Two *Lochners*: The Untold History of Substantive Due Process and the Idea of Fundamental Rights," *California Law Review* 97 (2009): 751–799.
10. Ibid., 65.
11. Ibid., 59.
12. Ibid.
13. Ibid.
14. Ibid., 70.
15. Ibid.
16. Ibid.
17. Ibid., 53, 61.
18. Ibid., 53, 62, 57.
19. Ibid., 69.
20. Ibid., 73.
21. Ibid., 67.
22. Ibid., 54.

23. Ibid., 55–56.
24. Ibid., 56.
25. Ibid., 67.
26. Ibid., 66.
27. Ibid., 75.
28. Ibid., 54.
29. Ibid., 56.
30. Ibid., 54.
31. Ibid., 64.
32. Ibid., 66.
33. Ibid., 67.
34. Ibid., 68.
35. Ibid.
36. Ibid., 57.
37. Ibid., 59–60.
38. Ibid., 71–72.
39. Ibid., 73.
40. Ibid., 76.
41. Ibid., 75.
42. Ibid.

Chapter 9

The Value of Interdependence v. Value of a Private and Independent Economic Sphere

Wickard v. Filburn

NARRATIVE IN A (SLIGHTLY LARGER) NUTSHELL

The legal players were Ohio farmer Roscoe Filburn and Secretary of Agriculture Claude Wickard.

What was the extent of Filburn's farming venture?

He had a herd of dairy cattle and raised poultry, and sold milk, poultry, and eggs. Each year, he raised a small acreage of winter wheat, which he harvested the following July and harvested it the following July. He sold part of the crop. Another part he fed to his poultry and livestock. Some of it he used to make flour for home consumption. Another part he kept for seeding.

Sounds like a plan.

A plan that broke the law.

How so?

Filburn received a wheat acreage allotment from the Department of Agriculture—and exceeded the quota. As such, he was subject to a penalty of $117.11. Filburn refused to pay the penalty, and entered a suit against the Secretary of Agriculture, Claude Wickard.

Why would such a law be on the books?

A great uncertainty gripped wheat farmers and farmers of all stripes as they struggled to make a profit during the Great Depression. If farmers harvested whatever they wanted, found nowhere to export their wheat, and the market was flooded with it, then these farmers could not turn a profit, which in turn would deepen the Great Depression. Images of congested railroad cars filled with wheat without a destination made a case for government intervention. Only the government had the reach to regulate these interacting markets for the good of both individuals and for the economy as a whole. The solution,

Table 9.1 Centralized Government and Failing Depression-Era Wheat Markets

1. The wheat industry was underperforming during the Great Depression. Wheat composed 25 percent of exports in the 1920s, dipping to 10 percent between 1931 and 1940.
2. The flailing wheat market impacted other markets: hindering railroad cars and inducing elevators to turn away grains and railroads to employ embargoes to stave off further congestion.
3. To relieve growers, Canada, Argentina, Australia, and the United States (the largest global exporters) used centralized government control to protect the domestic price received by producers.
4. The Agricultural Adjustment Act of 1938 (amended by the Act of May 26, 1941) restricted the amount of wheat on the market and determined how much wheat producers can use for their own needs.
5. The Agricultural Adjustment Act was designed to control interstate and foreign commerce for the purpose of avoiding surpluses and shortages in order to avoid surpluses and shortages and the abnormally low or high wheat prices and obstructions to commerce that arise from them.
6. Each year the Secretary of Agriculture was directed to ascertain and publicize a national acreage allotment for the next crop of wheat.
7. While one producer with a private stash of wheat would not harm the wheat market, many producers similarly acting would.
8. Because of a looming war, the government desired more wheat to be produced without penalizing farmers for producing it.
9. Marketing encompassed all that may be sold without penalty and what may be consumed on the premises.
10. The quota declared wheat produced on excess acreage could not be discarded or used without penalty except if stored according to the act and delivered to the Secretary of Agriculture.

Source: *Wickard v. Filburn*, 317 U.S. 111 (1942).

then, was simply to establish certain prices, which could only happen if there was a set amount of wheat in the marketplace. Thus, each farmer was allowed to grow only a certain amount of wheat, thereby steadying the supply side of the economic equation. A farmer could not grow more wheat to offset a potentially expensive season for wheat by growing his own; instead, he would be forced to partake in the market like everyone else and pay higher prices for what he still needed.

VALUE-INFUSED SCHOLARSHIP

Libertarians scapegoat *Filburn* and similar commodity programs for opening "the regulatory floodgates for the government to regulate anything and everything,"[1] which eventually destroyed the "agrarian dream."[2] More than that, the government invaded the privacy of farmers: "In *Wickard v. Filburn*, Congress even allowed Congress to delve into private, but not public behavior,[3] the "sad result" being "a government nearly limitless in its power."[4] A reading reared in the values of balance, complementarily, and interdependence understands the ruling according to "a careful balancing act between state sovereignty and federal supremacy,"[5] seeing, as the founders did, no contradiction between an energetic national government and "individual liberty" and considering their relationship as "mutually reinforcing and producing balanced governance."[6] Ultimately, *Filburn* is a classic value confrontation between interdependency and independence in a private sphere.

AT LEGAL LOGGERHEADS

Specifically, Filburn asserted that the Act exceeded the reach of the Commerce Clause (Article I, Section 8, Clause 3) and that the Act violated the Due Process Clause of the Fifth Amendment by taking his property. The question before the Court was whether the Commerce Clause gave Congress the power to prohibit an individual farmer from intra-state growing of wheat.

The Court held that it did. The Court collapsed the distinctions between indirect and direct effects and intrastate and interstate commerce. Virtually everything produced was considered to have a direct effect on the grand economic scheme, even making flour from one's wheat for home consumption. If virtually everything had a direct effect on the grand economic scheme, then the concept of intrastate commerce made no sense. No commerce could be contained within states, but spilled into other states. Only direct effects and interstate commerce existed in the mind of the court.

The Court argued that regulation curbed the self-interest of some so that others could reap the benefits: "It is of the essence of regulation that it lays a restraining hand on the self-interest of the regulated, and that advantages from the regulation commonly fall to others."[7] But this self-regulation did not deny Filburn and other farmers due process. Looking at the legislation as a whole and what was given to and taken away from farmers, it did nothing to deny due process. On the face of it, Filburn got a good deal, especially looking across the globe at wheat prices: "During 1941, producers who cooperated with the Agricultural Adjustment program received an average price on the farm of about $1.16 a bushel, as compared with the world market price of 40 cents a bushel."[8] Filburn wanted the advantages of government aid without complying with its rules to curb self-interest. For the Court, this situation exceeded the criteria of due process:

> That appellee is the worse off for the aggregate of this legislation does not appear; it only appears that, if he could get all that the Government gives and do nothing that the Government asks, he would be better off than this law allows. To deny him this is not to deny him due process of law.[9]

MAJORITY DECISION BY JUSTICE ROBERT JACKSON

Justice Jackson did not need to dredge up obscure authorities to make his case for near-absolute control of the market by the government. The pieces were already there in the Commerce Clause, the powerful Interstate Commerce Act, Sherman Anti-Trust Act, and the judgments of *Gibbons v. Ogden* and *Swift v. United States*. All of these gave Congress to regulate business. The fly in the ointment was the Fifth Amendment.

PIVOTAL AUTHORITIES

Commerce Clause of the Constitution, Article I, § 8, Clause 3

[The Congress shall have Power] To regulate Commerce with foreign Nations, and among the several States, and with the Indian Tribes;

Fifth Amendment (Due Process Clause)

"No person shall be . . . deprived of life, liberty, or property, without due process of law; nor shall private property be taken for public use, without just compensation."

Gibbons v. Ogden, 9 Wheat. 1, 22 U. S. 194 (1824)

Intrastate activity could be regulated under the Commerce Clause, if such activity is part of a larger interstate commercial scheme

Interstate Commerce Act (1887)

Made railroads first industry subject to government regulation, ushering in an era according to Judge Jackson when "interstate commerce power began to exert positive influence in American law and life"

The Sherman Anti-Trust Act of 1890

An act to protect trade and commerce against unlawful restraints and monopolies

Swift & Co. v. United States, 196 U. S. 375, 196 U.S. 398 (1905)

Congress had the authority to regulate local commerce, provided that activity partook of the continuous "current" of commerce involving the interstate movement of goods and services.

ARGUMENTATIVE FLASHPOINTS

One of the major points made by Justice Jackson was that the Agricultural Adjustment Act was in the best interest of farmers, providing a profit for farmers and ways to discharge surplus wheat:

> We do not agree. In its effort to control total supply, the Government gave the farmer a choice which was, of course, designed to encourage cooperation and

> discourage noncooperation. The farmer who planted within his allotment was, in effect, guaranteed a minimum return much above what his wheat would have brought if sold on a world market basis. Exemption from the applicability of quotas was made in favor of small producers. The farmer who produced in excess of his quota might escape penalty by delivering his wheat to the Secretary, or by storing it with the privilege of sale without penalty in a later year to fill out his quota, or irrespective of quotas if they are no longer in effect, and he could obtain a loan of 60 percent of the rate for cooperators, or about 59 cents a bushel, on so much of his wheat as would be subject to penalty if marketed. Finally, he might make other disposition of his wheat, subject to the penalty. It is agreed that, as the result of the wheat programs, he is able to market his wheat at a price "far above any world price based on the natural reaction of supply and demand." We can hardly find a denial of due process in these circumstances, particularly since it is even doubtful that appellee's burdens under the program outweigh his benefits. It is hardly lack of due process for the Government to regulate that which it subsidizes.[10]

Not only did Agricultural Adjustment Act aid individual farmers, but it also controlled a market, if left unchecked, would prove economically harmful:

> It is well established by decisions of this Court that the power to regulate commerce includes the power to regulate the prices at which commodities in that commerce are dealt in and practices affecting such prices. One of the primary purposes of the Act in question was to increase the market price of wheat, and, to that end, to limit the volume thereof that could affect the market. It can hardly be denied that a factor of such volume and variability as home-consumed wheat would have a substantial influence on price and market conditions. This may arise because being in marketable condition such wheat overhangs the market, and, if induced by rising prices, tends to flow into the market and check price increases. But if we assume that it is never marketed, it supplies a need of the man who grew it which would otherwise be reflected by purchases in the open market. Home-grown wheat in this sense competes with wheat in commerce. The stimulation of commerce is a use of the regulatory function quite as definitely as prohibitions or restrictions thereon.[11]

Quoting Justice Hughes from *Shreveport Rate Cases*, 234 U.S. 342 (1914), Justice Jackson emphasized the government can control commerce to keep it secure:

> matters having such a close and substantial relation to interstate traffic that the control is essential or appropriate to the security of that traffic, to the efficiency of the interstate service, and to the maintenance of conditions under which

interstate commerce may be conducted upon fair terms and without molestation or hindrance.[12]

OPERATIVE VALUES

The Absolute Value of Government Regulatory Power over Commerce

For all intents and purposes, intrastate commerce was collapsed into the category of interstate commerce and became merely a subsidiary of it. This was how the majority opinion read it, quoting from *United States v. Wrightwood Dairy Co.*, 315 U.S. 110, 315 U.S. 119 (1942), as the phrase "plenary and complete in itself" connoted:

> The commerce power is not confined in its exercise to the regulation of commerce among the states. It extends to those activities intrastate which so affect interstate commerce, or the exertion of the power of Congress over it, as to make regulation of them appropriate means to the attainment of a legitimate end, the effective execution of the granted power to regulate interstate commerce. . . . The power of Congress over interstate commerce is *plenary and complete in itself*, (our emphasis) may be exercised to its utmost extent, and acknowledges no limitations other than are prescribed in the Constitution. . . . It follows that no form of state activity can constitutionally thwart the regulatory power granted by the commerce clause to Congress. Hence, the reach of that power extends to those intrastate activities which in a substantial way interfere with or obstruct the exercise of the granted power.

The Value of Commercial Interdependence

The word "interdependence" will not be found in the ruling. However, it protruded by a process of elimination. If all effects were direct and intrastate commerce is interstate commerce, then no commercial activity was isolated from another and thus all commercial activities were interdependent. The zenith value of interdependence called for placing a high value on governmental regulation on this vast interconnected economic network:

> But if we assume that it is never marketed, it supplies a need of the man who grew it which would otherwise be reflected by purchases in the open market. Homegrown wheat in this sense competes with wheat in commerce. The stimulation of commerce is a use of the regulatory function quite as definitely as prohibitions or

> restrictions thereon. This record leaves us in no doubt that Congress may properly have considered that wheat consumed on the farm where grown, if wholly outside the scheme of regulation, would have a substantial effect in defeating and obstructing its purpose to stimulate trade therein at increased prices.[13]

The Value of Practicality

Government regulation was valued as practical, as a means for businesses to function: "Mr. Justice Holmes, in sustaining the exercise of national power over intrastate activity, stated for the Court that 'commerce among the States is not a technical legal conception, but a practical one, drawn from the course of business.'"[14]

The Value of Degree over the Value of Exactitude

Justice Jackson quoted Justice Hughes concerning the value of degree versus the value of exactitude:

> "direct" has been contrasted with "indirect," and what is "remote" or "distant" with what is "close and substantial." Whatever terminology is used, the criterion is necessarily one of degree, and must be so defined. This does not satisfy those who seek for mathematical or rigid formulas. But such formulas are not provided by the great concepts of the Constitution such as "interstate commerce," "due process," "equal protection."[15]

VALUE VIGNETTE

The value of government control was necessitated by the value of an interdependent commerce system and to a smaller extent by the values of practicality and degree, which served as buttressing values.

RECKONING OF THE ROGUE JUSTICES

No commerce is completely "local" or "indirect." Which means that all commerce is interconnected or interdependent. But there is a possible connection and probable connection. What could possibly impact a system and what could probably impact are distinctions that must be retrieved and reinstituted. If we make an apple pie wheat and sell it or give it as a gift to someone in our community, is that an interstate commerce? After all, we have purchased flour, sugar, molasses, and apples that could conceivably come from different states or even from different countries. Using things from the marketplace is not the same as impacting the marketplace. It is possible to conceive that our apple pie would impact the commerce system, as would say, the activities of corporations whose business is fundamentally interstate. Even if everyone in our neighborhood made apple pies and gifted others with them, what would that impact look like? Collapsing the distinction between direct and indirect commerce also collapses the distinction between private and public and independent and interdependent. Our actions in the privacy of our homes are subject to commercial regulation by the government. Does this also mean that everyone is a corporation? Because if the direct-indirect distinction collapses, everyone is involved in business in some way, shape, or form. And there would be no private productive space, as everything would be interdependent.

NOTES

1. "Cato Institute Scholar Reviews “worst” Supreme Court Decisions," Duke Law, News (September 15, 2008). https://law.duke.edu/news/cato-institute-scholar-reviews-worst-supreme-court-decisions/.
2. James Ming Chen, "The Story of *Wickard v. Filburn*: Agriculture, Aggregation, and Commerce," in *Constitutional Law Stories*, 2nd ed., ed. Michael C. Dorf (New York: Foundation Press, 2009), 36.
3. Thomas E. Travis, "Horne v. USDA: The Takings Clause, the Commerce Clause, and the 'World's Most Outdated Law,'" *Kentucky Journal of Equine, Agriculture, & Natural Resources Law* 7, 2 (2015): 422.
4. "Supreme Court Case That Gave the Federal Government Nearly Unlimited Power," Foundation for Economic Education (February 7, 2020) https://fee.org/articles/wickard-v-filburn-the-supreme-court-case-that-gave-the-federal-government-nearly-unlimited-power/.
5. Casey L. Westover, "Structural Interpretation and the New Federalism: Finding the Proper Balance Between State Sovereignty and Federal Supremacy," *Marquette Law Review* 88, 4 (2005): 750.
6. Keith Werham, "Checking Congress and Balancing Federalism: A Lesson from Separation-of-Powers Jurisprudence," *Washington and Lee Law Review* 57, 4 (2000): 1217.
7. *Wickard v. Filburn*, 317 U.S. 111, 129 (1942).
8. Ibid., 126.
9. Ibid., 133.
10. Ibid., 130–131.
11. Ibid., 128.
12. Ibid., 123.
13. Ibid., 128–129.
14. Ibid., 122.
15. Ibid., 317.

Chapter 10

The Sacred Value of Privacy in Marriage v. Traditionalism

Griswold v. Connecticut

NARRATIVE IN NUTSHELL

Where did this take place?

The New Haven Center of Planned Parenthood in New Haven Connecticut.

What services did this facility offer?

The Executive Director, Estelle Griswold, and Dr. Charles Lee Burton, a licensed physician and a professor at the Yale Medical School, met with *married* [italicized in the majority ruling] persons and offered them information, instruction, and medical advice regarding pregnancy prevention.

How long was this facility opened?

From November 1, 1961–November 10, 1961.

Were Griswold and Burton arrested with the closing of the facility?

Yes.

What was the charge?

Breaking a Connecticut statute stipulating people assisting, abetting, causing, hiring, or commanding another to use contraceptives would be prosecuted and punished the same as those who actually used contraceptives.

What was punishment for breaking the law?

A fine of at least fifty dollars and a jail term between sixty days and one year.

What was the justification for the Connecticut law?

The state statute was issued from moral concern. The use of contraceptives by married couples might encourage infidelity. Eliminating the risk of pregnancy, so the state reasoned, would encourage married people to have sex outside marriage.

VALUE-INFUSED SCHOLARSHIP

In 1967, two years after the verdict, Ernest Katin admitted "judicial inclination"[1] or values would determine how the marital privacy principles of *Griswold* would unfold. In 2015 Joanna L. Grossman pointed out how those values played out, assessing the legacy of *Griswold* in terms of its value to women's rights: "The legacy of a landmark ruling like *Griswold v. Connecticut* goes far beyond increasing the accessibility of contraception. *Griswold* was part and parcel of an era that gave women—through legal, social, and technological developments—greater control over reproduction. And that control, in turn, facilitated their greater integration into the labor force—and access to better economic security."[2] One of the value schemes of a pluralistic society is that the state does not have power over what individual choices people make in the privacy of their homes. The value of individual choice in private spheres takes precedence unless it "disturb[s] the public peace or adversely affect the social well-being."[3] Regarding penumbras and the use of metaphor in general, value claims were made. "Penumbra" was a poor choice because it depicted fundamental affirmative rights as "degrees of darkness," suggesting something shadowy or disreputable or negative about them.[4] Spatial metaphors like penumbras are the choice for those valuing the visual and imaginable.[5] Yet metaphors add flexibility to the law by allowing it to change and evolve."[6] The following axiological inquiry on this verdict places a premium of value on ideas in the vicinity of the penumbra rather than the penumbra itself.

THE MAJORITY OPINION BY JUSTICE WILLIAM DOUGLAS

The Zenith Value of Privacy Within Marriage

> We deal with a right of privacy older than the Bill of Rights—older than our political parties, older than our school system. Marriage is a coming together for better or for worse, hopefully enduring, and intimate to the degree of being sacred. It is an association that promotes a way of life, not causes; a harmony in living, not political faiths; a bilateral loyalty, not commercial or social projects. Yet it is an association for as noble a purpose as any involved in our prior decisions.[7]

The last paragraph of the majority opinion revealed the catalyst value of the Court. The majority opinion of this case boiled down to the "sacred" value of marriage, buttressed by another value: "noble a purpose" to defend it. Neither the Constitution nor the Bill of Rights contained the word "marriage." But the concept of liberty in the Bill of Rights could be molded to gain that result. The value of a living and flexible Constitution was instrumental in achieving this result, and penumbras were a manifestation of such a Constitution. Marriage received coverage from the shadow liberty casted, its penumbra. Whether marriage was or wasn't implied by liberty-endowed Amendments, it doesn't take a penumbra to show that Justice Douglas's shadowy legal rationale actually stemmed from the sacred or zenith value of marriage. Without a shadow of a doubt, *Griswold* became the poster child for the operation of values in jurisprudence. Not simply were values fully operational in the majority decision, but also in the dissent by Justice Black, who, in exposing the hand of values of the majority decision, revealed his own hand.

The sacred value of the intimacy of marriage deeply woven into the tradition of American culture and perhaps even beyond that into the human condition eclipsed the value of a state law interfering in it. In one sense, this was a case of catching up with the times and in another, it wasn't. The catching up with the times' aspect of the case concerned including the new technologies of birth control into the intimacy of married life and of professionals rather than clergy who could guide married couples to use this new technology. On the other hand, *Griswold* was an affirmation of a sacred value that practically transcended time. Thus, the case was about changing times and timeless truths.

THE CONNECTICUT LAWS

The majority opinion addressed the following two Connecticut laws originated from the sexually repressed Victorian era:

> Any person who uses any drug, medicinal article or instrument for the purpose of preventing conception shall be fined not less than fifty dollars or imprisoned not less than sixty days nor more than one year or be both fined and imprisoned.[8]
>
> "Any person who assists, abets, counsels, causes, hires or commands another to commit any offense may be prosecuted and punished as if he were the principal offender."[9]

A JUSTIFICATION FOR PENUMBRAS

Toward the end of the majority opinion, Justice Douglas made a case for penumbras, asserting the "specific guarantees in the Bill of Rights have penumbras, formed by emanations from those guarantees that help give them life and substance."[10] "Without those peripheral rights," he contended, "the specific rights would be less secure."[11] The penumbras were the practical applications of the specific guarantees of the Bill of Rights in real time. This was the only way such guarantees become lived in and lived out (giving life and substance). The specific guarantees in the Bill of Rights and the penumbras were valued for their interdependency.

Second, the Court was not seen as a "super-legislature" to correct bad laws. But in this case, Connecticut laws overreached by interfering with the intimate marriage relationship (including the physician's role in prescribing birth control) considered a sacred value:

> We do not sit as a super-legislature to determine the wisdom, need, and propriety of laws that touch economic problems, business affairs, or social conditions. This law, however, operates directly on an intimate relation of husband and wife and their physician's role in one aspect of that relation.[12]

Third, since the Connecticut laws invaded zone of privacy created by several penumbras from several Amendments, causing maximum damage, it could not stand:

> The present case, then, concerns a relationship lying within the zone of privacy created by several fundamental constitutional guarantees. And it concerns a law which, in forbidding the use of contraceptives, rather than regulating their manufacture or sale, seeks to achieve its goals by means having a maximum destructive impact upon that relationship. Such a law cannot stand in light of the familiar principle, so often applied by this Court, that a "governmental purpose to control or prevent activities constitutionally subject to state regulation may not be achieved by means which sweep unnecessarily broadly and thereby invade the area of protected freedoms."[13]

The profane nadir disvalue of "invasion" cannot be overestimated, especially when coupled with "maximum destructive impact." It was akin to using destructive weaponry to invade a country, undermining its sovereignty, which in this case was the sovereignty of a land of intimate privacy.

THE AUTHORITIES AND THEIR PENUMBRAS

The First Amendment's penumbra was grounded by a plethora of authorities, while the penumbras of the Third, Fourth, Fifth, and Ninth Amendments were far less grounded.

The First Amendment

> Congress shall make no law respecting an establishment of religion, or prohibiting the free exercise thereof; or abridging the freedom of speech, or of the press; or the right of the people peaceably to assemble, and to petition the Government for a redress of grievances.

The Case for the Penumbra

"The association of people was not mentioned in the Constitution nor in the Bill of Rights,"[14] Justice Douglas declared. "The right to educate a child in a school of the parents' choice—whether public or private or parochial—is also not mentioned. Nor is the right to study any particular subject or any foreign language. Yet the First Amendment has been construed to include certain of those rights."[15] Furthermore: "In other words, the State may not, consistently with the spirit of the First Amendment, contract the spectrum of available knowledge. The right of freedom of speech and press includes not only the right to utter or to print, but the right to distribute, the right to receive, the right to read."[16] The scope of the First Amendment was extensive. It is the right of parents to choose how to educate their children[17]; the right to study all subjects and languages[18]; the right of assembly regardless of race or ideology; the right to not only utter or say, but to distribute, receive, and read; the right to share one's views by being a member of a group; freedom of inquiry, thought, and freedom to teach; the freedom of the whole university; the impermissibility of disbarring a lawyer who had once been a member of the Communist party; protections of nonpolitical associations pertaining to the social, legal, and economic benefits of its members.[19] Since the First Amendment reached into so many spheres of our lives, it was not an overreach to affirm it also reached into the private sphere as well, to the intimacy inherent in marriage. This was the expansive value of the First Amendment.

The Third Amendment

"No Soldier shall, in time of peace be quartered in any house, without the consent of the Owner, nor in time of war, but in a manner to be prescribed by law."

The Case for the Penumbra

A single line sufficed to explain this penumbra: "The Third Amendment, in its prohibition against the quartering of soldiers 'in any house' in time of peace without the consent of the owner, is another facet of that privacy."[20] The Third Amendment's prohibition against invading the privacy of citizens by quartering soldiers in their residences (other than in war) could be extended to the state invading the bedrooms of married people by being an unwanted presence in their intimate aspects of their relationships. While the First Amendment penumbra was one of pure expansion, the Third Amendment penumbra was one of excluding the state from the intimacies of marriage.

The Fourth Amendment

> The right of the people to be secure in their persons, houses, papers, and effects, against unreasonable searches and seizures, shall not be violated, and no Warrants shall issue, but upon probable cause, supported by Oath or affirmation, and particularly describing the place to be searched, and the persons or things to be seized.

The Case for the Penumbra

Mapp v. Ohio, 367 U.S. 643 (1961)—created a "'right to privacy, no less important than any other right carefully an particularly reserved to the people.'"[21]

The case for this penumbra continues below under the Fifth Amendment.

The Fifth Amendment

> No person shall be held to answer for a capital, or otherwise infamous crime, unless on a presentment or indictment of a Grand Jury, except in cases arising in the land or naval forces, or in the Militia, when in actual service in time of War or public danger; nor shall any person be subject for the same offence to be twice put in jeopardy of life or limb; nor shall be compelled in any criminal case to be a witness against himself, nor be deprived of life, liberty, or property, without due process of law; nor shall private property be taken for public use, without just compensation.

The Case for the Penumbras of Fourth and Fifth Amendments

Justice Douglas employed *Boyd v. United States*, 116 U.S. 616, 116 U.S. 630 (1886) to invoke the zenith values of the sanctity of one's home and "privacies of life."[22] As cited in a footnote by Justice Douglas, the *Boyd* majority opinion drew its values from a pivotal case in English law, *Entick v. Carrington*, 19 Howell's State Trials 1029 (1765):

> "The principles laid down in this opinion [by Lord Camden in *Entick v. Carrington*, 19 How.St.Tr. 1029] affect the very essence of constitutional liberty and security. They reach farther than the concrete form of the case then before the court, with its adventitious circumstances; they apply to all invasions

> on the part of the government and its employees of the sanctity of a man's home and the privacies of life. It is not the breaking of his doors and the rummaging of his drawers that constitutes the essence of the offence, but it is the invasion of his indefeasible right of personal security, personal liberty, and private property, where that right has never been forfeited by his conviction of some public offence—it is the invasion of this sacred right which underlies and constitutes the essence of Lord Camden's judgment."[23]

Additionally, according to Justice Douglas, "[t]he Fifth Amendment, in its Self-Incrimination Clause enabled the citizen to create a zone of privacy which government may not force him to surrender to his detriment."[24] This established yet another private zone in which the government was excluded.

The Ninth Amendment

"The enumeration in the Constitution, of certain rights, shall not be construed to deny or disparage others retained by the people."

The Case for the Penumbra

No explanation was given for Ninth Amendment penumbra. Its value consisted of giving the green light to enumerate certain rights, like the privacy of the intimacies of marriage, as long as they did not negatively impact other rights.

CONCURRENCE BY JUSTICE ARTHUR GOLDBERG

Marriage as a Zenith Value

Justice Goldberg echoed the majority opinion, asserting that liberty encompassed marital privacy and fundamental personal rights are not explicitly articulated in the Bill of Rights. As in the majority opinion, the value of the sanctity of marriage proved to be the catalyst zenith value, and once again declared in the final paragraph: "In sum, I believe that the right of privacy in the marital relation is fundamental and basic—a personal right 'retained by the people' within the meaning of the Ninth Amendment."[25] Marriage was also "basic" and "deep-rooted in our society."[26] Quoting Justice Harlan from *Poe v. Ullman*, 367 U.S. 497 (1961), Justice Goldberg viewed marriage as something society must protect and foster and the intimacies of marriage belonging within privacies inherent in the "preeminence" of the home.[27] Another telling sign that marital privacy was a zenith value concerned its relationship to the necessary law. While some laws were rationally related to the realization of state policies, others were of a necessary nature.[28] When fundamental personal liberties such as marital privacy were involved, their zenith value could not be abridged by state law.[29] Without zenithing marital privacy and allowing the Connecticut law to prevent married people from using contraceptives, that opened the door for a rationally related law for compulsory birth control:

> The logic of the dissents would sanction federal or state legislation that seems to me even more plainly unconstitutional than the statute before us. Surely the government, absent a showing of a compelling subordinating state interest, could not decree that all husbands and wives must be sterilized after two children have been born to them. Yet, by their reasoning, such an invasion of marital privacy would not be subject to constitutional challenge, because, while it might be "silly," no provision of the Constitution specifically prevents the government from curtailing the marital right to bear children and raise a family. While it may shock some of my Brethren that the Court today holds that the Constitution protects the right of marital privacy, in my view, it is far more shocking to believe that the personal liberty guaranteed by the Constitution does not include protection against such totalitarian limitation of family size, which is at complete variance with our constitutional concepts. Yet if, upon a showing of a slender basis of rationality, a law outlawing voluntary birth control by married persons is valid, then, by the same reasoning, a law requiring compulsory birth control also would seem to be valid. In my view, however, both types of law would unjustifiably intrude upon rights of marital privacy which are constitutionally protected.[30]

Yet according to Justice Goldberg, he was not simply giving his personal or private opinion about the sanctity of marriage, but obtaining it from deeply rooted traditions and the collective conscience of the people.[31] On the contrary, values steer people toward one deeply valued tradition over another and also this aspect of the collective conscience over another. We cherry-pick channels of traditions.

LEGAL RATIONALE

Whereas the majority decision employed the First, Third, Fourth, Fifth, and Ninth Amendments to produce multiple penumbras of privacy that justified marriage intimacy, Justice Goldberg contended "[t]he entire fabric of the Constitution" and its specific guarantees demonstrate marital privacy.[32] Also, the Ninth Amendment allowed for additional fundamental rights not mentioned in the first eight amendments.[33] For Justice Goldberg, marital intimacy was not justified by mere shadows, but by dint of the totality of the Constitution empowered by the Ninth Amendment.

CONCURRENCE BY JUSTICE JOHN MARSHALL HARLAN II

For Justice Harlan, the Connecticut law infringed on the Due Process Clause of the Fourteenth Amendment, violating the "basic values" inherent in the idea of ordered liberty.[34] Justice Harlan obviously came down on the side of liberty. He also rejected the incorporation approach advocated by Justice Black. By restraining the Due Process Clause to the protection of rights found in other places of the Constitution, the incorporation approach presumably directs jurists to a single area of "specific constitutional provisions," preventing them from injecting their own views by exercising judicial restraint.[35] Even if this was true, however, specific constitutional provisions could still reflect the personal views of jurists.[36] The better way of instituting judicial restraint, he argued, would be by respecting history, recognizing our society's basic values, and appreciating federalism, especially the separation of powers.[37] For both justices, judicial restraint was a zenith value, with each having a different way of achieving it.

CONCURRENCE BY JUSTICE BYRON WHITE

The Connecticut law interfered with the liberty of married couples, denying due process of law inherent in the Fourteenth Amendment.[38] In Justice White's eyes, banning married people from using contraception would not deter them from committing adultery.[39] Furthermore, the state offered no evidence for this causal relationship.[40]

DISSENT BY JUSTICE HUGO BLACK

Noticeably absent from Justice Black's dissent was the sacred value of marriage. Yet this did not mean values were absent from the dissent. A cluster of values that included positivism, stability, state autonomy, judicial restraint (against the disvalue of judicial overreach), and slow rather rapid change catalyzed the interpretive dye in a particular direction. Justice Black didn't much care for the Connecticut law, calling it "offensive," but refused to see it as unconstitutional because of alleged evil qualities seen in it.[41] He disvalued the law as offensive, but offensiveness did not rise to the profane nadir value of evil. Privacy was not a zenith value, but could be routinely abridged by the government: "I like my privacy as well as the next one, but I am nevertheless compelled to admit that government has a right to invade it unless prohibited by some specific constitutional provision."[42]

The value of positivism impacted his dissent. This led Justice Black away from penumbras. When synonyms for crucial words were used, specifically the "right of privacy, the meaning of the text changes:

> One of the most effective ways of diluting or expanding a constitutionally guaranteed right is to substitute for the crucial word or words of a constitutional guarantee another word or words, more or less flexible and more or less restricted in meaning. This fact is well illustrated by the use of the term "right of privacy" as a comprehensive substitute for the Fourth Amendment's guarantee against "unreasonable searches and seizures."[43]

True to positivist bent, he declaimed against finding a scientific way to assess collective conscience and tradition: "Our Court certainly has no machinery with which to take a Gallup Poll. And the scientific miracles of this age have not yet produced a gadget which the Court can use to determine what traditions are rooted in the "[collective] conscience of our people."[44]

Another protuberant value structure in this dissent concerned two interlocked values: the value of state autonomy and the disvalue of judicial overreach:

> The adoption of such a loose flexible. uncontrolled standard for holding laws unconstitutional, if ever it is finally achieved, will amount to a great unconstitutional shift of power to the courts which I believe and am constrained to say will be bad for the courts, and worse for the country. Subjecting federal and state laws to such an unrestrained and unrestrainable judicial control as to the wisdom of legislative enactments would, I fear, jeopardize the separation of governmental powers that the Framers set up, and, at the same time, threaten to take away much of the power of States to govern themselves which the Constitution plainly intended them to have.[45]

Self-quoting from *Adamson v. California, 332 U.S. 46 (1947)*, Justice Black signaled his disdain for the judicial review established by *Marbury v. Madison*, which the Supreme Court was stuck with "for better or worse."[46] The Amendments should not be stretched.[47] He hearkened back to Supreme Court ruling in 1798, authored by Justice James Iredell:

> It has been the policy of all the *American states* which have individually framed their state constitutions since the revolution, and of the people of the *United States* when they framed the Federal Constitution, to define with precision the objects of the legislative power, and to restrain its exercise within marked and settled boundaries. If any act of Congress, or of the Legislature of a state, violates those constitutional provisions, it is unquestionably void, though I admit that, as the authority to declare it void is of a delicate and awful nature, the Court will never resort to that authority but in a clear and urgent case. If, on the other hand, the Legislature of the Union, or the Legislature of any member of the Union, shall pass a law within the general scope of their constitutional power,

> the Court cannot pronounce it to be void, merely because it is, in their judgment, contrary to the principles of natural justice. The ideas of natural justice are regulated by no fixed standard: the ablest and the purest men have differed upon the subject, and all that the Court could properly say in such an event would be that the Legislature (possessed of an equal right of opinion) had passed an act which, in the opinion of the judges, was inconsistent with the abstract principles of natural justice.[48]

Judicial overreaching caused societal instability, a negative value:

> The Due Process Clause, with an "arbitrary and capricious" or "shocking to the conscience" formula, was liberally used by this Court to strike down economic legislation in the early decades of this century, threatening, many people thought, the tranquility and stability of the Nation.[49]

A core value of the dissent embraced the value of tradition as means of maintaining a separation of powers. Justice Black embraced the value of tradition for his reasoning for diminishing judicial influence:

> The idea is that the Constitution must be changed from time to time, and that this Court is charged with a duty to make those changes. For myself, I must, with all deference, reject that philosophy. The Constitution makers knew the need for change, and provided for it. Amendments suggested by the people's elected representatives can be submitted to the people or their selected agents for ratification. That method of change was good for our Fathers, and, being somewhat old-fashioned, I must add it is good enough for me.[50]

RECKONING OF THE ROGUE JUSTICES

The penumbra business is both a dubious and legitimate enterprise. It's legitimate to draw inferences from the Constitution and all reasoning demands inferring. The question becomes to what degree? It depends on the value system. For those like Justice Black, penumbras were disvalued because they stretched out and distorted the Constitution and were indicative of judicial unrestraint. For those like Justice Douglas and Justice Goldberg, penumbras were valued as the full flowering of the Constitution and jurists as the enablers of this efflorescence.

But Justice Black cannot escape from values. Impacted by a cluster of zenith values that included positivism, stability, and state autonomy (against the disvalue of judicial overreach), Justice Black saw the majority opinion and Goldberg concurrence as natural law. But was it natural law or daringly drawing inferences from the Constitution? A strong investment in a cluster of zenith values polarized the value experience, preventing spectral thinking that would have provided various options. This is roughly the same thing that happens when right-wingers see every government program as socialism or left-wingers see every military action as fascism. Justice Black's natural law allegation fit neatly into this category.

NOTES

1. Ernest Katin, "*Griswold v. Connecticut*: The Justices and Connecticut's Uncommonly Silly Law," *Notre Dame Law Review* 42, 5 (1967): 706.
2. Joanna L. Grossman, "Griswold v. Connecticut: The Start of the Revolution," *Verdict* (June 8, 2015): https://scholarlycommons.law.hofstra.edu/faculty_scholarship/943.
3. Katin, "*Griswold v. Connecticut*: The Justices and Connecticut's Uncommonly Silly Law," 705.
4. Henry T. Greely, "A Footnote to 'Penumbra' in *Griswold V. Connecticut*," *Constitutional Quarterly* 6 (1989): 251.
5. Burr Henly, "Penumbra: The Roots of a Legal Metaphor," *Hastings Constitutional Law Quarterly* 15, 1 (Fall 1987): 82.
6. Chris Rideout, "Penumbral Thinking Revisited: Metaphor in Legal Argumentation," *Legal Communication & Rhetoric* 7 (2010): 189.
7. *Griswold v. Connecticut*, 381 U.S. 479, 486 (1965).
8. Ibid., 481.
9. Ibid., 481.
10. Ibid., 484.
11. Ibid., 483–484.
12. Ibid., 482.
13. Ibid., 485.
14. Ibid., 482.
15. Ibid., 481.
16. Ibid., 482.
17. Ibid.
18. Ibid.
19. Ibid., 482–484.
20. Ibid., 484.
21. Ibid., 585.
22. Ibid., 484
23. Ibid., 486.
24. Ibid., 484.
25. Ibid., 489.
26. Ibid., 491.
27. Ibid., 495.

28. Ibid.
29. Ibid.
30. Ibid., 496–497.
31. Ibid., 493.
32. Ibid., 495.
33. Ibid., 380.
34. Ibid., 499.
35. Ibid., 500–502.
36. Ibid., 500.
37. Ibid., 501.
38. Ibid., 502.
39. Ibid., 506.
40. Ibid., 507.
41. Ibid.
42. Ibid., 510.
43. Ibid., 509.
44. Ibid.
45. Ibid., 521.
46. Ibid., 525.
47. Ibid., 508.
48. Ibid., 525.
49. Ibid.
50. Ibid., 527, 529, 531.
51. Ibid.

Chapter 11

Malicious Free Speech v. Libel of a Government Official

New York Times Co. v. Sullivan

NARRATIVE IN NUTSHELL

"In Montgomery, Alabama, after students sang 'My Country, 'Tis of Thee' [false: actually the national anthem] on the State Capitol steps [false: never happened], their leaders were expelled from school [false: expelled for demanding service at a lunch counter], and truckloads of police armed with shotguns and tear-gas ringed [false: actually deployed near campus] the Alabama State College Campus. When the entire student body protested to state authorities by refusing to reregister, their dining hall was padlocked [never happened] in an attempt to starve them into submission" [only non-registered students and those with temporary meal plans were denied access to cafeteria].

"Again and again, the Southern violators have answered Dr. King's peaceful protests with intimidation and violence. They [L.B. Sullivan under whom the police were deployed] have bombed his home, almost killing his wife and child. They [L.B. Sullivan under whom the police were deployed] have assaulted his person. They [L.B. Sullivan under whom the police were deployed] have arrested him seven times [false: four times]—for 'speeding,' 'loitering' and similar 'offenses.' And now they [L.B. Sullivan under whom the police were deployed] have charged him with 'perjury'—a *felony* under which they could imprison him for *ten years.*"

The above was a paid advertisement from 1960 in *The New York Times* dramatizing violence against Blacks and civil rights workers and represents a copyeditor's nightmare. Falsehood after falsehood after falsehood. In the second excerpt from the advertisement, what was the meaning of "They"? On the surface, "They" apparently referred to the police, but in Birmingham, the police were under the leadership of L.B. Sullivan. Criticism of the police was actually criticism of L.B. Sullivan and criticism of L.B. Sullivan actually constituted libeling L.B. Sullivan. "They became associated with "me." Sullivan saw any attack on the police as an attack on him and his leadership.

This was the 1960s and the beginning of the civil rights movement in the United States of America. Tensions ran high in a polarized political environment in which citizens are out in the streets protesting racial injustice. An Alabama jury awarded Sullivan $500,000 for libel and this was upheld by the Supreme Court of Alabama.

VALUE-INFUSED SCHOLARSHIP

"A world without any protection against defamation," one commentator assesses, "is a world with too much defamation, too much misinformation-in a word, too much public fraud."[1] What is the threshold of fraud and how can that be determined without a value? *Sullivan* was a tool to bludgeon racial segregation and bring about a just society[2]: "There can be no doubt that the libel action in *Sullivan* was instituted to punish and suppress expressions of support for the cause of racial equality."[3] To counter "the racially charged Alabama court system," an evil in his mind, Justice Brennan created a new rule on constitutional malice.[4] On another front, "statements [that have expressive value] are designed to point at some larger truth in the world or serve some other legitimate, valuable, expressive purpose."[5]

> "We live in a democracy, yet the Court has failed to ask what the needs of democratic government are and how free expression meets these needs. . . . Does free expression conflict with and jeopardize other values? If so, what are the other values and how important are they in furthering the ideal of a democracy of individuals, for individuals, and by individuals? What harms can result from free expression? What harms can result from the allowance of civil libel suits?"[6]

The value of free speech falls under the sacred zenith value of American democracy, but what if falsehoods and mutual distrust from speech are detrimental to the existence of such a democracy?[7] Axiological analysis spins out in another direction, identifying specific elements of freedom of speech valued by the Court.

MAJORITY OPINION BY JUSTICE WILLIAM BRENNAN

At the outset of this case, axiology demands fine-tuning of freedom of speech, discovering the catalyst or animating value. A generic value analysis of freedom of speech will do little to understand its force in this case.

From the case, the following terms were used to describe freedom of speech, whether from Justice William Brennan's pen or what he approvingly quoted. Freedom of speech was described with the following words:

- robust
- wide-open
- widest possible dissemination
- uninhibited
- a plurality of voices rather than an authoritarian few
- rejection of self-censorship
- bad taste
- half-truths
- falsehoods
- misinformation
- exaggeration
- vilification

These words clearly demonstrated the wide scope of freedom of speech. The boundaries of free speech were pushed out by values of robustness, inhibition, and a denial of self-censorship (which today we might call "unfiltered"). The embracing of these three values entailed the inclusion of a plurality of voices (and rejection of authoritarianism), bad taste, misinformation, half-truths, falsehoods, exaggeration, and vilification. More than this: without freedom of speech as encapsulated in these values, a stable government cannot be secured.

As animated by these values, freedom of speech became a sacred zenith value. The value of the speaker acceded, while the value of the listener receded. What mattered most, what is of most significance, is the speechmakers and not the speech recipients. Not only how speech was to occur—with force and pervasively—but also not concerning oneself with its truth content places the speaker on a higher level than the recipient of the speech.

Taking all this into account, the bar for proving "actual malice" and libel was going to be exceedingly high, over which even Olympian barristers could not leap:

> A State cannot, under the First and Fourteenth Amendments, award damages to a public official for defamatory falsehood relating to his official conduct unless he proves "actual malice"—that the statement was made with knowledge of its falsity or with reckless disregard of whether it was true or false.[8]

The standard for actual malice consisted of knowingly making falsehoods and having a reckless disregard for the truth. "Knowingly?" One could easily argue ignorance. "Recklessly?" One could easily argue what that vague term means in various contexts. For example, in the production of a newspaper ad what could be seen as a reckless disregard for truth could be seen as simply getting the paper out on time.

So animated, freedom of speech could not be prohibited when criticizing government officials or that which was under the supervision of government officials. Thus, the argument that "they" referred to Commissioner Sullivan and thus libeled him could be seen as a patent infringement on free speech. It would allow any criticism of a government agency to be a de facto criticism of the person running the agency and potentially liable. If such were the case, then people would be wary of criticizing any government agency:

> The present proposition would sidestep this obstacle by transmuting criticism of government, however impersonal it may seem on its face, into personal criticism, and hence potential libel, of the officials of whom the government is composed. There is no legal alchemy by which a State may thus create the cause of action that would otherwise be denied for a publication which, as respondent himself said of the advertisement, "reflects not only on me but on the other Commissioners and the community." Raising as it does the possibility that a good faith critic of government will be penalized for his criticism, the proposition relied on by the Alabama courts strikes at the very center of the constitutionally protected area of free expression. We hold that such a proposition may not be constitutionally utilized to establish that an otherwise impersonal attack on governmental operations was a libel of an official responsible for those operations. Since it was relied on exclusively here, and there was no other evidence to connect the statements with respondent, the evidence was constitutionally insufficient to support a finding that the statements referred to respondent.[9]

To buttress his legal case, Justice Brennan made the usual pilgrimages to the First and Fourteenth Amendments:

> The question before us is whether this rule of liability, as applied to an action brought by a public official against critics of his official conduct, abridges the freedom of speech and of the press that is guaranteed by the First and Fourteenth Amendments.[10]

Together, these Amendments put a padlock on libel-chargers who were government officials.

The First and the Fourteenth Amendments were invigorated by the eloquent fireworks from the man with best name in history of jurisprudence, Learned Hand. The First Amendment "'presupposes that right conclusions are more likely to be gathered out of a multitude of tongues than through any kind of authoritative selection. To many, this is, and always will be, folly, but we have staked upon it our all.'"[11]

Also, Justice Brennan appropriated Justice Brandeis's compelling analysis of free speech in 1927's *Whitney v. California*:

> Those who won our independence believed . . . that public discussion is a political duty, and that this should be a fundamental principle of the American government. They recognized the risks to which all human institutions are subject. But they knew that order cannot be secured merely through fear of punishment for its infraction; that it is hazardous to discourage thought, hope and imagination; that fear breeds repression; that repression breeds hate; that hate menaces stable government; that the path of safety lies in the opportunity to discuss freely supposed grievances and proposed remedies, and that the fitting remedy for evil counsels is good ones. Believing in the power of reason as applied through public discussion, they eschewed silence coerced by law—the argument of force in its worst form. Recognizing the occasional tyrannies of governing majorities, they amended the Constitution so that free speech and assembly should be guaranteed.[12]

Order for society was a sacred zenith value. Its realization came not simply from fear of punishment but also through the values of thought, hope, and imagination. Free discussion of grievances and suggested remedies were much preferred to coercive silence.

Finally, from one of the Founders, James Madison, came a reminder that the people and not the government have absolute sovereignty:

> His premise was that the Constitution created a form of government under which "The people, not the government, possess the absolute sovereignty." The structure of the government dispersed power in reflection of the people's distrust of concentrated power, and of power itself at all levels. This form of government was "altogether different" from the British form, under which the Crown was sovereign and the people were subjects.[13]

> [T]he censorial power is in the people over the Government, and not in the Government over the people.[14]

RECKONING OF THE ROGUE JUSTICES

Government officials can be libeled. It cannot be called "libel," of course. However, if one can vilify a public official (speak or write about in an abusively disparaging manner), how much different is that than libeling them? If there is a difference, it can only be a difference to the most infinitesimal degree and hardly significant. If we spread misinformation, half-truths, falsehoods about a person and speak about them abusively and disparagingly, how different is that from libel?

"Actual malice" was the basis for libel. Yet that standard is extraordinarily difficult to prove. To prove that someone "knowingly" made a falsehood would entail what? Writings or conversations in which the person stated: "Yeah, I know I'm lying and I'm doing it because I hate this person." Such documentation would seem to be as hard to collect as lightning in a bottle. The notion of recklessness is also fraught with ambiguity. For the cautious person, recklessness might mean not dotting every i or crossing every t, while for others once over is enough. These standards—if you want to call them that—are largely inapplicable and window dressing.

The majority opinion amounted to open season on public officials. Libel will be as difficult to prove as it is for a rich person to go to heaven through the eye of the needle. Freedom of speech became a sacred zenith value when applied to government officials.

The value of freedom of speech was so important that collateral damage was accepted for its maintenance. That collateral damage included falsehoods, half-truths, misinformation, and vilification. Free speech comes at a price, but its value is so important that the price must be paid. Public officials are forewarned that being at the center of this war of words is a central element of their job descriptions. And if the agencies they run are maligned and they think the criticism it extends to them, then so be it.

Also, freedom of speech placed a premium value on the speechmaker and much less value on the speech recipient. Freedom of speech protected the speechmaker and left the recipient of speech vulnerable to speech. The First Amendment as articulated by Justice Brennan spoke to citizens protecting themselves with speech rather than be prey to the speech of others.

The First Amendment values action and activity on the part of people and not passivity. It promotes an attitude of engagement rather than disengagement. It is all about people finding their voices not in an echo chamber or in a silent meditation but with or against others. Resistance was inherent in freedom of speech, and compliance is never coerced.

Protecting freedom of speech entailed supporting a never-ending war of words. This right was not meant for the faint-hearted or those craving civility. Human beings have deep-seated views on the world and each person believes wholly in their worldview. These are the "fighting faiths" of which Justice Holmes spoke. Because of this, hostilities break out. The First Amendment allows for these outbreaks or wars of words and ideologies. Such hostilities are part and parcel of a free society. Moreover, as Justice Brandeis pointed out, the First Amendment acted as a safety valve for expressions that are better done in intellectual rather than in physical welfare. It is better to character-assassinate than assassinate our public officials.

The nature of truth must also be understood. Truth does not come out fully as Athena was said to spring from the head of Zeus. It comes out piecemeal and sometimes parts of it or the whole of it are later considered to be false. This holds not only in law but also in science. Do we degrade a scientist from an earlier era because the theory is shortsighted in some way, improved upon by a successor? Truth is often elusive and even in good faith, humans are usually only able to apprehend the world in one-sided ways as this and that emerges and the human mind only fits and starts grasping it. By valuing truth-bearing in this way, we can value humans as mistake-prone always and malicious maybe.

NOTES

1. Richard A. Epstein, "Was New York Times v. Sullivan Wrong?," *University of Chicago Law Review* 53 (1986): 799.
2. Bruce L. Ottley, John B. Lewis and Younghee J. Ottley, "*New York Times v. Sullivan*: A Retrospective Examination," *DePaul Law Review* 33, 4 (Summer 1984): 779.
3. Samuel R. Pierce Jr., "The Anatomy of an Historic Decision: *New York Times Co. v. Sullivan*," *North Carolina Law Review* 43, 2 (1965): 363.
4. Carlo A. Pedrioli, "*New York Times v. Sullivan* and the Rhetorics of Race: A Look at the Briefs, Oral Arguments, and Opinions," *Georgetown Journal Law and Modern Critical Race Perspectives* 7 (2015): 135.
5. Ashley Messenger, "The Problem with *New York Times and Co. v. Sullivan*: An Argument for Moving from a Falsity Model of Libel Law to a Speech Act Model," *First Amendment Law Review* 11, 1 (2012): 175.
6. Jerome Lawrence Merin, *The Supreme Court and Libel*, *William and Mary Law Review* 11, 2 (1969): 421.
7. David Andrew Logan, "Rescuing Our Democracy by Rethinking *New York Times Co. v. Sullivan Ohio State Law Journal*," Forthcoming: 815. SSRN: https://ssrn.com/abstract=3761438.
8. *New York Times Co. v. Sullivan*, 376 U.S. 254 (1964).
9. Ibid., 292.
10. Ibid., 268.
11. Ibid., 270.
12. Ibid., 270.
13. Ibid., 274.
14. Ibid., 282.

Chapter 12

The Subjective Turn of the Fourteenth Amendment v. Separate but Equal

Brown v. Board of Education of Topeka

NARRATIVE IN A NUTSHELL

> Segregation of white and colored children in public schools has a detrimental effect on colored children. The impact is greater when it has the sanction of the law, for the policy of separating the races is usually interpreted as denoting the inferiority of the negro group. A sense of inferiority affects the motivation of a child to learn. Segregation with the sanction of law, therefore, has a tendency to [retard] the educational and mental development of negro children and to deprive them of some of the benefits they would receive in a racial[ly] integrated school system.[1]

Brown v. Board of the Education—the Supreme Court decision that struck down segregation in public schools. That is the boilerplate narrative. However, much more in terms of values was going on. The scope was breathtaking. A good portion of American legal history was biopsied, deemed malignant, and excised by this decision. Second, education emerged as a protuberant value. Third, social science and psychology appeared as buttressing values. Finally, an amazing transformation of the Fourteenth Amendment occurred, like the ugly duckling transforming into a swan. It took a subjective turn, extended from political equality to psychological equality. It moved from objectivity to subjectivity. *Brown* struck down separate but equal, struck down a pillar of American law and the racial assumptions embedded in American history. *Brown v. Topeka Board of Education of Topeka* pertained not just separate but equal public schooling in Kansas but also in South Carolina, Virginia, and Delaware. Because those cases came from the same legal grounding, the Court decided to consolidate them in this single ruling. Each case consisted of Black children (through legal representation) seeking the courts' aid to go to school with Caucasian children. Each case ended up in the same segregated pile: the courts denied these Black children admission to all-white schools on the basis of laws that either required or permitted segregation according to race.

VALUE-INFUSED SCHOLARSHIP

Brown can be depreciated for giving false hope about a postracial world. Letting go of *Brown* or depreciating its value from the iconic plateau makes us face intractable elements of race and explore equality as its driving value.[2] Rather than seeing Brown as a stake in the heart of racism, it may be seen as retarding social justice. *Brown* promised much more than it delivered and overvaluing Brown's significance masks racial and social inequalities entrenched in the American way of life.[3] Less negatively, it would naive to believe that one ruling "could on its own do all the heavy lifting of transforming a racially divided nation into a racially harmonious one" or eliminate racial stigmas.[4] Looked at more broadly and outside of public education, *Brown* had a positive impact serving as "a constitutional precedent against state-mandated segregation" in later Court rulings by declaring the unconstitutionality of other publicly mandated forms of segregation, such as at municipal golf courses, in bus transportation, and at public beaches were also unconstitutional.[5] It was a catalyst for many civil rights movements as well as elevating the national conscience regarding civil rights.[6] Other positive impacts also emerged:

> One result of Brown I that had not been anticipated was its psychological impact on African-American communities around the South. This psychological effect manifested itself in a grass-roots anti-segregation revolt that took everyone by surprise in Montgomery, Alabama in 1956 with the bus boycott initiated by Rosa Park's refusal to move to the back of the bus.[7]

Its value can be seen to appreciate because it considered both tangible and intangible elements of racism and its larger impact:

> With regard to assessing the value of Brown, we need to engage in a similar exercise. If we limit our focus to objective measures of matters such as the degree to which the public schools of this country are meaningfully integrated, Brown admittedly falls woefully short. It is when we shift our focus to include broader, "intangible" considerations that we discover "what makes for greatness" in a legal opinion. [8]

Racial progressive gradualism is steeped in values:

> (1) the salience of societal, historical, and present-day racism and discrimination in shaping the interactions between African Americans and Whites; (2) the necessity of an active role of government, especially the Federal government, in the disestablishment of the values of racism and the inequalities premised on white supremacy and segregation; (3) the employment of race conscious measures and terminology to describe and address the values, significations and traditions that advantage Whites and disadvantaged African Americans; and (4) an emphasis on the harmful and persistent consequences of racism and its expressions on the lives of African Americans.[9]

For those who expected *Brown* to be a panacea to all social ills and elevated it to the level of great moral awakening as a prelude to the end of racism, this was not the landmark case, but a letdown. In this value scheme, a one-to-one causal relationship is valued rather than a multifaceted causal relationship. However, as axiological analysis will show, the addition of a subjective dimension of the Fourteenth Amendment deepened and extended it.

MAJORITY OPINION BY CHIEF JUSTICE EARL WARREN

The main legal target for Chief Justice Warren was the "separate but equal" mantra of the 1896 ruling *Plessy v. Ferguson*. In that case, segregation in transportation was justified by saying the accommodations in segregated train cars were separate, but equal. The majority opinion understood that Plessy was the head of the monster and it had to be chopped off so that its body (rulings using it as a precedent) would also perish. Against this multi-tentacled monster, the most potent power had to be unleashed: the Fourteenth Amendment. This was not the Fourteenth Amendment that had been enslaved by tradition and pre–civil war precedent. This newly minted and valued, potent Fourteenth Amendment would now like Hercules, capable of heroic labors, specifically, slay racism embedded in the legal mechanisms of the United States of America.

THE *PLESSY* PROGENY

In the four cases consolidated in this ruling, *Plessy* remained untouched and the Fourteenth Amendment stood mute on the sidelines. The Courts found ways to weasel out of the Fourteenth Amendment, basically by ordering equalization of Black schools and denying Black children admittance to schools during the equalization process or in the case of the Delaware ruling, ordering desegregation while simultaneously suggesting a back door to counteract it.

Kansas

Brown v. Board of Education of Topeka, 98 F. Supp. 797 (D. Kan. 1951)
District Court argued that while segregation negatively impacted Black children, Negro and Caucasian schools were equal in terms of buildings, transportation, curricula, and educational qualifications of teachers.

South Carolina

Briggs v. Elliott, 342 U.S. 350 (1952)
District Court admitted Negro schools were inferior and ordered defendants to equalize facilities, but denied Black children admission to Caucasian schools during the equalization process.

Delaware

Gebhart v. Belton, 33 Del. Ch. 144, 87 A.2d 862, aff'd, 91 A.2d 137 (1952)
Chancellor ordered Immediate admission of Black children to all-white schools on grounds of inferiority of Black schools based on teacher training, student-teacher ratio, extracurricular activities, facilities, and transportation challenges (time and distance). Supreme Court of Delaware affirmed Chancellor's decision, but diluted it by suggesting the decree could be modified once equalization had occurred.

Virginia

Davis v. County School Board (1954)
Ordered immediate equalization of curricula and transportation and equalization of physical plant with "due diligence," but denied Black children admission to Caucasian schools.

The cases consolidated in *Brown* reflected a pattern of court decisions regarding educational equality in which the Fourteenth Amendment was ignored.

Cumming v. County Board of Education, 175 U.S. 528 (1899) Black taxpayers sought injunction to discontinue operation of white schools until resumption of operation of Black schools.

Gong Lum v. Rice, 275 U.S. 78 (1927) Chinese youth contended misapplication of doctrine that classified him as Negro and compelled him to attend a Negro school.

Missouri ex rel. Gaines v. Canada, 305 U.S. 337 (1938) Inequalities in graduate school manifested themselves in specific benefits enjoyed by white students denied to Negro students of the same educational qualifications.
Sipuel v. Oklahoma, 332 U.S. 631 (1948) Inequalities in graduate school manifested themselves in specific benefits enjoyed by white students denied to Negro students of the same educational qualifications.
Sweatt v. Painter, 339 U.S. 629 (1950) Inequalities in graduate school manifested themselves in specific benefits enjoyed by white students denied to Negro students of the same educational qualifications.
McLaurin v. Oklahoma State Regents, 339 U.S. 637 (1950) Inequalities in graduate school manifested themselves in specific benefits enjoyed by white students denied to Negro students of the same educational qualifications.

ADMISSION OF VALUATION OF FOURTEENTH AMENDMENT

> This discussion and our own investigation convince us that although these sources cast some light, it is not enough to resolve the problem with which we are faced. At best, they are inconclusive. The most avid proponents of the postwar amendments undoubtedly intended them to remove all legal distinctions among "all persons born or naturalized in the United States." Their opponents, just as certainly, were antagonistic to both the letter and the spirit of the Amendments and wished them to have the most limited effect. What others in Congress and the state legislatures had in mind cannot be determined with any degree of certainty.[10]

This was coy. Of course, the legislatures knew what they were doing, and so did the judges. The Fourteenth Amendment could serve the purposes of liberating or enslaving Blacks. In the hands of segregationists, the Fourteenth Amendment was circumscribed by racist laws, traditions, and institutions and enfeebled. In the hands of integrationists, it became the master of racist laws, traditions, and institutions. Depreciated, the Fourteenth Amendment died on the vine. Appreciated, it could flower into the full bloom of freedom.

To revivify the Fourteenth Amendment, the majority opinion drew from *Strauder v. West Virginia*, 100 U.S. 303, 307–308 (1880):

> The words of the amendment, it is true, are prohibitory, but they contain a necessary implication of a positive immunity, or right, most valuable to the colored race—the right to exemption from unfriendly legislation against them distinctively as colored—exemption from legal discriminations, implying inferiority in civil society, lessening the security of their enjoyment of the rights which

> others enjoy, and discriminations which are steps towards reducing them to the condition of a subject race.[11]

OPERATIVE VALUES

Value of Education

Had the Court not elevated education to high value, its case would have been significantly weaker. The value of education was measured in the court's eyes in a number of ways. It acquired value because the law deemed it mandatory. It acquired value because of how much money American society spent on it. It acquired value for teaching public responsibilities, which were the basis for being good citizens. It acquired value for cultivating an awareness of cultural values, preparing children for professional training down the line, and facilitating a normal adjustment to the environment. Public education was deemed valuable for both individual children and for society as a whole. Americans deemed public education valuable by how much money was given to it. Projects receiving money were deemed more valuable than those not receiving money.

> Today, education is perhaps the most important function of state and local governments. Compulsory school attendance laws and the great expenditures for education both demonstrate our recognition of the importance of education to our democratic society. It is required in the performance of our most basic public responsibilities, even service in the armed forces. It is the very foundation of good citizenship. Today, it is a principal instrument in awakening the child to cultural values, in preparing him for later professional training, and in helping him to adjust normally to his environment. In these days, it is doubtful that any child may reasonably be expected to succeed in life if he is denied the opportunity of an education. Such an opportunity, where the state has undertaken to provide it, is a right which must be made available to all on equal terms.[12]

Value of the Social Sciences

Rather than valuing tradition, the Court depended upon psychological and psychological research to overturn *Plessy*:

- B. Clark, *Effect of Prejudice and Discrimination on Personality* Development (Mid-century White House Conference on Children and Youth, 1950);
- Witmer and Kotinsky, *Personality in the Making*;

- Deutscher and Chein, "The Psychological Effects of Enforced Segregation A Survey of Social Science Opinion";
- Chein, "What are the Psychological Effects of Segregation Under Conditions of Equal Facilities";
- Brameld, *Educational Costs, in Discrimination and National Welfare*;
- Frazier, *The Negro in the United States*;
- Myrdal, *An American Dilemma.*

Valuing this research lead to revaluing the Fourteenth Amendment. From this research came the following conclusion of the impact of segregated schools on black children:

> Such considerations apply with added force to children in grade and high schools. To separate them from others of similar age and qualifications solely because of their race generates a feeling of inferiority as to their status in the community that may affect their hearts and minds in a way unlikely ever to be undone. The effect of this separation on their educational opportunities was well stated by a finding in the Kansas case by a court which nevertheless felt compelled to rule against the Negro plaintiffs.[13]

This interest in the social and psychological states of oppressed Black children contributed to seeing the issue from the perspective of the oppressed Black children, from the inside out rather than from the outside in.

Disvalue of Feelings of Inferiority

The Court deemed schooling valuable for American society and for students. In this list of valuables, there was no mention of something in the order of self-esteem or a positive mindset. But the Court asserted that segregated schools fostered feelings of inferiority in the minds of black children.

Value the Subjective Dimension of the Fourteenth Amendment

> No state shall make or enforce any law which shall abridge the privileges or immunities of citizens of the United States; nor shall any state deprive any person of life, liberty, or property, without due process of law; nor deny to any person within its jurisdiction the equal protection of the laws.

Deprivation of life now included feelings of inferiority or liberty from feelings of inferiority. This revalued the Fourteenth Amendment. Now, the subjective mind, the perspective of young U.S. citizens, came into play. The

Fourteenth Amendment was violated not by social constraints, but by how social situations affected young, impressionable minds. When the subjectivity of another human being was taken into account, they were no longer lifeless blocks, or property, and so different to be not human. They were persons and as persons deserve dignity. In *Brown*, we find full expression of the Fourteenth Amendment. Human life was more than objective fact. It inhered in perspective. Once human perspective was valued, so, too, was dignity. The energy the Fourteenth Amendment received depended entirely on whether the justices valued Blacks as people, understood and commiserated with their subjectivity.

> We come then to the question presented: does segregation of children in public schools solely on the basis of race, even though the physical facilities and other "tangible" factors may be equal, deprive the children of the minority group of equal educational opportunities?[14]

Beyond what was objectively measurable, such as transportation, facilities, and teachers, there was another dimension of equality. That dimension resided in the headspace of young Black schoolchildren.

VALUE VIGNETTE

The majority opinion valued education and the findings of the social science, disvalued feelings of inferiority, and revalued the Fourteenth Amendment to include subjectivity. If education was a prime value for both children and society, then it followed that all educational facilities must be first rate. Valuing the findings of the social sciences was preferred to being ignorant of them. To understand where the impact of the disvalue of feelings of inferiority stood and their permanence was to be distinguished from the feeling of inferiority being a choice. Finally, the reimagined Fourteenth Amendment allowed for seeing both the objective and subjective ramifications of racism.

RECKONING OF THE ROGUE JUSTICES

Brown v. the Board of Educations reoriented and revalued the Fourteenth Amendment by investing it with subjectivity. It was more than the inadequate conditions of the schools that resulted in separate but equal, but the mindset of African-American children. Separate and equal were the same as different and depreciated. White public schools were "normal" and this otherworld of education was for the nonhumans. In the minds of those students in the otherworld and underworld of education, they were not as good as those in elite white schools. If this seems strange, it is not, for example, the stigma of mentally challenged people being segregated. This was beyond people being able to go wherever they want to or occupy certain physical spaces. This concerned the headspace of African-American children and how that headspace had been violated. This was about the trauma of racism as it affected the development of children, a vulnerable segment of the population. The American way of life at its core was rotten. It subsisted on a strict parallelism of the races except for exploitation at the tangents. It wasn't the case that this or that ruling was rotten, but that America had something rotten right at its core. Racism was still entrenched and *Brown* had to take extreme measures to remove its blot from American life. Under separate but equal, racism could continue to reproduce and appear "natural." *Brown* put us on the road to seeing racism as unnatural in the sense of that to be comfortable with or accepted carte blanche or as an article of faith. Desegregating the schools meant more than moving bodies into the same space. It meant shaping the minds of Black children in positive ways. Racism was damaging to the psyches of young Black Americans. The other part of such segregation was that it promoted racial superiority of whites, who never have to interact with blacks and never come to understand them in real time. While the students in one school system suffered in inferiority, the students in the other reveled in their superiority. *Brown* unleashed the full power of the Equality Clause of the Fourteenth Amendment by confronting the psychological dimensions of inferiority. Wearing a badge of inferiority for all to see had stigmatized Blacks and made them feel inferior. *Brown* was an acknowledgment of this shaming and the psychological harm it caused and the integration of schools was meant in no small part a way to remedy it.

NOTES

1. *Brown v. Board of Education of Topeka*, 347 U.S. 483, 494 (1954).
2. Geraldo Lopez and Rebecca Burciago, "The Troublesome Legacy of *Brown v. Board of Education*," *Educational Administration Quarterly* 50, 5 (December 2014): 796.
3. Derrick A. Bell Jr., "The Unintended Lessons in *Brown v. Board of Education*," *New York Law School Law Review* 49, 4 (2004–2005): 1066.
4. Sabrina Zrkel, "Ongoing Issues of Racial and Ethnic Stigma in Education 50 Years after *Brown v. Board*," *The Urban Review* 37, 2 (June 2005): 108.
5. James T. Patterson, "Brown v. Board of Education and the Civil Rights Movement," 420, https://www.stetson.edu/law/lawreview/media/brown-v-board-of-education-and-the-civil-rights-movement.pdf.
6. Ibid.

7. Constance Baker Motley, "Symposium: *Brown v. Board of Education* and Its Legacy: A Tribute to Justice Thurgood Marshall, The Historical Setting of Brown and Its Impact on the Supreme Court's Decision," *Fordham Law Review* 61, 1 (1992): 16.

8. Neil G. Williams, "*Brown v. Board of Education* Fifty Years Later: What Makes for Greatness in a Legal Opinion?," *Loyola University Chicago Law Journal* 36 (2004): 198.

9. Michael W. Combs and Gwendolyn Combs, "Revisiting *Brown v. Board of Education*: A Cultural, Historical Legal, and Political Perspective," *Management Department Faculty Publications* (2005): 677, https://digitalcommons.unl.edu/managementfacpub/48.

10. *Brown v. Board of Education of Topeka*, 489.

11. Ibid., 496.

12. Ibid., 493.

13. Ibid., 494.

14. Ibid., 493.

Chapter 13

Collective Safety Net v. Individualistic Self-Defense

District of Columbia v. Heller

NARRATIVE IN A NUTSHELL

Who was Dick Anthony Heller?

Heller was a District of Columbia special police officer.

In his job, was Heller authorized to use a handgun?

Yes.

But according to Washington, D.C. Code, was he allowed to keep his handgun at home?

Yes, on a year-to-year basis, provided he obtained a license.

Was he denied that license?

Yes.

What was the D.C. Code in question?

D. C. Code §§7–2501.01(12), 7–2502.01(a), 7–2502.02(a)(4) (2001) illegalized carrying unregistered firearms *and* prohibited the registration of handguns *unless* according to §§22–4504(a), 22–4506, the chief of police issued a license. Unless the weapon was kept in a place of business or was being used for legal recreational purposes, §7–2507.02 required owners of lawfully registered firearms either to keep their firearms unloaded and disassembled or bound by a trigger lock or some equivalent device.

Why did Washington, D.C. legislators pass these provisions?

Because gun violence was particularly bad in their urban center.

And Heller thought his Second Amendment rights were being violated by the D.C. code?

"A well regulated Militia, being necessary to the security of a free State, the right of the people to keep and bear Arms, shall not be infringed."

VALUE-INFUSED SCHOLARSHIP

Heller is castigated for potentially eroding Fourth Amendment privacy, as it could prompt police officers to run roughshod over privacy rights to find guns before their bullets find them.[1] In the same vein, the verdict could conceivably encourage reactionaries to overthrow the government.[2] Why "the Second Amendment should protect the 'lineal descendants' of commonly used Framing-era weapons-rather than, as Justice Scalia suggested, weapons in common use at some ever-changing 'present' time"[3] can only be determined by the scope of the implication, whether a narrow or broader range of implication is valued. "Among other things, the majority opinion basically nullified any operative importance of the 'militia'-oriented preamble and, instead, viewed the amendment entirely from what might be termed a private, individualized perspective of self-defense."[4] In other words, self-defense becomes an absolute value: there is no standard by which the D.C. law cannot be a violation of the Second Amendment in terms of self-defense,[5] in effect making the Second Amendment an absolute value. The verdict can be seen as a call to collective action, a "need to combine the regulation of weapons and greater resources for law enforcement with preventive intervention strategies aimed at high-risk populations and communities."[6] Looked through a novel civil rights lens, the positive aspects of *Heller* can be articulated as "the beginning of a new chapter of civil rights constitutionalism animated by a new convergence of white and black interests around the kinds of civil rights that deserve constitutional protection."[7] By embracing a

> popular constitutionalism view, the Court itself is deciding whether handgun bans are consistent with the best understanding of our constitutional tradition; the determination is made in the present and responds to the beliefs and values of living Americans who identify with the commitments and traditions of their forbears.[8]

This demonstrates the nuances of values as the majority opinion hyper-values one aspect of the Second Amendment to the level of a sacred zenith value while virtually ignoring everything else.

SELF-DEFENSE AS A SACRED ZENITH VALUE; COLLECTIVE SAFETY AS A PREFERRED VALUE

In the majority opinion written by Justice Antonin Scalia, there was a sense of urgency to save the Second Amendment from extinction:

> Undoubtedly some think that the Second Amendment is outmoded in a society where our standing army is the pride of our Nation, where well-trained police

> forces provide personal security, and where gun violence is a serious problem. That is perhaps debatable, but what is not debatable is that it is not the role of this Court to pronounce the Second Amendment extinct.[9]

When a species is on the verge of extinction, the rescuers of that species see the issue as a life-and-death matter. The endangered species must be vigorously protected, lest it perish. For Justice Scalia, this profane nadir value of the extinction of a sacred zenith value of the Second Amendment catalyzed his majority opinion. The thicket of history concerning firearm laws and a detailed grammatical analysis of the Second Amendment justified the self-defense dimension of the Second Amendment. Justice Scalia saw "the inherent right of self-defense" as "central to the Second Amendment right"[10]:

> The First Amendment contains the freedom-of-speech guarantee that the people ratified, which included exceptions for obscenity, libel, and disclosure of state secrets, but not for the expression of extremely unpopular and wrong-headed views. The Second Amendment is no different. Like the First, it is the very product of an interest-balancing by the people—which Justice Breyer would now conduct for them anew. And whatever else it leaves to future evaluation, it surely elevates above all other interests [values] the right of law-abiding, responsible citizens to use arms in defense of hearth and home.[11]

However—while the self-defense dimension of the Second Amendment was an absolute, there were limitations on who could possess weaponry:

> Although we do not undertake an exhaustive historical analysis today of the full scope of the Second Amendment, nothing in our opinion should be taken to cast doubt on longstanding prohibitions on the possession of firearms by felons and the mentally ill, or laws forbidding the carrying of firearms in sensitive places such as schools and government buildings, or laws imposing conditions and qualifications on the commercial sale of arms.[12]

The dissents from Justice Breyer and Justice Stevens did not value self-defense as essential to the Second Amendment and if not essential, then not absolute. From their perspectives, the self-defense dimension could be justified by neither the original text nor the history of firearm laws. According to Justice Breyer:

> The second independent reason is that the protection the Amendment provides is not absolute. The Amendment permits government to regulate the interests that it serves. Thus, irrespective of what those interests are—whether they do or do not include an independent interest in self-defense—the majority's view cannot

> be correct unless it can show that the District's regulation is unreasonable or inappropriate in Second Amendment terms.[13]

The negative value that drove Justice Stevens' dissent was that the self-defense justification at home could become a gateway justification, legitimizing self-defense in any conceivable venue:

> Given the presumption that most citizens are law abiding, and the reality that the need to defend oneself may suddenly arise in a host of locations outside the home, I fear that the District's policy choice may well be just the first of an unknown number of dominoes to be knocked off the table.[14]

Another operative disvalue in Justice Stevens' dissent concerned how the majority decision will cause a "dramatic upheaval in the law."[15] The same disvalue of upheaval of the law occurred in Justice Breyer's dissent:

> Far more important are the unfortunate consequences that today's decision is likely to spawn. Not least of these, as I have said, is the fact that the decision threatens to throw into doubt the constitutionality of gun laws throughout the United States. I can find no sound legal basis for launching the courts on so formidable and potentially dangerous a mission. In my view, there simply is no untouchable constitutional right guaranteed by the Second Amendment to keep loaded handguns in the house in crime-ridden urban areas.[16]

Additionally, Justice Breyer contended, the value of saving lives and diminishing harm outweighed individual self-defense:

> Assume, for argument's sake, that the Framers did intend the Amendment to offer a degree of self-defense protection. Does that mean that the Framers also intended to guarantee a right to possess a loaded gun near swimming pools, parks, and playgrounds? That they would not have cared about the children who might pick up a loaded gun on their parents' bedside table? That they . . . would have lacked concern for the risk of accidental deaths or suicides that readily accessible loaded handguns in urban areas might bring?[17]

Justice Scalia, in what sounded in part like an infomercial for handguns, embraced the value of individual self-defense, while Justice Breyer preferred a collective safety net approach:

Table 13.1 An Infomercial for Handguns

Justice Scalia	*Justice Breyer*
It is enough to note, as we have observed, that the American people have considered the handgun to be the quintessential self-defense weapon. There are many reasons that a citizen may prefer a handgun for home defense: It is easier to store in a location that is readily accessible in an emergency; it cannot easily be redirected or wrestled away by an attacker; it is easier to use for those without the upper-body strength to lift and aim a long gun; it can be pointed at a burglar with one hand while the other hand dials the police. Whatever the reason, handguns are the most popular weapon chosen by Americans for self-defense in the home, and a complete prohibition of their use is invalid.[1]	Even so, a legislature could reasonably conclude that the law will advance goals of great public importance, namely, saving lives, preventing injury, and reducing crime.[2] [T]he District's regulation, which focuses upon the presence of handguns in high-crime urban areas, represents a permissible legislative response to a serious, indeed life-threatening, problem.[3]

Source: *District of Columbia v. Heller*, 554 U.S. 570, 636 (2008).
[1]Ibid, 680.
[2]Ibid, 682.
[3]Ibid, 681–82.

LINGUAL VIVISECTION ACCORDING TO THE VALUE OF ORDINARY AND NORMAL USAGE OF LANGUAGE

The majority opinion penned that Justice Scalia leaned on a lingual vivisection of the Second Amendment and heavy historical analysis preceding and following its ratification in 1791. "Self-defense" as intrinsic to Second Amendment popped from the majority opinion and constituted the single protuberant value. The value of ordinary and normal language buttressed the protuberant value to justify that "self-defense" could be gleaned from the original wording of the Second Amendment.

Justice Scalia placed premium value on the normal and ordinary usage of language in contrast to the disvalue, technical, or stealth language:

> In interpreting this text, we are guided by the principle that "[t]he Constitution was written to be understood by the voters; its words and phrases were used in their normal and ordinary as distinguished from technical meaning. . . ." Normal meaning may of course include an idiomatic meaning, but it excludes secret or technical meanings that would not have been known to ordinary citizens in the founding generation.[18]

The lingual vivisection exposed many subtle valuations. Most notably, the prefatory clause: "A well regulated Militia, being necessary to the security of a free State. . ."

The winds were taken away from the sails of the prefatory clause. For Justice Scalia, the prefatory clause was neutral,[19] tilting toward neither expanding nor limiting the operative clause: "the right of the people to keep and bear Arms, shall not be infringed." The term "well-regulated" referred to the proper discipline and training and did not pertain to the government.[20] The "free state" did not pertain to specific states of the Union, but generally to the country at large.[21] For Justice Scalia, the term "the people" transcended the Militia and included "all members of a political community."[22] The term "to keep and bear arms" related "to weapons that were not specifically designed for military use and were not employed in a military capacity."[23] "Defending our own person or home was a matter of self-preservation."[24] Justice Scalia admitted his own value preferences: "We start therefore with a strong presumption that the Second Amendment right is exercised individually and belongs to all Americans."[25]

This reading of the Second Amendment valued integration of the military and ordinary citizens. The Militia and the people were not two distinct categories but merged. Militarization was not concentrated into militias, but spread to individual Americans to "hold and bear arms" to protect their country and their homes. Only with the depreciation of the prefatory clause could the value of integration work. The value of integration functioned as means to the real prize, individual rights, in particular, the right of self-defense.

In contrast, Justice Stevens saw the prefatory clause as binding and the operative clause under its aegis, claiming the majority "tries to denigrate the importance of this clause."[26] He understood the Militia and the people as segregated. Since Congress was "to organize, arm, and discipline the militia" and the states could appoint officers and train the militia, government regulated the militia well.[27] Then, "to keep and bear arms" confirmed "that the Framers' single-minded focus in crafting the constitutional guarantee "to keep and bear Arms" was on military uses of firearms, which they viewed in the context of service in state militias.[28] The Founders preferred militias to the threat of a standing army.[29] Segregating the Militia from the people undercut and devalued the individual right to bear arms and "self-defense" therein. The value of segregation functioned as a means to the real prize, namely, government-led security of the nation in contrast to individual security efforts:

> When each word in the text is given full effect, the Amendment is most naturally read to secure to the people a right to use and possess arms in conjunction with service in a well-regulated militia. So far as appears, no more than that was contemplated by its drafters or is encompassed within its terms.[30]

This was in direct contrast to "the Court's overwrought and novel description of the Second Amendment" in which defending one's home and hearth was preferred to the exclusion of other interests or values.[31]

AUTHORITIES, HISTORIES, AND SCIENTIFIC DATA

As much as cherry-picking is construed as a negative value, it cannot be avoided and thus does not deserve its lowly position in intellectual life. In developing an argument, what does not fit the narrative is eliminated, just as painters exclude brushstrokes that fail to fit the theme of the painting.

In some axiological analyses of law, an arc of authorities and histories can be beneficial as a bird's-eye view. Our axiological analysis in this case will feature a head-to-head clash of interpretation, which we think will underscore the central point of our text, that values rule the day.

Beginning with histories, Justice Scalia played the long game, starting over one hundred years before the ratification of the First Amendment, taking through the American Revolution and Civil War and dropping us on the doorstep of the 2000s. His long game took us back to England in 1669 and the Bill of Rights. Because the Bill of Rights guaranteed Protestants the right of self-defense, Justice Scalia saw it as a precursor to the Second Amendment. Justice Stevens depreciated the value of the Bill of Rights, saying that the right pertained to only some Protestants and not universally.

Table 13.2 The English Bill of Rights and the Second Amendment

Justice Scalia	*Justice Stevens*
These experiences caused Englishmen to be extremely wary of concentrated military forces run by the state and to be jealous of their arms. They accordingly obtained an assurance from William and Mary, in the Declaration of Right (which was codified as the English Bill of Rights), that Protestants would never be disarmed: "That the subjects which are Protestants may have arms for their defense suitable to their conditions and as allowed by law."[1]	This grant did not establish a general right of all persons, or even of all Protestants, to possess weapons. Rather, the right was qualified in two distinct ways: First, it was restricted to those of adequate social and economic status ("suitable to their Condition"); second, it was the only available subject to regulation by Parliament ("as allowed by Law").[2] The Court may well be correct that the English Bill of Rights protected the right of *some* English subjects to use *some* arms for personal self-defense free from restrictions by the Crown (but not Parliament). But that right—adopted in a different historical and political context and framed in markedly different language—tells us little about the meaning of the Second Amendment.[3]

Source: *District of Columbia v. Heller*, 554 U.S. 570, 636 (2008).
[1]Ibid., 593.
[2]Ibid., 664.
[3] Ibid., 664–665.

Let's turn to Blackstone's *Commentaries*, the shibboleth of jurisprudence.

Table 13.3 The Voice of Blackstone

Justice Scalia	*Justice Stevens*
Blackstone, whose works, we have said, "constituted the preeminent authority on English law for the founding generation. . . ." cited the arms provision of the Bill of Rights as one of the fundamental rights of Englishmen. . . . His description of it cannot possibly be thought to tie it to militia or military service. It was, he said, "the natural right of resistance and self-preservation. . . ." "The right of having and using arms for self-preservation and defence."[1]	*The Court's reliance on Blackstone's Commentaries on the Laws of England is* unpersuasive for the same reason as its reliance on the English Bill of Rights. . . . The excerpt from Blackstone offered by the Court, therefore, is, like Article VII itself, of limited use in interpreting the very differently worded, and differently historically situated, Second Amendment.[2]

Source: District of Columbia v. Heller, 554 U.S. 570, 636 (2008).
[1]Ibid., 593–594.
[2]Ibid., 665.

Let's now proceed to a flashpoint case in gun control, *United States v. Miller*, 307 U.S. 174 (1939). Justice Scalia expressly stated that Justice Stevens placed too much emphasis on this case, while Justice Stevens suggested that the majority dismissed *Miller* because they did not agree with the outcome.

Table 13.4 *Miller*: Monumental or Minutiae

Justice Scalia	*Justice Stevens*
Justice Stevens places overwhelming reliance upon this Court's decision in *United States v. Miller*. . . . Nothing so clearly demonstrates the weakness of Justice Stevens' case. *Miller* did not hold that and cannot possibly be read to have held that. The judgment in the case upheld against a Second Amendment challenge two men's federal convictions for transporting an unregistered short-barreled shotgun in interstate commerce, in violation of the National Firearms Act, 48 Stat. 1236. It is entirely clear that the Court's basis for saying that the Second Amendment did not apply was *not* that the defendants were "bear[ing] arms" not "for . . . military purposes" but for "nonmilitary use," *post,* at 2. Rather, it was that the *type of weapon at issue* was not eligible for Second Amendment protection: "In the absence of any evidence tending to show that the possession or use of a [short-barreled shotgun] at this time has some reasonable relationship to the preservation or efficiency of a well regulated militia, we cannot say that the Second Amendment guarantees the right to keep and bear *such an instrument.*" 307 U. S., at 178 (emphasis added).[1]	The majority cannot seriously believe that the Miller Court did not consider any relevant evidence; the majority simply does not approve of the conclusion the Miller Court reached on that evidence. Standing alone, that is insufficient reason to disregard a unanimous opinion of this Court, upon which substantial reliance has been placed by legislators and citizens for nearly seventy years.[2] [T]he Miller Court unanimously concluded that the Second Amendment did not apply to the possession of a firearm that did not have "some reasonable relationship to the preservation or efficiency of a well regulated militia."[3]

Source: District of Columbia v. Heller, 554 U.S. 570, 636 (2008).
[1]Ibid., 675.
[2]Ibid., 679.
[3]Ibid., 677.

Let's now turn to statistics:

Table 13.5 Data Doesn't Matter

Justice Scalia	*Justice Breyer (sample, not comprehensive)*
	From 1993 to 1997, there were 180,533 firearm-related deaths in the United States, an average of over 36,000 per year. . . . [1]Fifty-one percent were suicides, 44 percent were homicides, 1 percent were legal interventions, 3 percent were unintentional accidents, and 1 percent were of undetermined causes. . . .[2] Over that same period there were an additional 411,800 nonfatal firearm-related injuries treated in U. S. hospitals, an average of over 82,000 per year. . . .[3] Of these, 62 percent resulted from assaults, 17 percent were unintentional, 6 percent were suicide attempts, 1 percent were legal interventions, and 13 percent were of unknown causes. . . . .[4] In over one in every eight firearm-related deaths in 1997, the victim was someone under the age of 20. . . .[5] Firearm-related deaths account for 22.5 percent of all injury deaths between the ages of 1 and 19. . . .[6] More male teenagers die from firearms than from all natural causes combined. . . .[7] Handguns are involved in a majority of firearm deaths and injuries in the United States.. . . .[8] From 1993 to 1997, 81 percent of firearm-homicide victims were killed by handgun. . . .[9]In the same period, for the 41 percent of firearm injuries for which the weapon type is known, 82 percent of them were from handguns. . . . [10]And among children under the age of 20, handguns account for approximately 70 percent of all unintentional firearm-related injuries and deaths. . . .[11] In particular, 70 percent of all firearm-related teenage suicides in 1996 involved a handgun.[12]

Source: *District of Columbia v. Heller*, 554 U.S. 570, 636 (2008).
[1]Ibid., 696.
[2]Ibid.
[3]Ibid.
[4]Ibid.
[5]Ibid.
[6]Ibid.
[7]Ibid.
[8]Ibid.
[9]Ibid.
[10]Ibid., 721.
[1]Ibid.
[2]Ibid.

The majority opinion ignored statistics on both sides of the violence-from-guns argument. Mountains of evidence existed on both sides. No matter the evidence, the self-defense component of the Second Amendment was set in stone, an article of faith.

RECKONING OF THE ROGUE JUSTICES

> A well-regulated Militia, being necessary to the security of a free state, the right of the people to keep and bear arms, shall not be infringed.

In the prefatory clause, "necessary to" stands in contrast to "important to" or "relevant to." "Necessary to" is essential for bringing about "the security of a free state." "A well regulated Militia" is essential to bring about the security of a free state. The prefatory clause as a whole represents an absolute value. What about "the right of people to keep and bear Arms, shall not be infringed?" If we assume that the absolutely valued prefatory clause covers the operant clause, then "people" would refer to people in the militia. If we assume the absolutely valued prefatory clause does not cover the operant clause and the operant clause somehow exists outside the domain of the prefatory clause, then "the people" would be free floating and malleable enough to include people outside of the militia. No matter how ingenious or forceful the arguments, the precise relationship between the prefatory and operative clause will remain shrouded in mystery. No matter how much thought is put into it, whether militia and the people are interchangeable or represent distinct groups will remain shrouded in mystery. The Second Amendment contains all the clarity of an obscure pronouncement of a crazed prophet or an E.E. Cummings's poem. What the Second Amendment means depends upon the values of the interpreters, what largely has been called their "agendas." But value agendas are necessary to interpret the Second Amendment in real time in a concrete societal context.

The battle in *Heller* had to do with extremely different values of safety. For Justice Scalia, safety was seen on an individual level and as an individual right in the form of self-defense. Self-defense was just another arm of individualism. For Justices Breyer and Stevens, safety was seen from a communitarian perspective and represented a shared societal responsibility. The communitarian position focused on stopping violence before it could be started—by limiting access to weapons. This was the difference between taking care of yourself and your own within the confines of the brick and mortar structure called home and looking out for the safety of everyone in the community. There was a big value difference between protecting oneself and protecting everybody.

NOTES

1. George M. Dery III, "*Unintended Consequences:* The Supreme Court's Interpretation of the Second Amendment in *District of Columbia V. Heller* Could

Water-Down Fourth Amendment Rights," *University of Pennsylvania Juvenile Law and Social Change* 13 (2009): 3.

2. Marc Spindelman, "Some Early Views on *District of Columbia v. Heller*," *Ohio State Law Journal* 69, 4 (2008): 607.

3. Enrique Schaerer, "What the Heller?: An Originalist Critique of Justice Scalia's Second Amendment Jurisprudence," *University Cincinnati Law Review* 82, 3 (2018): 801.

4. Sanford Levinson, "United States: Assessing *Heller*," *International Journal of Constitutional Law* 7, 2 (April 2009): https://academic.oup.com/icon/article/7/2/316/758653?login=true.

5. Andrew R. Gould, "The Hidden Second Amendment Framework within *District of Columbia v. Heller*," *Vanderbilt Law Review* 62 (2019): 1535–1576.

6. Joel Teitelbaum and Erica Spector, "*District of Columbia v. Heller*: Implications for Public Health Policy and Practice," *Public Health Reports* 124, 5 (Sep–Oct 2009): 10.1177/003335490912400519.

7. Walker Anders, "From Ballots to Bullets: *District of Columbia v. Heller* and the New Civil Rights," *Louisiana Law Review* 69 (2009): 512.

8. Revi Segal, "Dead or Alive: Originalism as Popular Constitutionalism in *Heller*," *Harvard Law Review* 122, 1 (November 2008): 192.

9. *District of Columbia v. Heller*, 554 U.S. 570, 636 (2008).

10. Ibid., 679.

11. Ibid., 683.

12. Ibid., 643.

13. Ibid., 681.

14. Ibid., 679–680.

15. Ibid., 686.

16. Ibid., 722.

17. Ibid.

18. Ibid., 648.

19. Ibid., 649.

20. Ibid., 660.

21. Ibid., 660.

22. Ibid., 650.

23. Ibid., 651.

24. Ibid., 653.

25. Ibid., 651.

26. Ibid., 643.

27. Ibid., 654–655.

28. Ibid., 643.

29. Ibid., 655.

30. Ibid., 651.

31. Ibid., 652.

Chapter 14

The Establishment Clause v. Spiritual Heritage

Engel v. Vitale

NARRATIVE IN A NUTSHELL

> Almighty God, we acknowledge our dependence upon Thee, and we beg Thy blessings upon us, our parents, our teachers, and our Country.[1]

Those twenty-two words don't seem to be controversial. Repeated in a place of worship or in the privacy of one's home, they don't seem out of place in a society with a long and established spiritual history. What happened, however, if these words were repeated on a daily basis in a public school? For the purposes of improving the moral outlook and deepening the spirituality of students, the New York State Regents mandated this prayer to be recited in the New York State public schools. A group of parents with students in New York state public schools filed suit, stating that these religious views were being forced on their children and were not their views. The law that loomed in this case was the Establishment Clause of the First Amendment:

> Congress shall make no law respecting an establishment of religion, or prohibiting the free exercise thereof; or abridging the freedom of speech, or of the press; or the right of the people peaceably to assemble, and to petition the Government for a redress of grievances.

The first sixteen words of the First Amendment were pitted against the twenty-two words of a prayer recited in New York state public schools.

VALUE-INFUSED SCHOLARSHIP

If national unity results from a "Christian understanding of brotherhood,"[2] that value takes precedence of the absolute wall between church and state justifying prayer in public schools. Observing a causal relationship between prayer leaving public schools (and secular humanism replacing it) and "anarchy" in educational institutions[3] reveals a Sacred Cow-Scapegoat Value Scheme that reduces complex social situations to simplistic causal rationales. *Engel* can also be disvalued because it compels people to ignore or be deprived of the sacred value of their religious heritage.[4] Further, the neutralized zone of the First Amendment can be seen as diminishing adherence to religion.[5] Being inclined toward the value of religion, one can see a distinction in the Establishment Clause between promoting religion in general terms and making one religion the official state religion.[6] Conversely, *Engel* can be esteemed as brave counter-majoritarian decision-making as well for incorporating dialogue with the American people as an element of judicial review.[7] From a religious standpoint, reverence emerges from instinct or revelation,[8] but the other option is the sacred zenith value. While school prayer could be justified in higher education because of the maturity of students, it can be counter-valued by virtue of the audience still being age-diverse, attendance being compulsory, and age and maturity not being an antidote for impressionability.[9] Our value inquiry leads to the idea that in the same way too many cooks spoil the broth, too many sacred cows spoil a democratic society.

MAJORITY OPINION BY JUSTICE HUGO BLACK

> [I]t is proper to take alarm at the first experiment on our liberties. . . . Who does not see that the same authority which can establish Christianity, in exclusion of all other Religions, may establish with the same ease any particular sect of Christians, in exclusion of all other Sects? That the same authority which can force a citizen to contribute three pence only of his property for the support of any one establishment may force him to conform to any other establishment in all cases whatsoever?[10]

This quote from James Madison appeared at end of the majority opinion, but it provided a leading value of the case. The Establishment Clause of the First Amendment was deemed a sacred zenith value. There could be no breaches between church and state, described as "the constitutional wall of separation between Church and State." Once these twenty-two words have the force of the state behind them, they are now favored by the state. These words have been established at the exclusion of other words:

> The petitioners contend, among other things, that the state laws requiring or permitting use of the Regents' prayer must be struck down as a violation of the Establishment Clause because that prayer was composed by governmental officials as a part of a governmental program to further religious beliefs. For this reason, petitioners argue, the State's use of the Regents' prayer in its public school system breaches the constitutional wall of separation between Church and State. We agree with that contention, since we think that the constitutional prohibition against laws respecting an establishment of religion must at least mean that, in this country, it is no part of the business of government to compose official prayers for any group of the American people to recite as a part of a religious program carried on by government.[11]

From an axiological standpoint, the current of the majority opinion ran toward the value of social harmony. While speaking about how the Book of Common Prayer provoked discord in England, Justice Black revealed how breaching the wall between church and state even with twenty words could threaten societal peace:

> The controversies over the Book and what should be its content repeatedly threatened to disrupt the peace of that country as the accepted forms of prayer in the established church changed with the views of the particular ruler that happened to be in control at the time.

In looking at the history of the breaches between church and state, Justice Black pointed out that in addition to societal harmony, freedom of individuals to worship would also be endangered:

> By the time of the adoption of the Constitution, our history shows that there was a widespread awareness among many Americans of the dangers of a union of Church and State. These people knew, some of them from bitter personal experience, that one of the greatest dangers to the freedom of the individual to worship in his own way lay in the Government's placing its official stamp of approval upon one particular kind of prayer or one particular form of religious services. They knew the anguish, hardship and bitter strife that could come when zealous religious groups struggled with one another to obtain the Government's stamp of approval from each King, Queen, or Protector that came to temporary power. The Constitution was intended to avert a part of this danger by leaving the government of this country in the hands of the people, rather than in the hands of any monarch. But this safeguard was not enough. Our Founders were no more willing to let the content of their prayers and their privilege of praying whenever they pleased be influenced by the ballot box than they were to let these vital matters of personal conscience depend upon the succession of monarchs.[12]

The adoption of the Book of Prayer in England served as a cautionary tale regarding the breach of church and state and how the religious freedom of individuals could be taken away:

> The Founders knew that, only a few years after the Book of Common Prayer became the only accepted form of religious services in the established Church of England, an Act of Uniformity was passed to compel all Englishmen to attend those services and to make it a criminal offense to conduct or attend religious gatherings of any other kind.[13]

It was not out of hatred of religion that the Establishment Clause arose, but out to protect the value of each individual being able to worship their way:

> They knew, rather, that it was written to quiet well-justified fears which nearly all of them felt arising out of an awareness that governments of the past had shackled men's tongues to make them speak only the religious thoughts that government wanted them to speak and to pray only to the God that government wanted them to pray to.[14]

Religious intolerance was practiced in the United State by the very groups that had been persecuted in England:

> It is an unfortunate fact of history that, when some of the very groups which had most strenuously opposed the established Church of England found themselves sufficiently in control of colonial governments in this country to write their own prayers into law, they passed laws making their own religion the official religion of their respective colonies.[15]

The combination of the First and Fourteenth Amendments secured the rights of individuals from state-sponsored religious exercises:

> The First Amendment was added to the Constitution to stand as a guarantee that neither the power nor the prestige of the Federal Government would be used to control, support or influence the kinds of prayer the American people can say—that the people's religions must not be subjected to the pressures of government for change each time a new political administration is elected to office. Under that Amendment's prohibition against governmental establishment of religion, as reinforced by the provisions of the Fourteenth Amendment, government in this country, be it state or federal, is without power to prescribe by law any particular form of prayer which is to be used as an official prayer in carrying on any program of governmentally sponsored religious activity.[16]

Even assuming the prayer was "denominationally neutral" and noncoercive did not allow it to wriggle out the constraints of the First and Fourteenth Amendments. The value of the Establishment clause was to protect both government and religion: "Its first and most immediate purpose rested on the belief that a union of government and religion tends to destroy government and to degrade religion."[17] The Establishment Clause "is violated by the enactment of laws which establish an official religion whether those laws operate directly to coerce non-observing individuals or not."[18] Contrary to the claim of non-coercion, this prayer with the support of the government behind it is coercive:

> This is not to say, of course, that laws officially prescribing a particular form of religious worship do not involve coercion of such individuals. When the power, prestige and financial support of government is placed behind a particular religious belief, the indirect coercive pressure upon religious minorities to conform to the prevailing officially approved religion is plain.[19]

Freedom for the individual to worship as they please and social harmony were the leading values of the majority opinion as well as the concurrence by Justice Douglas.

CONCURRENCE BY JUSTICE WILLIAM DOUGLAS

Justice Douglas was a hardliner on this matter. While agreeing with the majority opinion, Justice Douglas went further. Not only was it unconstitutional to introduce prayer in public schools, all other breaches in the church-state constitutional wall embedded in American society—including the national anthem, the pledge of allegiance, and the president's oath of office—were also equally unwarranted.

> The point for decision is whether the Government can constitutionally finance a religious exercise. Our system at the federal and state levels is presently honeycombed with such financing. Nevertheless, I think it is an unconstitutional undertaking whatever form it takes.[20]

Justice Douglas saw through language that assured this twenty-two-word prayer would not be pushed down students' throats, even with safeguards in place. The act overtly stated that teachers would assume neutrality regarding student participation: teachers and administrators were not supposed to comment about participation or lack thereof in the prayer. Nor were they to suggest what clothes were to be worn or postures assumed.[21] Additionally, students could be excused from the prayer:

> Provision is also made for excusing children, upon written request of a parent or guardian, from the saying of the prayer or from the room in which the prayer is said. A letter implementing and explaining this regulation has been sent to each taxpayer and parent in the school district. As I read this regulation, a child is free to stand or not stand, to recite or not recite, without fear of reprisal or even comment by the teacher or any other school official.[22]

As Justice Douglas espied, this did not remove the element of coercion. Students were captive audiences, no matter how short the prayer, just as audience members of Supreme Court rulings were captive when the chaplain opens proceedings with a prayer. Public officials on public payrolls in public venues conducting religious exercises breach the wall between church and state:

> In New York, the teacher who leads in prayer is on the public payroll, and the time she takes seems minuscule as compared with the salaries appropriated by state legislatures and Congress for chaplains to conduct prayers in the legislative halls. Only a bare fraction of the teacher's time is given to reciting this short 22-word prayer, about the same amount of time that our Crier spends announcing the opening of our sessions and offering a prayer for this Court. Yet, for me, the principle is the same, no matter how briefly the prayer is said, for, in each of the instances given, the person praying is a public official on the public payroll, performing a religious exercise in a governmental institution. It is said that the element of coercion is inherent in the giving of this prayer. If that is true here, it is also true of the prayer with which this Court is convened, and of those that open the Congress. Few adults, let alone children, would leave our courtroom or the Senate or the House while those prayers are being given. Every such audience is in a sense a "captive" audience.[23]

Echoing the majority opinion, the concurrence contends that "once government finances a religious exercise, it inserts a divisive influence into our communities."[24] There was a deep concern that breaching the Establishment Clause would lead to social unrest: "The end of such strife cannot be other than to destroy the cherished liberty. The dominating group will achieve the dominant benefit; or all will embroil the state in their dissensions."[25] The Establishment Clause was considered an instrumental value in achieving the ultimate aim, social concordance.

As generic as this prayer appeared, Justice Douglas concurred with the New York Court that "the prayer given does not conform to all of the tenets of the Jewish, Unitarian, and Ethical Culture groups." The prayer was not inclusive.

The biggest legal obstacle in this case, according to Justice Douglas, was *Everson v. Board of Education*, 330 U.S. 1 (1947). In it, the Court allowed taxpayers to fund bus fares for needy children attending parochial and public schools. Justice Douglas saw the merit of helping such children even with the government financing lunches, books, and tuition of such parochial students. However, the value of aiding such students was eclipsed by the overarching value of absolutely maintaining the Establishment Clause of the First Amendment. Quoting Justice Rutledge, Justice Douglas affirmed:

> The reasons underlying the Amendment's policy have not vanished with time or diminished in force. Now, as when it was adopted, the price of religious freedom is double. It is that the church and religion shall live both within and upon that freedom. There cannot be freedom of religion, safeguarded by the state, and intervention by the church or its agencies in the state's domain or dependency on its largesse.[26]

The high value of religious freedom could not be realized without valuing the Establishment Clause. Like the most fervent religious zealot, Justice Douglas valued the church-state separation as absolute, its absolute nature being assured by the absolute neutrality of the state in religious matters. The high value of religious freedom was but one of the overarching values in this dissent, the other being the avoidance of a "divisive force" issue by breaching the Establishment Clause:

> The First Amendment leaves the Government in a position not of hostility to religion, but of neutrality. The philosophy is that the atheist or agnostic—the nonbeliever—is entitled to go his own way. The philosophy is that, if government interferes in matters spiritual, it will be a divisive force. The First Amendment teaches that a government neutral in the field of religion better serves all religious interests.[27]

In the final axiological analysis, the sacred zenith values of religious freedom and social harmony catalyze this concurrence.

DISSENT BY JUSTICE POTTER STEWART

Justice Stewart did not see the Establishment Clause as an absolute. He appreciated "the deeply entrenched and cherished spiritual traditions of our Nation."[28] The value of the separation of church and state was pitted against the value of the spiritual tradition of the country.

Justice Stewart rejected the assessment that the twenty-two words in question established an official religion. According to Justice Stewart, these twenty-two words represented a continuance of spiritual traditions of the United States:

> I do not believe that this Court, or the Congress, or the President has, by the actions and practices I have mentioned, established an "official religion" in violation of the Constitution. And I do not believe the State of New York has done so in this case. What each has done has been to recognize and to follow the deeply entrenched and highly cherished spiritual traditions of our Nation—traditions which come down to us from those who almost two hundred years ago avowed their "firm Reliance on the Protection of divine Providence" when they proclaimed the freedom and independence of this brave new world.[29]

How could this interfere with anybody's religion, since the prayer session was voluntary and free from embarrassment and pressures?

> The Court does not hold, nor could it, that New York has interfered with the free exercise of anybody's religion. For the state courts have made clear that those who object to reciting the prayer must be entirely free of any compulsion to do so, including any "embarrassments and pressures."[30]

For Justice Stewart, the vital value was religious traditions reflected in our governmental institutions:

> What is relevant to the issue here is not the history of an established church in sixteenth century England or in eighteenth century America, but the history of the religious traditions of our people, reflected in countless practices of the institutions and officials of our government.[31]

He pointed out salient examples:

> At the opening of each day's Session of this Court we stand, while one of our officials invokes the protection of God. Since the days of John Marshall, our Crier has said, "God save the United States and this Honorable Court." Both the Senate and the House of Representatives open their daily Sessions with prayer. [Each of our Presidents, from George Washington to John F. Kennedy, has, upon assuming his Office, asked the protection and help of God.][32]

> In 1954, Congress added a phrase to the Pledge of Allegiance to the Flag so that it now contains the words "one Nation *under* God, indivisible, with liberty and justice for all." In 1952, Congress enacted legislation calling upon the President each year to proclaim a National Day of Prayer. Since 1865, the words "IN GOD WE TRUST" have been impressed on our coins.[33]

"The Star Spangled Banner" manifested this religious tradition:

Blest with victory and peace, may the heav'n rescued land
Praise the Pow'r that hath made and preserved us a nation,
Then conquer we must, when our cause it is just.
And this be our motto "In God is our Trust."

Justice Stewart differentiated between an official religion and religious tradition. The first he disvalued; the second he embraced. The affirmation of embracing a religious tradition diminished the Establishment Clause, making it easily pregnable to whatever falls under the category of religious tradition.

RECKONING OF ROGUE JUSTICES

We begin with the evidence against an absolute wall between church and state: the appearance of the divine in public spaces. The divine in a sense already has squatting rights in the public arena. Yet should this continue?

From the perspective of an atheist or agnostic, this seemingly innocuous twenty-two-word prayer does not speak to their spiritual worldview. From a humanistic perspective, this prayer assumes the existence of a God that the atheist would certainly dispute and on which an agnostic would not wish to decide.

> Almighty God, we acknowledge our dependence upon Thee, and we beg Thy blessings upon us, our parents, our teachers and our Country.

For those who value spiritual self-sufficiency or believe an impersonal force started the universe and has no interest in human beings, the notion of dependence of God would be reciting something against their beliefs. This notion of God is also monotheistic, excluding polytheists. This underscores another point why religion should be excluded from the public domain. Monotheists are going to see religion in a monotheistic way, even if they are in good faith attempting to come up with a concept of God applicable to all. One usually only has eyes for own religious faith to the exclusion of others.

This prayer was not, then, a one-size-fits-all spiritual garb. Atheists, agnostics, deists, and polytheists were excluded. "Neutrality" was viewed as a positive value, suggesting that the prayer was general and thus applicable to all faiths. But it failed to live up to that billing.

This prayer represented an official religion. One could not identify these twenty-two words as deriving from a particular creed. It was an amalgamation. If that was the litmus test as an official religion, then it certainly did not meet the criteria. However, it becomes an official new religion in being an amalgam of different faiths. The fact that these twenty-two words were not borrowed from one specific faith does not mean it isn't an "official religion." By invoking God and prayer, these twenty-two words became a religion. These twenty-two words became the gospel for an "official religion," its followers being the administrators and faculty and the students at New York public schools. The fact that it is a new religion does not preclude its being official. The New York state regents in authorizing this prayer made it official.

The next point concerned the claim of noncoercion. Nobody put a gun to the heads of students to recite the prayer. They had the option of remaining silent or leaving the room. But coercion does not have to been seen as physical, but psychological as well. People can be coerced to doing something because everyone else is doing it or because if they don't join in, they will be thought of not part of the group or as heathens and excluded from other social groups or activities on that basis. The coercion of the majority to conform can be especially effective on young people who are insecure and attempting to find their social and spiritual identities. The fact most people were praying exposes them as out by themselves as possible objects of ridicule, although this was not the intent. Not wanting that, they conform, reciting the prayer. It does not play out well for young atheists or budding polytheists this coercive environment doesn't.

The most compelling evidence against the wall between church and state was the prevalence of divinity embedded in the public sphere. As Justice Stewart remarked, look around and you will see manifested everywhere divinity:

- national anthem
- pledge of allegiance
- president's oath of office
- currency
- introduction of Supreme Court justices
- introduction of Senate and House of Representatives

The wall between church and state has been repeatedly breached and another breaching was not going to matter, so goes the argument. What's another tiny breach in the wall?

The Rogue Justices embrace sacred-zenith value of everyone having a space to worship as they wish. To achieve this value, coercion cannot occur. Any hint of the state associating with religion is taboo by the absolute standard. In this case, guilt is assumed by association. The state must be excessively hands-off as to give no indication of favoring one religion over another. This must be scrupulous and pervasive. Must the presence of the divine be excluded from all public spaces, taken off our money and not mentioned in our national anthem, pledge of allegiance ("one nation under God" added in 1954 to contrast our nation with godless communist Russia), excised from the President's oath and from the introduction of Supreme Court and Congressional meetings? Can there be a way to justify the appearance of these divine signs and still adhere to a strict separation of state and church?

The fact that the prayer was public publicized and promulgated a divine being. The government was not a bullhorn for God. The government must remain mum on religion. This is why its presence must be removed from money, the national anthem, pledge of allegiance, and all of the three branches of government. Early in this nation's history, President George Washington urged neutrality in foreign affairs, knowing that any entanglement could endanger the fledgling nation. So, too, the government must have no entanglements with religion. It must not in any way, shape, or form or give any appearance of favoring one religious view over another. Such entanglements breaching the absolute wall between church and state could promote one religious perspective undermining others and increasing hostilities in the country. Government must have a completely hands-off view. It must stay out of the business of religion, not put one finger in it.

Without this chance to pray at school, you may miss an opportunity to join the spiritual heritage. It makes it sounds as if this was the only opportunity to see Haley's Comet or the Taj Mahal on a trip of a lifetime. One can easily visit any number of religious organizations in one's area. They are abundant as supermarkets or department stores. Prayer also does not need to be expressed publicly. It can be a private matter and if the student needs to pray, it can be done in the confines of their minds. If the person who argues that nonbelievers could have a moment of silence during prayer and basically do their thing in their heads, so, too, could believers do silent prayer. The exclusion of prayer in public schools does not entail the exclusion of prayers generally. Numerous opportunities are afforded for prayer, and they are readily available in a place of workshop near you.

Religion tends to deal in absolutes, in sacred zenith values. For a democratic society and a plurality of ideas to persist, sacred zenith values must be stored in hermeneutically sealed spaces known as houses of worship or homes. Their unleashing into the public arena opens up the gates of hell and endangers democracy, which is characterized by a give-and-take dialogue of higher and lower but not absolute values, except those that guard against one group imposing its views on another—like the Establishment Clause.

NOTES

1. *Engel v. Vitale*, 370 U.S. 421, 423 (1962).
2. Robert E. Rodes, "The Passing of Nonsectarianism—Some Reflections on the School Prayer Case," *Notre Dame Law* 38, 2 (1963): 120.
3. John H. Garvey, "Comment on Church and State in Seventeenth and Eighteenth Century America," *Journal Law and Religion* 7 (1989): 276.
4. James F. Janz, "Church and State: Prayer in Public Schools," *Marquette Law Review*, 46 (1962): 237.
5. William W. Van Alstyne, "Constitutional Separation of Church and State: The Quest for a Coherent Position," *Faculty Publications* (1963): 881, https://scholarship.law.wm.edu/facpubs/775.
6. Dallin Lewis, "Flaws and Repercussions of *Engel v. Vitale*," *Brigham Young University Prelaw Review* 21 (2007): 65.
7. Corinna Barrett Lain, "God, Civic Virtue, and the American Way: Reconstructing *Engel*," *Stanford Law Review* 67 (2015): 479.
8. Rodes, "The Passing of Nonsectarianism—Some Reflections on the School Prayer Case," 136.
9. Deanna N. Pihos, "Assuming Maturity Matters: The Limited Reach of the Establishment Clause at Public Universities," *Cornell Law Review* 90, 5 (July 2005): 1375.
10. *Engel v. Vitale*, 437.
11. Ibid., 426.
12. Ibid., 430.
13. Ibid., 432.
14. Ibid., 435.
15. Ibid., 427.
16. Ibid., 429–430.
17. Ibid., 432.
18. Ibid., 431.
19. Ibid., 430–431.
20. Ibid., 437.
21. Ibid., 438.
22. Ibid.
23. Ibid., 441–442.
24. Ibid., 442.
25. Ibid., 444.
26. Ibid., 443–444.
27. Ibid., 443.
28. Ibid., 450.
29. Ibid., 450.
30. Ibid., 445.
31. Ibid., 446.
32. Ibid., 448.
33. Ibid., 449.

Chapter 15

Liberty and Privacy in the Bedroom v. the Stability of Homophobia

Lawrence v. Texas

NARRATIVE IN A NUTSHELL

What happened?

Two people had sex.

What were their names?

John Lawrence and Tyrone Gardner.

When did it happen?

1998.

Where did it happen?

Near Houston, Texas.

Where these people adults?

Yes.

Was the sex consensual?

Yes.

Was the act done in public or private?

Private.

If the act was private, how did police find out about it?

The police received a phone call that a "crazed" black man had a gun and after storming the residence *apparently* caught the two in the act.

What law did Mr. Lawrence and Mr. Gardner break?

They broke Texas statute 21:01, which made sodomy a felony.

VALUE-INFUSED SCHOLARSHIP

Lawrence has been seen as a landmark, but also as a roadblock to gay rights. It stands against the "aggressively negative" Traditional Family Values campaign oriented around disgust and contagion devalues and dehumanizes gay people.[1] The negative emotions find their correlation in the negative values of ugliness and sickness. From the standpoint of sexual freedom or liberty as zenith values, *Lawrence* ranks as a disappointment. The sexual freedom or liberty in *Lawrence* is geographically confined to a domestic locale (the bedroom) rather than extending to the public sphere.[2] "I believe that gay people cannot rest on the decision in *Lawrence* or be content with protections of private life. They must embrace visibility in order to demonstrate how private discrimination has a profoundly public impact."[3] In the aftermath of *Lawrence*, in the push for equal marriage, marriage is considered as sacred or a zenith value while other forms of family, intimate, sexual, or kin formations are peripherally valued.[4] For those invested in liberty, this ruling represents a first step to maximize liberties in other spheres.[5] The "ordered liberty approach and the history and tradition method reflect a court's prejudice,"[6] but no less than an approach from classical liberal thought.[7] From the perspective of sex-equality theorists:

> What Lawrence and the commentary about the case have given victims and survivors of sexual abuse so far is nothing—unless silence counts as something when it reaffirms the longstanding preference that victims of sexual abuse, along with their injuries, remain closeted. [8]

Our value analysis takes another direction, investing itself in the value maneuvers at hand.

VALUE CLUSTERS IN PLAY

- Kennedy Majority Opinion: Liberty (Sacred Zenith Value Focalized Around Values of Dignity and Privacy)
- O'Connor Concurrence: Equality (Zenith value clustered with Politically Unpopular Groups)
- Scalia Dissent: Stability (Sacred Zenith Value, in tandem with the Values of Tradition and Certainty)

MAJORITY OPINION BY JUSTICE ANTHONY KENNEDY

We did not have to wade far into Justice Kennedy's Opinion to discover the overriding valuation in his verdict: "Liberty protects the person from unwarranted government intrusions into dwellings or other private places."[9] But to understand liberty in a pedestrian sense would be to miss its ascendance to a high-ranking value:

> Freedom extends beyond spatial bounds. Liberty presumes an autonomy of self that includes freedom of thought, belief, expression, and certain intimate conduct. The instant case involves liberty of the person both in its spatial and more transcendent dimensions.[10]

This freedom or liberty of the person concerned both freedom of intimacy in physical private space and freedom in the transcendent sense. This intimate space transcended state control because to deprive persons from making their own decisions regarding intimate relationships and stripping them of self-determination would be demeaning:

> The petitioners are entitled to respect for their private lives. The State cannot *demean their existence or control their destiny* [our emphasis] by making their private sexual conduct a crime. Their right to liberty under the Due Process Clause gives them the full right to engage in their conduct without intervention of the government.[11]

The absolute value of human beings—as autonomous and therefore transcendent beings—with respect to making choices regarding their private sexual choices grounded a transcendent space for them to engage in such acts.

According to Justice Kennedy, three aspects arose:

1. Whether the Texas statute was fair to both heterosexuals and homosexuals
2. Whether the liberty and privacy entailed in the Fourteenth Amendment was violated
3. Whether the controlling case, *Bowers v. Hardwick*, should be overturned[12]

Having received a phone call about a possible weapons disturbance, police entered a Harris County, Texas apartment to find Lawrence Geddes and Tyron Garner "engaging in a sexual act," the complaint reading "'deviate sexual intercourse, namely anal sex, with a member of the same sex (man).'" The men's actions violated Texas Penal Code §21.06 (a). The Court of Appeals of the Texas Fourteenth District dismissed the petitioners' arguments based on "the Equal Protection and Due Process Clauses of the Fourteenth Amendment."

The narrative following the opening salvos fell in line with the value of liberty interests concerning private human moments in private places—for the most part. The arc of authorities utilized to support the transcendent human beings in transcendent places consisted of

- *Griswold v. Connecticut*, 381 U.S. 479 (1965)—Transcendent space and transcendent liberty for married couples to acquire contraceptives from third parties.
- *Eisenstadt v. Baird*, 405 U.S. 438 (1972)—Transcendent space and transcendent liberty for unmarried couples to acquire contraceptives.
- *Roe v. Wade*, 410 U.S. 113 (1973)—Transcendent space for women's reproductive freedom and speaking to the destiny of women to make their own decisions.
- *Carey v. Population Services Int'l*, 431 U.S. 678 (1977)—Invalidation of the law prohibiting the sale and distribution of contraceptives to people under 16 (the expansion of privacy from married people, to single people, and now to people under 16).

These four cases formed the basis for the *Lawrence* Court to expand liberty to the private acts of homosexuals. *Bowers v. Hardwick* in which a police officer witnessed two men engaged in a sexual act in the privacy of their home stood in the way. Unlike the Texas statute, the Georgia statute prohibited sodomy for both same-sex and different-sex partners. The *Bowers* opinion saw no fundamental right for homosexuals to engage in sodomy. But *Lawrence*, with *Griswold*, *Eisenstadt*, *Roe*, and *Carey* in tow to buttress the value of liberty, attacked *Bowers*, criticizing "the Court's own failure to appreciate the *extent* [our emphasis] of the liberty at stake."[13] The word "extent" spoke to the appreciation of the value of liberty from being state-controlled to transcendent. This had much more than prohibiting a sexual act. It concerned dignity and its "demeaning," reducing a free choice between human beings to a mere sexual act, akin to marriage being a right to have sexual intercourse. The sacred zenith value consisted of people's liberty to be together in private spaces to have a personal relationship without that relationship being criminalized:[14] "It suffices for us to acknowledge that adults may choose to enter upon this relationship in the confines of their homes and their own private lives and still retain their dignity as free persons."[15] Here, the idea of "dignity" resounded in the discourse. The heightened sense of liberty entailed the dignity of human beings to self-determination, to make their own decisions without state interference. According to the philosopher credited with reinventing the concept, dignity transcended price and thus cannot be exchanged for anything.

To buttress the heightened sense of liberty defended in this case, the Court challenged the history of sodomy as presented in *Bowers*. An axiological analysis divulges more than a difference of opinion regarding history, revealing a strategy the Kennedy Court believed necessary to make its case for legalizing sodomy. Whereas the *Bowers* majority saw a clear-cut moral condemnation of sodomy in America, *Lawrence* either airbrushed or offered a nuanced account of history to soften the image of sodomy. The *Lawrence* Majority described no longstanding prohibition against homosexual conduct, explaining that early sodomy laws mainly focused on nonprocreative activity. Since the categorization of homosexual did not emerge until the late nineteenth century, laws could not be aimed at a category of people who did not yet exist. Early American sexual prohibitions constrained both same-sex and different-sex relationships. Also, they did not usually pertain to private matters. Not until the last third of the twentieth century did states criminally prosecute same-sex acts.[16] While it may be true the *Lawrence* Majority saw that the history of homosexuality was more complex than *Bowers* claimed, from a public relations standpoint, sodomy had to be cast in a more positive light, to be valued as something that, though perhaps not savory to the majority, nonetheless represented one option of among the array of personal choices for consenting adult sexual partners to practice in private.

America was reconceiving sexuality and *Lawrence* crystallized these new notions. In 1960 all fifty states outlawed sodomy. By the 1980s the number dwindled twenty-five. By 2003, twenty-five shrunk to thirteen. The *Lawrence* Majority could justifiably proclaim: "These references show an emerging awareness that liberty gives substantial protection to adult persons in deciding how to conduct their private lives in matters pertaining to sex."[17]

In contemporary America and also in contemporary Europe, a growing awareness could be discerned concerning the morality of homosexuality. If *Bowers* went for the "ancient roots" route, *Lawrence* would instead value Western Europe from which America had sprung. The Wolfenden Report of 1957, for example, delivered to the British Parliament, requested a repeal law punishing private same-sex acts. In the same vein, the European Court for Human Rights ruled much the same way. *Bowers* pointed to Old Europe and Old America to devalue same-sex behavior; *Lawrence* pointed to New Europe and New America to value it.

In other words, sodomy never constituted an evil in the past and in modern times even less so. That's what the majority of Americans thought as the repeal of sodomy laws in state after state suggested. And Europe, which shared many of our values and from which our nation sprung, tilted in that direction. This softer image of same-sex sodomy allowed it to be put under the heightened liberty umbrella. Unless softened, it could not go under that umbrella.

Romer v. Evans 517 U.S. 620 (1996), which nullified a Colorado law that discriminated against homosexuals as a class and was decided by the Equal Protection Clause of the Fourteenth Amendment, had to be sidestepped. The

Lawrence Court realized *Romer* did not fit neatly under their heightened sense of liberty argument, diminishing its value because its application could jeopardize the liberty of both gays and straights: "Were we to hold the statute invalid under the Equal Protection Clause some might question whether a prohibition would be valid if drawn differently, say, to prohibit the conduct both between same-sex and different-sex participants."[18]

The coup de grâce of the elevation of sodomy to a heightened sense of liberty occurred near the conclusion of the Majority Opinion with the severing of same-sex conduct from aspects that would make it unsavory, for example, if it involved minors, people being injured or forced into it, public conduct, prostitution, or formal government recognition of people who engage in the act (marriage). Once severed from the historical onus and negative values, private homosexual conduct could be safely tucked under the umbrella of a heightened sense of liberty:

> To say that the issue in *Bowers* was simply the right to engage in certain sexual conduct demeans the claim the individual put forward, just as it would demean a married couple were it to be said marriage is simply about the right to have sexual intercourse. The laws involved in *Bowers* and here are, to be sure, statutes that purport to do no more than prohibit a particular sexual act. Their penalties and purposes, though, have more far-reaching consequences, touching upon the most private human conduct, sexual behavior, and in the most private of places, the home. The statutes do seek to control a personal relationship that, whether or not entitled to formal recognition in the law, is within the liberty of persons to choose without being punished as criminals.[19]

The isle of intimacy between consenting adults ascended to a sacred zenith value in the sense of being impervious to state control. The space for these intimate acts ascended to sacred-zenith valued transcendent status only because of the special status of the human beings engaged in these acts, also deemed sacred.

CONCURRENCE BY JUSTICE SANDRA DAY O'CONNOR

In the concurrence by Justice O'Connor, equality protruded as the leading value:

> Rather than relying on the substantive component of the Fourteenth Amendment's Due Process Clause, as the Court does, I base my conclusion on the Fourteenth Amendment's Equal Protection Clause.[20]

Justice O'Connor attached the value of equality to the disvalue of animus toward a "politically unpopular group." While in the *Lawrence* Majority Opinion a heightened sense of liberty (attached to the dignity of the person) reigned as the zenith value, for O'Connor equality as it applied to politically unpopular groups ranked highest. Her views followed accordingly in line with this track or arc of precedents:

- *Eisenstadt v. Baird*, 405 U.S. 488 (1972)—overturned law discriminating against sexually active unmarried people denied contraception.
- *Department of Agriculture v. Moreno* 413 U.S. 528 (1973)—overturned law discriminating against hippies by not allowing them to procure government benefits.
- *Plyer v. Doe* 457 U.S. 202 (1982)—overturned law denying state funding for education to undocumented immigrant children and charging them an additional tuition fee to compensate for lost state funding.
- *Cleburne v. Cleburne Living Center, Inc.*, 473 U.S. 432 (1982)—overturned law discriminating against mentally challenged people denied housing.
- *Romer v. Evans*, 517 U.S. 620 (1996)—overturned law discriminating against gay people as a class.

In each case, statutes denied equality to a politically unpopular group (people engaging in premarital sex, hippies, undocumented immigrant children, mentally challenged, and gay people). The rider of a "politically unpopular group" animated the value of equality in O'Connor's concurrence:

> The statute at issue here makes sodomy a crime only if a person engages in deviate sexual intercourse with another individual of the same sex. Tex. Penal Code Ann. ß21.06(a) (2003). Sodomy between opposite-sex partners, however, is not a crime in Texas. That is, Texas treats the same conduct differently based solely on the participants. Those harmed by this law are people who have a same-sex sexual orientation and thus are more likely to engage in behavior prohibited by ß21.06.[21]

Whereas the legal penalty for same-sex sodomy represented a slap on the wrist (class-C misdemeanor punishable by a fine not exceeding $500.00), other consequences accompanied such a conviction, for example, being unable to work in certain professions and being considered sex offenders if people convicted of sodomy moved to some states:

> Indeed, Texas itself has previously acknowledged the collateral effects of the law, stipulating in a prior challenge to this action that the law legally sanctions

> discrimination against [homosexuals] in a variety of ways unrelated to the criminal law, including in the areas of employment, family issues, and housing.[22]

O'Connor zeroed in on the value of the Texas sodomy statute: it aimed not at crime prevention, but expressed antipathy toward gay people: "And because Texas so rarely enforces its sodomy law as applied to private, consensual acts, the law serves more as a statement of dislike and disapproval against homosexuals than as a tool to stop criminal behavior."

The Texas Court claimed it did not discriminate against gay people as a class, only against homosexual conduct. In Texas, however, calling someone a homosexual could be deemed slanderous because of the criminalization of same-sex sodomy. This stigmatized gay people as a class. The Texas statute, which made the same acts legal for one group of citizens and illegal for another, could only be seen as an expression of inequality and arbitrariness. From an axiological viewpoint, not abstract equality, but equality in terms of unfair treatment of politically unpopular groups became the protuberant value in O'Connor's Concurrence. In the Majority Opinion, the dignity of human beings to engage in intimate conduct in private spaces emerged as the leading value cluster. In Justice O'Connor's Concurrence, the impact of the Texas statute to legitimize unequal treatment for a politically unpopular group in public spaces emerged as the leading value.

DISSENT BY JUSTICE ANTONIN SCALIA

Only seventeen years after *Bowers* upheld sodomy laws, Justice Scalia lamented, *Lawrence* overturned them. This galled Justice Scalia because in *Planned Parenthood of Southeastern Pa. v. Casey* 505 U.S. 833 (1992), the Court pronounced the importance of certainty in jurisprudence gained from following precedence. Justice Scalia espied the inconsistency and remarked: "The need for stability and certainty presents no barrier [to the *Lawrence* Majority]."[23] Though he maintained "I do not myself believe in rigid adherence to *stare decisis* in constitutional cases; but I do believe that we should be consistent rather than manipulative in invoking the doctrine,"[24] in his dissent, he decidedly embraced stability and certainty. He approvingly quoted not happiness but of the "'orderly pursuit of happiness by free men'"[25] as well as "traditionally protected" interests and most importantly, rights "'deeply rooted in this Nation's history and tradition"[26]—*Moore v. East Cleveland*, 262 U.S., 494, 503 (1977) and liberty interests "'so rooted in the traditions and conscience of our people to be ranked as fundamental'"[27]—*Reno v. Flores*, 507 U.S. 232, 303 (1993). He may well have been in favor of discarding *stare decisis* in other areas, but in the case of traditional sexual morality, his value-bent toward stability framed his concern for "far-reaching implications beyond this case,"[28] including equal marriage ("Today's opinion dismantles the structure of constitutional law that has permitted a distinction to be made between heterosexual and homosexual unions, insofar as formal recognition in marriage is concerned"[29]) as well as sexual matters:

> It seems to me that the "societal reliance" on the principles confirmed in *Bowers* and discarded today has been overwhelming. Countless judicial decisions and legislative enactments have relied on the ancient proposition that a governing majority's belief that certain sexual behavior is "immoral and unacceptable" constitutes a rational basis for regulation.[30]

The rulings that depended on *Bowers* were not simply aimed at LGBT people, although many do, as we examine the arc or path of precedents marshaled by Justice Scalia:

- *High Tech Gays v. Defense Industrial Security Clearance Office*, 895 F. 2d 563, 570–571 (CA9 1988)—*allowing the Defense Department to conduct deeper investigations into backgrounds of gay and lesbian applicants seeking secret and top-secret security clearances*
- *Charles v. Baesler*, 910 F. 2d 1349, 1353 (CA6 1990)—rejecting fire department captain's fundamental right for promotion
- *Henne v. Wright*, 904 F. 2d 1208, 1214–1215 (CA8 1990)—restricting giving surnames at birth is not an implication of a fundamental right
- *Walls v. Petersburg*, 895 F. 2d 188, 193 (CA4 1990)—*allowing police department to ask prospective employees if they had same-sex relationships*
- *Barnes v. Glen Theatre, Inc.*, 501 U. S. 560, 569 (1991)—allowing government to have an interest in protecting order and moral judgment
- *Schowengerdt v. United States*, 944 F. 2d 483, 490 (CA9 1991)—*upholding a bisexual's dismissal from armed forces*
- *Doe v. Wigginton,* 21 F. 3d 733, 739–740 (CA6 1994)—*rejecting of prisoner's fundamental right for on-demand HIV testing*
- *Mullins v. Oregon,* 57 F. 3d 789, 793–794 (CA9 1995)—denying grandparents a fundamental liberty interest to adopt their grandchildren
- *Sherman v. Henry,* 928 S. W. 2d 464, 469–473 (Tex. 1996)—denying a constitutional right to adultery
- *Holmes v. California Army National Guard,* 124 F. 3d 1126, 1136 (CA9 1997)—*upholding federal and state and regulations banning same-sex participants from military service*
- *Milner v. Apfel,* 148 F. 3d 812, 814 (CA7 1998)—justifying moral legislation by the harm it prevents

- *Owens v. State,* 352 Md. 663, 683, 724 A. 2d 43, 53 (1999)—rejecting constitutional right to have sexual intercourse outside of marriage
- *Williams v. Pryor,* 240 F. 3d 944, 949 (CA11 2001)—prohibiting sale of sex toys
- *Marcum v. McWhorter,* 308 F. 3d 635, 640–642 (CA6 2002)—rejecting adultery as a fundamental right
- 10 U. S. C. § 654(b)(1)—*supporting the removal members of the armed forces who engage in sodomy*

Without *Bowers* as their legal bulwark, these decisions could fall to the wayside and jeopardize stability: "What a massive disruption of the current social order, therefore, the overruling of *Bowers* entails [expression of value of stability and certainty]."[31]

Not only the cases stated above but also the laws prohibiting numerous sexual offenses would be jeopardized:

> State laws against [1] bigamy, [2] same-sex marriage, [3] adult incest, [4] prostitution, [5] masturbation, [6] adultery, [7] fornication, [8] bestiality, and [9] obscenity are likewise sustainable only in light of *Bowers'* validation of laws based on moral choices. Every single one of these laws is called into question by today's decision; the Court makes no effort to cabin the scope of its decision to exclude them from its holding.[32]

Scalia assigned the same degree of disvalue to each of the deadly nine offenses, putting them in the same basket of opprobrium. Apparently, he valued them as equally horrible. Same-sex sodomy between consenting adults as horrible as bestiality? Masturbation a crime? Here, we see more clearly the value dimensions of coherence. Scalia lumped these acts together through a coherence rooted in the value of precedents. But that need not be the only way for coherence to function. It could also function equally as well by homogenizing according to criteria other than precedents. Other ways could have been found to discriminate between same-sex sodomy and other sexual acts deemed immoral, a point clearly made in the Majority Opinion. Sodomy in private places between consenting adults does not constitute a public act; an act between an adult and a minor; if not photographed and placed in a public domain like a magazine or the Internet, not pornography; not coercion; not about a married person who is legally married to another person; not masturbation. Same-sex sodomy between consenting adults may be distinguished between coercive and age-inappropriate activities and those that are consensual and age-appropriate activities. Rape, statutory rape, and adult-child incest, absent from Scalia's list of sexual horribles, apparently did not fit into this circle of coherence and prevented him from concluding that in fact there existed a clear line to be drawn between same-sex sodomy and sexual horribles. This underscored the difference between coherences: what falls in and out of the circle depended on what the adjudicator valued or disvalued. If you value authorities, your circle of inclusion would be drawn differently than if you value new discoveries and findings. Scalia's coherence, animated by valuing stability and whatever could bolster that value (authorities), could never break these time-honored offenses apart from each other.

Coherence also admits of degrees. A text, legal system, or social situations can exhibit a tight or condensed coherence or a loose or diffuse coherence. Texts, legal systems, and social situations can function according to different degrees of coherence depending on the situation. Tight coherence represents only one type of coherence. By valuing tight coherence, which offers maximum stability, Justice Scalia believed that without *Bowers* the whole house of cards would come tumbling down, ignoring the fact that those cases relied on precedents other than *Bowers* and that many of those used *Bowers* to discriminate against queer folk.

At the same time Justice Scalia hyper-valued stability, he denied the transcendent value of liberty (when it comes to intimate relations in private places): "Texas Penal Code Ann. §21.06(a) (2003) undoubtedly imposes constraints on liberty. So do laws prohibiting prostitution, recreational use of heroin, and, for that matter, working more than 60 hours per week in a bakery."[33] Intimate acts in intimate places constituted a garden-variety type of liberty and did not ascend to the level of transcendence. By claiming that same-sex sodomy could only be legally justified if the practice were "deeply rooted in this Nation's history and tradition," Justice Scalia denied the transcendent space of the bedroom for sexual intimacy as well as the dignity of free persons to engage in those acts and defined its worth through tradition.

Not only did Justice Scalia dispense with freedom in the transcendent bedroom but also jettisoned equal treatment of heterosexuals and homosexuals:

> To be sure, §21.06 does distinguish between the sexes insofar as concerns the partner with whom the sexual acts are performed: men can violate the law only with other men, and women only with other women. But this cannot itself be a denial of equal protection, since it is precisely the same distinction regarding partner that is drawn in state laws prohibiting marriage with someone of the same sex while permitting marriage with someone of the opposite sex.[34]

At the time of *Loving v. Virginia*, sixteen states had anti-miscegenation laws. To justify the illegality of same-sex sodomy on the illegality of same-sex marriage could be seen as analogous to justifying the illegality of miscegenation on the basis of the illegality of racial intermarriage. It represented a case of justifying a bad law by precedents that also constituted bad law.

Justice Scalia held tight to the value of coherence based on authorities as an expression of the leading value of stability, and with *his* coherence everything fit in the bag just fine. He consistently found more value in tradition than in an "emerging awareness" in which the American people began to understand the concept and value of heteronormativity and its ill effects on the LGBT community. Justice Scalia opted for precedent and the deep roots of tradition, clearly marked, rather than the less clearly marked (emerging awareness). In the end, he valued custom over comprehension.

An axiological analysis can also illuminate other contours of the dissent. For instance, in a frank admission, Scalia spoke for the homophobic American Everyman:

> Many Americans [Justice Scalia among them, perhaps speaking for them?] do not want persons who openly engage in homosexual conduct as partners in their business, as scoutmasters for their children, as teachers in their children's schools, or as boarders in their home. They view this as protecting themselves and their families from a lifestyle that they believe to be immoral and destructive.[35]

It is hard to excuse this comment from the charge of homophobia. Homophobia stems from hetero*normativity*. Normal is hyper-valued; abnormal hyper-disvalued. The hyper-valued normal stands as far away from the hyper-valued abnormal as the mind can imagine (as heaven is from hell)—each at the extreme edge of the value spectrum. In the parlance of twentieth-century phenomenology and existentialism, gay people are the Other. Regarding the Other as only a single bloc of identity is as simple-minded as regarding oppressed people without intersectionality. Otherness can be experienced as mild, being uncomfortable with some aspects of another being (Near-Other). Or it can be extreme, fearing or hating the whole of another being, as in the case of a homophobia (Far-Other). The hyper-valuation of heteronormativity cast the hyper-valued disvalue of homosexuality to the far edge of Otherness, abnormality (in the value equivalence of pure negation or hell), and of course, demons inhabit hell. With the emergence of a new sexual morality, as the net of accepted sexual practices expanded, gay people could no longer be demonized. However, normal and abnormal as values will remain and the vast value difference between them maintained. The value of normalcy, as usual, typical, or expected, protruded as another aspect of the predominant value for Justice Scalia—stability.

In a less forthright moment, Justice Scalia devalued the culture war, but instead of coming out and stating that he, too, had an ideological ax to grind, he blamed the other side for participating in the conflict:

So imbued is the Court with the law profession's anti-anti-homosexual culture, that it is seemingly unaware that the attitudes of that culture are not obviously "mainstream"; that in most States what the Court calls "discrimination" against those who engage in homosexual acts is perfectly legal.[36]

The value of democracy also protruded from Justice Scalia's Dissent:

Let me be clear that I have nothing against homosexuals, or any other group, promoting their agenda through normal democratic means. Social perceptions of sexual and other morality change over time, and every group has the right to persuade its fellow citizens that its view of such matters is the best. That homosexuals have achieved some success in that enterprise is attested to by the fact that Texas is one of the few remaining States that criminalizes private, consensual homosexual acts. But persuading one's fellow citizens is one thing, and imposing one's views in absence of democratic majority will is something else.[37]

In the case of whether to legalize homosexual sodomy, Justice Scalia valued the process of the democratic majority and disvalued judicial intervention. However, as he himself admitted, he agreed with court intervention when it came to anti-miscegenation laws, although in 1967 racial equality undoubtedly still constituted an "emerging awareness" and certainly could not be seen as rooted deeply in our country's traditions and history (far to the contrary). Why not wait for the democratic process to work in that case? Because he marked off Blacks as a class of oppressed individuals, but did not do the same for LGBTQI people. LGBTQI people could be valued as individuals committing crimes instead of being valued as an oppressed group being denied their liberty. He saw the illegalization of homosexual sodomy in the same way he perceived curbing the liberty of any individual, whether they be prostitutes, heroin users, or people working more than sixty hours per week.

Justice Scalia's adherence to the value of tradition (as an instrument to bring about the values of stability and the certainty that resulted from it) disclosed that his dissent aimed at social results no less than the *Lawrence* Majority did. Justice Scalia saw himself above the culture wars and posed as the neutral judge par excellence. But this became another case that by doing nothing you get the desired result of maintaining the status quo because the wheels of justice grind slowly, so slowly that they grind down and dishearten challengers of law by putting them through an amendment process that virtually promises by its Olympian standards that change will be minimized to perpetuate marginalization. Through the democratic process, Scalia argued, sodomy could be decriminalized, but not until the majority had spoken. Vaguely valued majority rule stood against vividly valued stability and its attendants, certainty and prediction. We see in Justice Scalia velleity toward democratic action and volition toward stability. The values of stability and democratic action could not camouflage the disvalue of homophobia that steered his dissent.

RECKONING OF THE ROGUE JUSTICES

1. Law in question

Tex. Penal Code Ann. §21.06(a) (2003). "A person commits an offense if he engages in deviate sexual intercourse with another individual of the same sex." [Accordingly,] "[d]eviate sexual intercourse" [is]: "(A) any contact between any part of the genitals of one person and the mouth or anus of another person; or "(B) the penetration of the genitals or the anus of an-other person with an object" §21.01(1).

2. Constitutional focal points

Constitution, Preamble

We the People of the United States, in Order to form a more perfect Union, establish Justice, insure domestic Tranquility, provide for the common defence, promote the general Welfare, and secure the *Blessings of Liberty* [our emphasis] to ourselves and our Posterity, do ordain and establish this Constitution for the United States of America.

Fourteenth Amendment Section 1

All persons born or naturalized in the United States, and subject to the jurisdiction thereof, are citizens of the United States and of the State wherein they reside. No State shall make or enforce any law which shall abridge the privileges or immunities of citizens of the United States; nor shall any State deprive any person of life, liberty, or property, without due process of law; nor deny to any person within its jurisdiction the equal protection of the laws.

3. *Prima facie* value assessment

a. For one who values equality, the Texas statute is patently unjust:

The same sexual acts are legal for heterosexuals and illegal for gay people.

b. For one who values liberty in its transcendent sense, the law is patently unjust:

The private sexual acts of consenting adults are beyond government jurisdiction and thus transcendent. This implies a transcendent space (private space, isle of intimacy) in which consenting adults have the dignity to make their own choices concerning intimacy. This path did not begin in 1965, but extended back to the due process elaborated in the Fourteenth Amendment and in the U.S. Constitution. We commit a category mistake by claiming the case concerns liberty over one's sexual decisions. Rather, the protruding value concerns the dignity of autonomous beings to make such choices.

c. For one who values knowledge over tradition, when an "emerging awareness" illustrates that deeply rooted traditions are mistaken or pernicious, this new comprehension is valued over adherence for the sake of adherence, tradition for the sake of tradition, and so on.
d. For one who values epiphanies, fundamental rights do not necessarily have to be found in the past, but can emerge at any time or place in history, depending on the degree of perspicacity.

4. Rationale and rejoinders

Having introduced authorities and valuations, the investigation is deepened.

a. The path or arc of authorities

On the basis of rather recent precedents (*Griswold*, *Eisenstadt*, *Baird*, and *Roe*), a legal path of liberty regarding private sexual matters has been established. However, this path or arc actually extends back to the Due Process Clause of the Fourteenth Amendment and beyond that to the "blessings [protection] of liberty" in the Preamble of the Constitution. Not to have the state interfering with our sex lives is a blessing of liberty. Placing a premium on liberty entails an absolutely free space where government cannot dictate private matters concerning reproduction and intimacy of dignified beings. The more such places we have in our society, the more liberty we shall have in it.

b. The values of liberty and equality

In this case, liberty and equality do not clash. Striking down all sodomy laws covers the actions of both heterosexuals and homosexuals, expanding liberty in private spaces while not taking away anything from either group. It treats all consensual adult partners the same. The fact that a gay couple next door practices sodomy does not force the heterosexual missionary-position loving couple next door from ever engaging in that act.

c. The disvalue of choice

The presumption that gay people choose the same way as heroin users, nudists, and people working overtime choose entails gay people become valued as individuals and not as a group. This prevents gay people from being seen as an oppressed class. Usually, choice is valued, but in this case, choice becomes disvalued to the extent it prevents LGBT people from being deemed an oppressed class and thus covered by the Equal Protection Clause of the Fourteenth Amendment.

d. The value of tradition

Tradition is a double-edged sword. Good and bad (beneficial/harmful) traditions exist. Sodomy laws we put in the category of bad traditions because they interfere with the liberty of consenting adults to conduct themselves as they wish in private spaces and violate equality because of unequal treatment. Same-sex sodomy misses out of being fundamentally grounded in America's tradition and history because of heteronormative valuing of sexuality. Thus, we reject the fundamental tradition as anything but a diversion and never applicable. Also, there can be conflicting traditions, especially distant and near traditions. We value the near tradition that values full sexual freedom over the distant tradition that values traditional sexual values.

e. Comment on the disvaluing of the gay lifestyle

In this case, the term "lifestyle" demands strict axiological scrutiny. Justice Scalia reduced lifestyle to its sexual value without considering that "lifestyle" entailed more than one's sexual acts and can be affected by as one's occupation, one's socioeconomic class, one's tastes, one's religion, or even one's dietary prohibitions. "Lifestyles" could be as various as religious or political views and also can be the result of combinations of various factors. Therefore, to single out the "gay lifestyle" on the basis of a single act leads one to consider the existence of a single Jewish lifestyle, Catholic lifestyle, Republican lifestyle, Democratic lifestyle, and also if we can reduce these lifestyles to their sexual acts, for example, would it be fair or accurate to say that a Catholic's lifestyle be reduced to the rhythm method? As demeaning as it would to a Catholic to reduce his whole lifestyle to the way he performs sex, it would be equally as demeaning to reduce the lifestyle of a gay person to his or her acts of sodomy. Lifestyle, if such an animal exists, can only be expressed by a plurality of values. Hence, it could be argued that if a gay person and straight person engage in similar types of activities and differ only to the extent that one engaged in sodomy and the other didn't, they could be living similar lifestyles. The politically loaded term "lifestyle" stigmatizes gay people as promiscuous, child molesters, deviants, engagers in sexual acts against nature and God, and therefore people who need to be kept away from our children and out of our safe, hetero-nuclear-familied communities. Yet many gay people live monogamous lifestyles and many heterosexuals live promiscuous lifestyles. This disvaluing of the mythical gay lifestyle slips in a heteronormative value and a corresponding homophobic disvalue intimating the agenda at hand. If using the word "lifestyle" in a negative context has nothing to with the culture war, the bombing of Dresden had nothing to do with World War II.

NOTES

1. William N. Eskridge, Jr., "Body Politics: *Lawrence v. Texas* and the Constitution of Disgust and Contagion," *Florida Law Review* 57, 5 (December 2005): 1013.
2. Katherine M. Franke, "The Domesticated Liberty of *Lawrence v. Texas*," *Columbia Law Review* 104 (2004): 1400.
3. Danaya C. Wright, "The Logic and Experience of Law: *Lawrence v. Texas* and the Politics of Privacy," *University Florida Journal Law Public Policy* 15 (2004): 409.
4. Ibid., 1425.
5. Randy E. Barnett, "Justice Kennedy's Libertarian Revolution: *Lawrence v. Texas*," *Georgetown Law Faculty Publications and Other Works* (2003): 21, https://scholarship.law.georgetown.edu/facpub/838.
6. Davin J. Hall, "Not So LandmarkvAfter All? *Lawrence v. Texas*: Classical Liberalism and Due Process Jurisprudence," *William and Mary Bill Rights Journal* 13 (2004): 650.
7. Matt Coles, "*Lawrence v. Texas* and the Refinement of Substantive Due Process," *Stanford Law and Policy Review* 16 (2005): 47.
8. Marc Spindelman, "Surviving *Lawrence v. Texas*," *Michigan Law Review* 102 (2004): 1666.
9. *Lawrence v. Texas*, 539 U.S. 558, 562 (2003).
10. Ibid.
11. Ibid., 578.
12. Ibid., 564.
13. Ibid., 567.
14. Ibid.
15. Ibid.
16. Ibid., 568–569.
17. Ibid., 572.
18. Ibid., 575.
19. Ibid., 567.

20. Ibid., 579.
21. Ibid.
22. Ibid., 581–582.
23. Ibid., 586.
24. Ibid., 587.
25. Ibid., 593.
26. Ibid., 588.
27. Ibid., 593.
28. Ibid., 586.
29. Ibid., 604.
30. Ibid., 589.
31. Ibid., 591.
32. Ibid., 590.
33. Ibid., 592.
34. Id, 599–600.
35. Ibid., 602.
36. Ibid..
37. Ibid., 603.

Chapter 16

Weaponized Words v. the Fruition of Conscience in Action

Brandenburg v. Ohio

NARRATIVE IN A NUTSHELL

Clarence Brandenburg was a member of the Ohio KKK.

And he wanted publicity?

Yes. So he phoned a Cincinnati TV station and invited an announcer-reporter to a Klan rally.

And the announcer-reporter couldn't get out there fast enough, of course.

The announcer-reporter and a cameraperson showed up and the event was filmed.

Where was this rally held?

In a field somewhere in the sticks.

How many audience members were there?

If you exclude Brandenburg and eleven other Klan-bedecked individuals, the gate was the average between negative 1 and 1, but it was broadcast and thus many people were exposed.

What kinds of activities were the twelve involved in?

Burning a cross.

Standard.

Although much of what they said was incomprehensible, they denounced the usual groups.

Standard.

And some had guns.

Standard. What did Brandenburg say?

From his own mouth: "'We're not a revengent organization, but if our President, our Congress, our Supreme Court, continues to suppress the white,

Caucasian race, it's possible that there might have to be some revengeance taken.'" And: "'Personally, I believe the nigger should be returned to Africa, the Jew returned to Israel.'" Other evidence from the film included "a pistol, a rifle, a shotgun, ammunition, a Bible, and a red hood worn by the speaker."

And what Ohio law did he break?

The Ohio Criminal Syndicalism stipulating that "advocat[ing] . . . the duty, necessity, or propriety of crime, sabotage, violence, or unlawful methods of terrorism as a means of accomplishing industrial or political reform" and for "voluntarily assembl[ing] with any society, group, or assemblage of persons formed to teach or advocate the doctrines of criminal syndicalism."

And the punishment for this crime?

$1,000.00 and a one-to-ten-year prison sentence.

VALUE-INFUSED SCHOLARSHIP

Calling the ruling a "major breakthrough for freedom of speech" that rejects "the fear and paranoia of the past," one commentator sees his work strengthening and thus valuing *Brandenburg* and the First Amendment.[1] Similarly, *Brandenburg* is useful because it encourages decision-makers to use restraint and not overact in perilous times when civil liberties are jeopardized.[2] The disvalue of fear should not compel us to diminish the First Amendment.[3] On the other hand, a "relaxed" or dminished *Brandenburg* standard could be used to restrict speech advocating, for instance, illegal drug use by giving school officials latitude to cultivate stability and order (positive values) essential requisite for an effective learning environment (intrinsic value).[4] Those who see freedom of speech entangled with the values of universal human rights and the norms of democratic discourse view the government censorship of online speech to be a highly negative value.[5] The value of the *Brandenburg* standard is the prevention of arbitrarily punishing "unpopular and outsider organizations."[6] Freedom of speech, a free press, and freedom to assemble are valued as means to hold free political discussions, which in turn helps government respond to the will of the people so that changes can be made in a peaceful manner, which in turn promotes the security of the republic, the very foundation of constitutional government.[7] Ultimately, freedom of speech is valued for providing security. Yet more qualifications put on the likelihood factor, the more diluted freedom of speech and the less it is exercised and valued.[8] An axiological analysis of this decision reveals another level of valuation centering on the sacred zenith value of conscience, which when repressed ranks as a profane nadir disvalue.

PER CURIAM MAJORITY OPINION

The Supreme Court, in a per curiam decision, struck down the Ohio Criminal Syndicalism statute, largely using the First Amendment as a blunt weapon. Seizing on *Noto v. United States*, 367 U.S. 290, 367 U. S. 297–298 (1961), the majority opinion reaffirmed: "'the mere abstract teaching . . . of the moral propriety or even moral necessity for a resort to force and violence is not the same as preparing a group for violent action and steeling it to such action.'"[9] Stated in a slightly different way, "mere advocacy not distinguished from incitement to imminent lawless action"[10] was the core problem with the Ohio statute. Wielding that bold differentiation, the majority concluded: "A statute which fails to draw this distinction impermissibly intrudes upon the freedoms guaranteed by the First and Fourteenth Amendments. It sweeps within its condemnation speech which our Constitution has immunized from governmental control."[11]

OPERATIVE AUTHORITIES WITH COMMENTS

First Amendment

> Congress shall make no law respecting an establishment of religion, or prohibiting the free exercise thereof; or abridging the freedom of speech, or of the press; or the right of the people peaceably to assemble, and to petition the government for a redress of grievances.

Government control assumed a nadir disvalue on a spectrum which freedom stood at the other end as zenith value.

Fourteenth Amendment (Section 1)

All persons born or naturalized in the United States, and subject to the jurisdiction thereof, are citizens of the United States and of the state wherein they reside. No state shall make or enforce any law which shall abridge the privileges or immunities of citizens of the United States; nor shall any state deprive any person of life, liberty, or property, without due process of law; nor deny to any person within its jurisdiction the equal protection of the laws.

The "liberty" aspect of Section 1 was tied back to the First Amendment.

Whitney v. California, 274 U.S. 357 (1927). Rejected because that Court upheld a statute affirming that advocating violence to achieve political and economic change was a danger to the state

Noto v. United States, 367 U.S. 290, 367 U. S. 297–298 (1961). The difference between teaching about violence and planning to be violent comes into bold relief in the light of the value of freedom

OPERATIVE VALUES

Value of Freedom

One does not just come to distinction between abstract teaching about violence and how-to-do lesson on violence without guidance from values. This distinction was guided by deep appreciation of freedom of speech for individuals. If, as the per curiam majority opinion stated, there was speech "which our Constitution has immunized from governmental control,"[12] government control was the disease for which immunization is intended. Government control obtrudes as a nadir disvalue at one end of the spectrum, with freedom of speech as zenith value on the other. The First Amendment was like an inoculation that protected people from the disease of government control.

CONCURRENCE BY JUSTICE WILLIAM DOUGLAS

Justice Douglas's concurrence appreciated free speech and the First Amendment to even a greater degree than what is found in the per curiam majority opinion. In contrast to seeing that freedom in functional terms as an immunization, Justice Douglas elevated it to a sacred zenith status. The inner world of beliefs was a sanctuary like a church, synagogue, or mosque, and that sanctuary was extended to speech and actions as expressions of beliefs—up to the point they proved to be dangerous.

CHRONOLOGY OF AUTHORITIES—WITH BRIEF COMMENTS

First Amendment. Emphasis on the inner world of beliefs and conscience.

Schenck v. United States, 249 U.S. 47, 249 U. S. 52 (1919). Charged with attempts to cause insubordination in armed forces and obstruction of the enlistment for distributing pamphlets denouncing conscription, and impugned motives of war advocates. This fell into the clear and present danger category. Rejected: "clear and present danger" test, thought by Justice Douglas to be too vague and because of its vagueness, a means to encroach upon the First Amendment.

Frohwerk v. United States, 249 U.S. 204 (1919). Prosecution and punishment for publication of articles very critical of the war effort in World War I/ Rejected: "clear and present danger" test, thought by Justice Douglas to be too vague and because of its vagueness a means to encroach upon the First Amendment.

Debs v. United States, 249 U.S. 211 (1919). Debs charged with language that could obstruct recruiting. Rejected: "clear and present danger" test, thought by Justice Douglas to be too vague and because of its vagueness, a means to encroach upon the First Amendment.

Whitney v. California, 274 U.S. 357 (1927). Rejected: advocacy endangers the state and justifies the state to outlaw it.

Dennis v. United States, 341 U.S. 494 (1951). Court supported prosecution that teaching Marxism was a conspiracy, distorting clear and present danger test by asserting the gravity of the evil (minus its improbability) justified infringement of free speech "as is necessary to avoid danger."

Noto v. United States, 367 U.S. 290, 367 U.S. 297–298 (1961). Agreed: Abstract teaching about violence ≠ preparation for violence and to fill a group with resolution and determination to enact such violence.

LEGAL REASONING

Because he valued freedom of speech as a sacred zenith value, Justice Douglas was inclined to enlarge the scope of the First Amendment. Rather than simply point to *Noto* and the distinction between abstract advocacy and a call to arms, he chose another target. His target was the "clear and present danger" test and mantra. Ostensibly, this test had enlarged freedom of speech such that only in rare circumstances could it be abridged. Douglas pushed back against the "clear and present danger" test, thinking it too restrictive.

Douglas dubbed *Schenk*, *Frohwerk*, and *Debs* as a trilogy of decisions from the 1918 term that constricted free speech and remarked of the clear and present danger test at the core of each:

> Those, then, were the World War I cases that put the gloss of "clear and present danger" on the First Amendment. Whether the war power—the greatest leveler of them all—is adequate to sustain that doctrine is debatable.[13]

> Though I doubt if the "clear and present danger" test is congenial to the First Amendment in time of a declared war, I am certain it is not reconcilable with the First Amendment in days of peace.[14]

> My own view is quite different. I see no place in the regime of the First Amendment for any "clear and present danger" test, whether strict and tight.[15]

There was a clear distinction "between ideas and overt acts." Shouting "Fire!" in a crowded theater was an overt act because speech and act are linked. However, teaching Marxism was not such an overt act, nor was even burning one's draft card: "Advocacy and teaching of forcible overthrow of government as an abstract principle is immune from prosecution."[16]

In most cases, the "clear and present danger" test was applied to those who simply lacked the power to cause any damage to society. Or during the Red Scare of the 1940s and 1950s, it was politicized to persecute teachers of Marxism:

> When one reads the opinions closely and sees when and how the "clear and present danger" test has been applied, great misgivings are aroused. First, the threats were often loud, but always puny, and made serious only by judges so wedded to the *status quo* that critical analysis made them nervous. Second, the test was so twisted and perverted in *Dennis* as to make the trial of those teachers of Marxism an all-out political trial which was part and parcel of the cold war that has eroded substantial parts of the First Amendment.[17]

In other words, a short speech by a Klansman in an open field to eleven other Klansman, vile as it was, even though it appeared on TV, did not constitute a clear and present danger.

OPERATIVE VALUES

Value of Inner World

For Justice Douglas, one's beliefs, ideas, and convictions were considered sacred, in his own words "sanctuaries":

> One's beliefs have long been thought to be sanctuaries which government could not invade. . . . The lines drawn by the Court between the criminal act of being an "active" Communist and the innocent act of being a nominal or inactive Communist mark the difference only between deep and abiding belief and casual or uncertain belief. But I think that all matters of belief are beyond the

reach of subpoenas or the probings of investigators. That is why the invasions of privacy made by investigating committees were notoriously unconstitutional. That is the deep-seated fault in the infamous loyalty security hearings which, since 1947, when President Truman launched them, have processed 20,000,000 men and women. Those hearings were primarily concerned with one's thoughts, ideas, beliefs, and convictions. They were the most blatant violations of the First Amendment we have ever known.[18]

[G]overnment has no power to invade that sanctuary of belief and conscience.[19]

The inner life of a person was treasured and actions of the state to monitor the inner life were considered "ransacking" it:

And so the investigator roams at will through all of the beliefs of the witness, ransacking his conscience and his innermost thoughts.[20]

Value of a Pluralistic Proliferation of Ideas

In Douglas's eyes, Holmes redeemed himself with his dissent in *Gitlow v. New York*, 268 U.S. 652, 268 U.S. 673 (1925) by enlarging free speech to include the expression of any, not just some, ideas:

Every idea is an incitement. It offers itself for belief, and, if believed, it is acted on unless some other belief outweighs it or some failure of energy stifles the movement at its birth. The only difference between the expression of an opinion and an incitement in the narrower sense is the speaker's enthusiasm for the result. Eloquence may set fire to reason. But whatever may be thought of the redundant discourse before us, it had no chance of starting a present conflagration. If, in the long run, the beliefs expressed in proletarian dictatorship are destined to be accepted by the dominant forces of the community, the only meaning of free speech is that they should be given their chance and have their way.

"We have never been faithful to the philosophy of that dissent," Justice Douglas remarked, which he saw "as closer to the First Amendment ideal."[21] Freedom of speech was valued for its pluralistic proliferation of ideas, with a premium of value placed on what might be construed as negative values.

The Value of the First Amendment's Extension to Actions

The First Amendment must be extended even to those expressions that manifest themselves in actions:

> Action is often a method of expression, and within the protection of the First Amendment.[22]
>
> Suppose one tears up his own copy of the Constitution in eloquent protest to a decision of this Court. May he be indicted? Suppose one rips his own Bible to shreds to celebrate his departure from one "faith" and his embrace of atheism. May he be indicted?[23]

This significantly increased the territory of the First Amendment, demonstrating Douglas's absolute adherence to its full breadth.

The Value of Ideas as the Agents of Social Change

More the valuing the inner life, Justice Douglas recognized the importance of ideas as a catalyst for changing society. Quoting Justice Brandeis in *Pierce v. United States*, 252 U.S. 239 (1920), he saw argument and discourse (even in times of war) as "[t]he fundamental right of free men to strive for better conditions through new legislation and new institutions."[24]

RECKONING OF THE ROGUE JUSTICES

Had Mr. Brandenburg led his sheeted comrades into a crowd, then goodbye to First Amendment. Mr. Brandenburg's speech, although vitriolic, did not cross the line. There was no crowd to be fomented as in the case of yelling fire in a crowded movie theater. The weaponry was concerning, but hardly a threat at an outdoor venue with no patrons. Did Brandenburg & Co. push the envelope of free speech? Revolting and evil ideas may push the envelope, but pushing the envelope does not mean sending a mail bomb. When we consider freedom of speech as a sacred zenith value, we are led to see its full potential, its genesis in thought and conscience, its articulation in words, and its connection to action. Sacred valuations eschew containment and are prone to universalization or full actualization. Believers find God everywhere. According to this value framework, both words and actions are expressions of and as sacred as thought and conscience. The curtailment of speech and action is tantamount to a curtailment of conscience.

NOTES

1. Thomas Healy, "*Brandenburg* in a Time of Terror," *Notre Dame Law Review* 84, 2 (2009): 731.

2. Martha Field, "*Brandenburg v. Ohio* and Its Relationship to *Masses Publishing Co. v. Patten*," *Arizona State Law Journal* 50 (2018): 800.
3. Chris Montgomery, "Can *Brandenburg v. Ohio* Survive the Internet and the Age of Terrorism?: The Secret Weakening of a Venerable Doctrine," *Ohio State Law Journal* 70, 1 (2009): 193.
4. Steven Penaro, "Reconciling *Morse* with *Brandenburg*," *Fordham Law Review* 77 (2008): 285.
5. Emerson J. Sykes, "In Defense of *Brandenburg*: The ACLU and Incitement Doctrine in 1919, 1969, and 2019," *Brooklyn Law Review* 85 (2019): 35.
6. Christina E. Wells, "Assumptions about Terrorism and the *Brandenburg* Incitement Test," *Brooklyn Law Review* 85 (2019): 147.
7. Margot Kaminski, "Incitement to Riot in the Age of Flash Mobs," *University Cincinnati Law Review* (2013): 84.
8. Clay Calvert, "First Amendment Envelope Pushers: Revisiting the Incitement-to-Violence Test with Messrs. *Brandenburg*, Trump, & Spencer," *Connecticut Law Review* 51 (2019): 153.
9. *Brandenburg v. Ohio*, 395 U.S. 444, 448 (1969).
10. Ibid., 449.
11. Ibid., 448.
12. Ibid., 448.
13. Ibid., 451.
14. Ibid., 452.
15. Ibid., 454.
16. Ibid., 453.
17. Ibid., 454.
18. Ibid., 456.
19. Ibid., 457.
20. Ibid., 454.
21. Ibid., 452.
22. Ibid., 454.
23. Ibid., 454–455.
24. Ibid., 452.

Chapter 17

Invidious Discrimination v. the Purity of White Supremacy

Loving v. Virginia

NARRATIVE IN A NUTSHELL

When were Richard and Mildred Loving married?

In 1958.

Where?

In the District of Columbia.

Did they stay there?

No. They moved to Caroline County, Virginia the same year they were married.

What noteworthy thing happened to them in Virginia?

They were arrested in July 1958 and a jury indicted them on January 6, 1959.

For what?

For violating Virginia's ban on interracial marriage.

And they plead guilty and received suspended sentences.

Yes and on the condition they would not return to Virginia until 1984.

Many states had a ban on interracial marriage, even when this case came to Supreme Court.

Yes, as of 1967, when the case reached the Supreme Court, seventeen states enforced laws prohibiting the marriage of whites and blacks. All these were southern states, including all the former slave states in addition to Oklahoma and West Virginia.

VALUE-INFUSED SCHOLARSHIP

The appropriation of *Loving* or any landmark case or any precedent or authority for that matter stems from the appropriator's value agenda, whether that is to further social justice, transracial families, same-sex families, or diverse sexual or familial arrangements. The "generational moral progress"[1] in *Loving* was evident by its departure from the nadir value of invidious discrimination. When a case like *Loving* becomes a landmark case, it assumes that status because it is anchored in the zenith value such as social justice: "We must affirm our common humanity by working to end the social injustices preserved by race."[2] This case has been cited as the point of departure and foundation for transracial families[3] as well as for same-sex families.[4] ["T] he imaginary value assigned to racial composition"[5] is not imaginary at all, but a specific value scheme. The Court recognized marriage as "important,"[6] assigning it a sacred zenith value. The premium value placed on marriage does not suit those who emphasize the end of marriage (erotic pleasures and communities of care), a catalyst value conducive to embracing "forms of sex and family unrecognized and/or prohibited by civil marriage regimes" and related to liberty interests concerning procreation, contraception, abortion, and sodomy.[7] Our value-driven analysis takes a wholly different path, showing how the sacred zenith value of marriage relates to the parallelism and tangents inherent in the purity and supremacy.

WHITE SUPREMACY APPROPRIATED FROM VIRGINIA LAW

On January 22, 1965, a judge had this to say about the Loving's marriage:

> Almighty God created the races white, black, yellow, malay and red, and he placed them on separate continents. And, but for the interference with his arrangement, there would be no cause for such marriage. The fact that he separated the races shows that he did not intend for the races to mix.[8]

This judge harnessed the value of white supremacy inherent in the Virginia anti-miscegenation laws:

> Leaving State to evade law.—If any white person and colored person shall go out of this State, for the purpose of being married, and with the intention of returning, and be married out of it, and afterwards return to and reside in it, cohabiting as man and wife, they shall be punished as provided in § 20-59, and the marriage shall be governed by the same law as if it had been solemnized in

> this State. The fact of their cohabitation here as man and wife shall be evidence of their marriage.[9]
>
> Punishment for marriage.—If any white person intermarry with a colored person, or any colored person intermarry with a white person, he shall be guilty of a felony and shall be punished by confinement in the penitentiary for not less than one nor more than five years.[10]

With distinctions worthy of a medieval philosopher or botanist, the Virginia law offered a number of nice racial distinctions:

> *Intermarriage prohibited; meaning of term "white persons."*—It shall hereafter be unlawful for any white person in this State to marry any save a white person, or a person with no other admixture of blood than white and American Indian. For the purpose of this chapter, the term "white person" shall apply only to such person as has no trace whatever of any blood other than Caucasian; but persons who have one-sixteenth or less of the blood of the American Indian and have no other non-Caucasic blood shall be deemed to be white persons. All laws heretofore passed and now in effect regarding the intermarriage of white and colored persons shall apply to marriages prohibited by this chapter. Va.Code Ann. § 20–54 (1960 Repl. Vol.)[11]
>
> The exception for persons with less than one-sixteenth "of the blood of the American Indian" is apparently accounted for, in the words of a tract issued by the Registrar of the State Bureau of Vital Statistics, by "the desire of all to recognize as an integral and honored part of the white race the descendants of John Rolfe and Pocathontas. . . ." Plecker, The New Family and Race Improvement, 17 Va.Health Bull., Extra No. 12, at 25–26 (New Family Series No. 5, 1925), cited in Wadlington, The *Loving* Case: Virginia's Anti-Miscegenation Statute in Historical Perspective, 52 Va.L.Rev. 1189, 1202, n. 93 (1966).[12]
>
> *Colored persons and Indians defined.*—Every person in whom there is ascertainable any Negro blood shall be deemed and taken to be a colored person, and every person not a colored person having one-fourth or more of American Indian blood shall be deemed an American Indian; except that members of Indian tribes existing in this Commonwealth having one fourth or more of Indian blood and less than one-sixteenth of Negro blood shall be deemed tribal Indians.[13]

AT LEGAL LOGGERHEADS

The legal battle could be summed up in the following chart, listing the legal precedents on both sides .

Table 17.1 Racial Integrity

Authorities Supporting Virginia Law	*Authorities Refuting Law*
Tenth Amendment The powers not delegated to the United States by the Constitution, nor prohibited by it to the States, are reserved to the States respectively, or to the people.	*Fourteenth Amendment* No state shall make or enforce any law which shall abridge the privileges or immunities of citizens of the United States; nor shall any state deprive any person of life, liberty, or property, without due process of law; nor deny to any person within its jurisdiction the equal protection of the laws.
Naim v. Naim, 197 Va. 80, 87 S.E.2d 749, (1955). The State had legitimate purposes to (1) preserve racial integrity, (2) prevent blood from being corrupted, and (3) prevent a mongrel breed of citizens from being born, and (4) prevent racial pride from being destroyed.	*Skinner v. Oklahoma*, 316 U.S. 535, 316 U. S. 541 (1942). Marriage is one of the basic civil rights of people.
Pace v. Alabama, 106 U. S. 583 (1883). Because the punishment for Whites and Blacks was the same for adultery and fornication under Alabama law, the Court upheld a conviction forbidding adultery or fornication between a white person and a Negro, although the penalty for the same conduct between people of the same races was not as great.	*McLaughlin v. Florida*, 379 U.S. 184 (1964) On the basis of the Equal Protection Law of Fourteenth Amendment, the Supreme Court reversed a Florida criminal statute prohibiting an unmarried interracial couple from being together in the same room at night while no such statute applied to members of the same race.

Source: Loving v. Virginia, 388 U.S. 1, 3 (1967).

Looking down both barrels of Section One of the Fourteenth Amendment, the Due Process Clause and the Equal Rights Clause, the Tenth Amendment was depreciated. Valuing marriage as a civil right (*Skinner*) eclipsed the notion of state interests in race purity (*Naim*). In two cases focused on interracial sexual activity, *McLaughlin* was preferred over *Pace* because equality was not valued for equal punishment, but for equal opportunity.

Virginia wanted to diminish the Fourteenth Amendment by equating equality with equal punishment:

> Thus, the State contends that, because its miscegenation statutes punish equally both the white and the Negro participants in an interracial marriage, these statutes, despite their reliance on racial classifications, do not constitute an invidious discrimination based upon race. The second argument advanced by the State assumes the validity of its equal application theory. The argument is that, if the Equal Protection Clause does not outlaw miscegenation statutes because of their reliance on racial classifications, the question of constitutionality would thus

> become whether there was any rational basis for a State to treat interracial marriages differently from other marriages. On this question, the State argues, the scientific evidence is substantially in doubt and, consequently, this Court should defer to the wisdom of the state legislature in adopting its policy of discouraging interracial marriages.[14]

But this equal punishment ploy was actually a means to reinforce invidious discrimination:

> In the case at bar, however, we deal with statutes containing racial classifications, and the fact of equal application does not immunize the statute from the very heavy burden of justification which the Fourteenth Amendment has traditionally required of state statutes drawn according to race.[15]
>
> There is patently no legitimate overriding purpose independent of invidious racial discrimination which justifies this classification. The fact that Virginia prohibits only interracial marriages involving white persons demonstrates that the racial classifications must stand on their own justification, as measures designed to maintain White Supremacy.[16]

MAJORITY OPINION BY CHIEF JUSTICE EARL WARREN

OPERATIVE VALUES

Values of Liberty and Equality

Against invidious discrimination, embedded in Virginia laws and a legal system that ordained racist rulings, the Supreme Court moved in with Article 1 of the Fourteenth Amendment, using both barrels, the Due Process Clause and the Equal Protection Clause:

> The fact that Virginia prohibits only interracial marriages involving white persons demonstrates that the racial classifications must stand on their own justification, as measures designed to maintain White Supremacy. We have consistently denied the constitutionality of measures which restrict the rights of citizens on account of race. There can be no doubt that restricting the freedom to marry solely because of racial classifications violates the central meaning of the Equal Protection Clause.[17]
>
> These statutes also deprive the Lovings of liberty without due process of law in violation of the Due Process Clause of the Fourteenth Amendment. The freedom to marry has long been recognized as one of the vital personal rights essential to the orderly pursuit of happiness by free men.[18]

Value of the Broader, Organic Value of the Fourteenth Amendment

> The State argues that statements in the Thirty-ninth Congress about the time of the passage of the Fourteenth Amendment indicate that the Framers did not intend the Amendment to make unconstitutional state miscegenation laws. Many of the statements alluded to by the State concern the debates over the Freedmen's Bureau Bill, which President Johnson vetoed, and the Civil Rights Act of 1866, 14 Stat. 27, enacted over his veto. While these statements have some relevance to the intention of Congress in submitting the Fourteenth Amendment, it must be understood that they pertained to the passage of specific statutes, and not to the broader, organic purpose of a constitutional amendment.[19]

The majority opinion understood the Fourteenth Amendment beyond the racist trappings of a century before and as a blossoming ideal, which once bloomed would reject any form of invidious discrimination. In other words, Justice Warren valued the Fourteenth Amendment as an ideal.

Disvalue of Invidious Racial Discrimination and the Value of Equality

The State of Virginia refused to acknowledge "the invidious racial discrimination" at the root of their racial classification scheme. This type of discrimination was unfair in the extreme, "invidious." The disvalue of unfairness and value of equality protrude from and propels this ruling:

> To deny this fundamental freedom [to marry who you want] on so unsupportable a basis as the racial classifications embodied in these statutes, classifications so directly subversive of the principle of equality at the heart of the Fourteenth Amendment, is surely to deprive all the State's citizens of liberty without due process of law.[20]

RECKONING OF THE ROGUE JUSTICES

Virginia embraced the separate but equal doctrine of White Supremacy. Separate meant the races living fundamentally parallel lives, intersections being rare and only if necessary. The Virginia anti-miscegenation laws preserved the purity of the white race by severing the races. This contradicted *e pluribus unum* and simultaneously liberty and equality, the essence of American life embodied in the ideals of the Fourteenth Amendment, which must be lived out in interaction rather than parallelism. The purity doctrine played out in the social world as a parallelism at tangents, with interactions only tolerated for exploitative purposes. Anti-miscegenation was an effective means to maintain this social, political, ideological, and psychological parallelism. Marriage was not only a union of two people but also of families as well, where religion, culture, and ideas could be united. Also, if marriage as a zenith value included interracial relationships, one of the most sacred institutions of the civilization would be despoiled. The parallelism of White Supremacy did much more than marginalize Black people. It put them in another plane of existence in which their rare appearance could only be seen from the White Supremacist viewpoint as barbarians outside the gates of civilized society.

NOTES

1. Linda McClain, "Prejudice, Constitutional Moral Progress, and Being 'On the Right Side of History': Reflections on *Loving v. Virginia* at Fifty," *Fordham Law Review* 86 (2018): 2702.
2. Dorothy Roberts, "*Loving v. Virginia* as a Civil Rights Decision," *New York Law School Law Review* 59, 1 (January 2015): 209.
3. Elizabeth Bartholet, "Race Separatism in the Family: More on the Transracial Adoption," *Duke Journal of Gender Law & Policy* 2 (Spring 1995): 105.
4. Joanna L. Grossman and John DeWitt Gregory, "The Legacy of *Loving*," *Howard Law Journal* 15 (2007): 27.
5. Justice Leah Ward Sears (Ret.) and Sasha N. Greenberg, "The Love in *Loving*: Overcoming Artificial Racial Barriers," *Notre Dame Law Review Online* 94 (2018): 30. https://scholarship.law.nd.edu/ndlr_online/vol94/iss1/6.
6. Robert A. Destro, "Law and the Politics of Marriage: Loving v. Virginia after 30 Years Introduction," *Catholic University Law Review* 47, 4 (Summer 1998): 1214.
7. Tucker Culbertson, "Arguments Against Marriage Equality: Commemorating & Reconstructing *Loving v. Virginia*," *Washington Law Review* 85, 3 (2007): 577.
8. *Loving v. Virginia*, 388 U.S. 1, 3 (1967).
9. Ibid., 4.
10. Ibid.
11. Ibid., 13.
12. Ibid.
13. Ibid.
14. Ibid., 8.
15. Ibid., 9.
16. Ibid., 11.
17. Ibid., 11–12.
18. Ibid., 12.
19. Ibid., 9.
20. Ibid., 12.

Chapter 18

Health v. Liberty

National Federation of Independent Business v. Sebelius

NARRATIVE IN A NUTSHELL

The Affordable Care Act (ACA, colloquially known as "Obamacare") was a lightning rod even before it became law in 2010.

Yes. The Affordable Care Act excited ire because it coerced individual states to comply with it and it taxed citizens who refused to purchase health insurance.

The ACA covered most Americans and prevented insurance companies from denying coverage to people with preexisting conditions, but it was not a favorite of business.

A coalition of health care providers, the National Federation of Independent Business, sued the face of the government, the Secretary of Human Health and Services, Karen Sibelius, over what they thought unconstitutional aspects of the ACA.

VALUE-INFUSED SCHOLARSHIP

Chief Justice Roberts's judicial style, drawing "clear boundary lines but that invites future litigation,"[1] can be understood as valuing clarity for the purpose of containment. Many commentators value or disvalue "the Machiavellian Roberts" who "shrewdly gave liberal Democrats an immediate victory, but advanced long-term conservative Republican interests by curtailing Congress's power under the Commerce, Necessary and Proper, and Spending Clauses."[2] One of the central aspects of the case is the Necessary and Proper Clause, to what degree Congress can control the states. One way of looking at this is valuing the Necessary and Proper Clause for its flexibility, but disvaluing it for giving Congress the power of national police.[3] The flexible is the functional. Beyond functionality is coercion and that is a nadir value. This case takes on a completely different value hue for those for whom health care is a zenith value. Advocates of universal health care value it holistically: "A holistic understanding of government in the United States reveals that, as is the case in many other developed countries, providing for the health, safety, and welfare of citizens is among the primary obligations of government. These obligations are so well established that they should be thought of as constitutional in character."[4]

THE CONSTITUTIONAL WISHBONE

The Supreme Court wrestled over The Commerce Clause of the Constitution (Article 1, Section 8, Clause 1):

> The Congress shall have Power To lay and collect Taxes, Duties, Imposts and Excises, to pay the Debts and provide for the common Defence and general Welfare of the United States; but all Duties, Imposts and Excises shall be uniform throughout the United States;

This case turned on how the Commerce Clause was interpreted. The three interpretations were guided by definitive values. Each revealed values in different ways. In the dissent by Justices Scalia, Kennedy, Thomas, and Alito, the values were ostensible. In fact, they were articulated in a bold manner, much like in an undergraduate paper when the student writes: "My thesis in this paper is . . ." In contrast to ostensible values in the majority, the values Justice Ginsburg concurrence and dissent were recessed. The values in the majority opinion by Chief Justice Roberts were also recessed and only an axiological kind of black light could detect its traces. Traces or not, values subsist and drive the decision.

MAJORITY OPINION BY CHIEF JUSTICE JOHN ROBERTS

Chief Justice Roberts gave a split decision to the ACA. He saw the taxing constitutional and the Medicaid expansion as unconstitutional:

> The Affordable Care Act is constitutional in part and unconstitutional in part. The individual mandate cannot be upheld as an exercise of Congress's power under the Commerce Clause. That Clause authorizes Congress to regulate

> interstate commerce, not to order individuals to engage in it. In this case, however, it is reasonable to construe what Congress has done as increasing taxes on those who have a certain amount of income, but choose to go without health insurance. Such legislation is within Congress's power to tax.
>
> As for the Medicaid expansion, that portion of the Affordable Care Act violates the Constitution by threatening existing Medicaid funding. Congress has no authority to order the States to regulate according to its instructions. Congress may offer the States grants and require the States to comply with accompanying conditions, but the States must have a genuine choice whether to accept the offer. The States are given no such choice in this case: They must either accept a basic change in the nature of Medicaid, or risk losing all Medicaid funding. The remedy for that constitutional violation is to preclude the Federal Government from imposing such a sanction. That remedy does not require striking down other portions of the Affordable Care Act.[5]

Taxing did not reach the status of depriving people of their individual choice or their liberty. On the other hand, the ACA allowed Congress to offer grants to states on the basis of complying with certain conditions. This was in effect coercing the states and not giving them a genuine choice. This amounted to a deprivation of liberty. Taxation did not interfere with liberty, while the states' so-called "compliance" with certain conditions did.

Chief Justice Roberts understood the ACA as a way of cost-shifting such that healthy people would pay more for their insurance than they need and that extra money would then subsidize unhealthy people who would not otherwise be able to afford health care:

> The individual mandate was Congress's solution to these problems. By requiring that individuals purchase health insurance, the mandate prevents cost-shifting by those who would otherwise go without it. In addition, the mandate forces into the insurance risk pool more healthy individuals, whose premiums on average will be higher than their health care expenses. This allows insurers to subsidize the costs of covering the unhealthy individuals the reforms require them to accept. The Government claims that Congress has power under the Commerce and Necessary and Proper Clauses to enact this solution.[6]

OPERATIVE VALUES

The Value of the Court to Interpret Law and the Disvalue of the Court Being Society's Protector

In this very heated issue at the center of an American political maelstrom, Justice Roberts revealed a penchant for keeping the Supreme Court out of the business of improving American life:

> Members of this Court are vested with the authority to interpret the law; we possess neither the expertise nor the prerogative to make policy judgments. Those decisions are entrusted to our Nation's elected leaders, who can be thrown out of office if the people disagree with them. It is not our job to protect the people from the consequences of their political choices.[7]

The valuing of neutrality can be seen clearly in the argumentation—in contrast to the concurrence and dissent by Justice Ginsburg and the dissent by Justice Scalia, Kennedy, Thomas, and Alito. In both, we find arguments that speak the consequences of adopting the ACA and how it would affect society. We find none of that in majority opinion, mainly because the driving value of non-entanglement with society. The focus was on interpreting the law and not "to protect the people from the consequences of their political choices." This value of non-interference in politics is what we call neutrality or not supporting either side:

> The Framers created a Federal Government of limited powers, and assigned to this Court the duty of enforcing those limits. The Court does so today. But the Court does not express any opinion on the wisdom of the Affordable Care Act. Under the Constitution, that judgment is reserved to the people.[8]

The Liberty of States and the Limits of Federal Power

Chief Justice read the Constitution as the protector of states' rights:

> The same does not apply to the States, because the Constitution is not the source of their power. The Constitution may restrict state governments—as it does, for example, by forbidding them to deny any person the equal protection of the laws. But where such prohibitions do not apply, state governments do not need constitutional authorization to act. The States thus can and do perform many of the vital functions of modern government—punishing street crime, running public schools, and zoning property for development, to name but a few—even though the Constitution's text does not authorize any government to do so. Our cases refer to this general power of governing, possessed by the States but not by the Federal Government, as the "police power." See, e.g., *United States v. Morrison*, 529 U. S. 598–619 (2000)

Also, in play here was the Necessary and Proper Clause of the Constitution:

> [Congress shall have the power] To make all laws which shall be <u>necessary and proper</u> for carrying into execution the foregoing powers, and all other powers vested by this Constitution in the government of the United States, or in any department or officer thereof.

To protect states rights, the value of the Commerce Clause and the Necessary and Proper Clause must be diluted:

> The lesson of these cases is that the Commerce Clause, even when supplemented by the Necessary and Proper Clause, is not carte blanche for doing whatever will help achieve the ends Congress seeks by the regulation of commerce. And the last two of these cases show that the scope of the Necessary and Proper Clause is exceeded not only when the congressional action directly violates the sovereignty of the States but also when it violates the background principle of enumerated (and hence limited) federal power.[9]

Congress did not have absolute control of the states. The tandem of state sovereignty and limited federal power prevented states from being compelled to accept the ACA.

The value of the state sovereignty was inextricably coupled with the value of limited government powers:

> Everyone will likely participate in the markets for food, clothing, transportation, shelter, or energy; that does not authorize Congress to direct them to purchase particular products in those or other markets today. The Commerce Clause is not a general license to regulate an individual from cradle to grave, simply because he will predictably engage in particular transactions. Any police power to regulate individuals as such, as opposed to their activities, remains vested in the States.[10]

State Accountability

Not only did Judge Roberts value state sovereignty but also the functionality of federalism, which he thought was threatened if states were dictated to by the federal government. Unless states could fit federal programs to the needs of their constituents and the challenges in their states, there would be no accountability and the federal programs would fail: "Permitting the Federal Government to force the States to implement a federal program would threaten the political accountability key to our federal system."[11] The functioning of the federal system depended upon leaving the states alone to determine how to implement federal programs.

Individual Liberty

The majority opinion clearly protects individual rights, but in the final analysis not from taxes. Chief Justice Roberts thought it an encroachment on individual liberty for federal regulations to compel people from being commercially inactive, in this case, from not purchasing health insurance.

> Every day individuals do not do an infinite number of things. In some cases they decide not to do something; in others they simply fail to do it. Allowing Congress to justify federal regulation by pointing to the effect of inaction on commerce would bring countless decisions an individual could potentially make within the scope of federal regulation, and—under the Government's theory—empower Congress to make those decisions for him.[12]
>
> But Congress has never attempted to rely on that power to compel individuals not engaged in commerce to purchase an unwanted product.[13]

Congress could not force people to do what is good for them, for example, to exercise or have a plant-based diet:

> People, for reasons of their own, often fail to do things that would be good for them or good for society. Those failures—joined with the similar failures of others—can readily have a substantial effect on interstate commerce. Under the Government's logic, that authorizes Congress to use its commerce power to compel citizens to act as the Government would have them act.[14]

This would allow the government to further trample individual liberties. To further buttress individual liberty, Chief Justice Roberts classifies the uninsured as not partaking of commercial activity and thus part of the commercially inactive who cannot be compelled by the government to act:

> The individual mandate's regulation of the uninsured as a class is, in fact, particularly divorced from any link to existing commercial activity. The mandate primarily affects healthy, often young adults who are less likely to need significant health care and have other priorities for spending their money. It is precisely because these individuals, as an actuarial class, incur relatively low health care costs that the mandate helps counter the effect of forcing insurance companies to cover others who impose greater costs than their premiums are allowed to reflect.[15]

Despite all this protection of individual liberty, Congress could tax, even those people who are commercially inactive:

> First, and most importantly, it is abundantly clear the Constitution does not guarantee that individuals may avoid taxation through inactivity. A capitation, after all, is a tax that everyone must pay simply for existing, and capitations

> are expressly contemplated by the Constitution. The Court today holds that our Constitution protects us from federal regulation under the Commerce Clause so long as we abstain from the regulated activity. But from its creation, the Constitution has made no such promise with respect to taxes.[16]

Disvalue of Ideational Evolution

Chief Justice Roberts looked at the Medicaid expansion as something completely new rather than altering and expanding Medicaid according to the original boundaries. This was a completely different animal:

> The Medicaid expansion, however, accomplishes a shift in kind, not merely degree. The original program was designed to cover medical services for four particular categories of the needy: the disabled, the blind, the elderly, and needy families with dependent children. See 42 U. S. C. §1396a(a)(10). Previous amendments to Medicaid eligibility merely altered and expanded the boundaries of these categories. Under the Affordable Care Act, Medicaid is transformed into a program to meet the health care needs of the entire nonelderly population with income below 133 percent of the poverty level. It is no longer a program to care for the neediest among us, but rather an element of a comprehensive national plan to provide universal health insurance coverage.[17]

Chief Justice Roberts saw legislation as ossified in time rather and its boundaries permanently defined. He failed to see that health care challenges had redefined neediness to include all those denied health care. For example, without it, one could lose one's home in order to pay for health care costs or go into bankruptcy. Or those with preexisting conditions could be denied life-saving care. These are the new needy. They are the needy because their lives are being undermined by health care instead of being assisted by it. The collective consciousness of neediness had shifted in the forty-five years since the legislation. "Why should The Chief Justice strive so mightily to hem in Congress' capacity to meet the new problems arising constantly in our ever-developing modern economy?"[18] is a great question.

VIGNETTE OF VALUES

The majority opinion defueled the Commerce Clause of the Constitution to allow for state rights, but not enough to prevent taxation of the commercially inactive. The value of judicial neutrality and the disvalue of idea evolution led to this split decision, which was one step forward and one step backward.

CONCURRENCE AND DISSENT BY JUSTICE GINSBURG

Justice Ginsberg valued the Commerce Clause differently than Chief Justice Roberts did. In the Commerce Clause, she saw potency to change to the life of Americans for the better. The Commerce Clause not only had powers but also powers to bring improve social welfare:

> The Framers' solution was the Commerce Clause, which, as they perceived it, granted Congress the authority to enact economic legislation "in all Cases for the general Interests of the Union, and also in those Cases to which the States are separately incompetent." . . . . ("[The commerce power] is an affirmative power commensurate with the national needs.")[19]

The Framers' solution was the Commerce Clause, which, as they perceived it, granted Congress the authority to enact economic legislation "in all Cases for the general Interests of the Union, and also in those Cases to which the States are separately incompetent."[20]

In the concurrence and dissent by Justice Ginsburg, the values don't jump up and hit you in the face as they do in the dissent. But they were there nonetheless, if not in black and white, then outlined and only having to be filled in.

LEADING VALUES

Value of Social Welfare of Individuals, Which Is Linked to the Social Welfare of a System

The overarching or animating value proved to be social welfare. Far more important than a dig at Chief Justice Roberts was the value of social welfare: "Since 1937, our precedent has recognized Congress' large authority to set the Nation's course in the economic and social welfare realm."[21] Justice Ginsburg chastised the decision of *Railroad Retirement Bd. v. Alton R. Co*, 295 U.S. 330 (1935) in which the Court ruled against a compulsory retirement and pension plan:

> The Chief Justice's crabbed reading of the Commerce Clause harks back to the era in which the Court routinely thwarted Congress' efforts to regulate the national economy in the interest of those who labor to sustain it. See, e.g., Railroad Retirement Bd. v. Alton R. Co., 295 U.S. 330, 362, 368 (1935) (invalidating compulsory retirement and pension plan for employees of carriers subject to the Interstate Commerce Act; Court found law related essentially "to

the social welfare of the worker, and therefore remote from any regulation of commerce as such"). It is a reading that should not have staying power.[22]

By invoking the Social Security Act that assisted wage earners and their survivors and adding that Congress could have done something analogous for health care, Justice Ginsburg placed a zenith value on social welfare:

> The provision of health care is today a concern of national dimension, just as the provision of old-age and survivors' benefits was in the 1930's. In the Social Security Act, Congress installed a federal system to provide monthly benefits to retired wage earners and, eventually, to their survivors. Beyond question, Congress could have adopted a similar scheme for health care. Congress chose, instead, to preserve a central role for private insurers and state governments. According to The Chief Justice, the Commerce Clause does not permit that preservation. This rigid reading of the Clause makes scant sense and is stunningly retrogressive.[23]

The social welfare zenith value impacted her view of the ACA and the Commerce Clause: Those people with preexisting conditions had to be protected from a healthcare industry unwilling to insure them:

> Before the ACA's enactment, private insurance companies took an applicant's medical history into account when setting insurance rates or deciding whether to insure an individual. Because individuals with preexisting medical conditions cost insurance companies significantly more than those without such conditions, insurers routinely refused to insure these individuals, charged them substantially higher premiums, or offered only limited coverage that did not include the preexisting illness.[24]

Individuals and society as a whole suffer because of ineffective systems. A vicious circle ensues. The uninsured person cannot obtain health care services that would prevent that illness and, once becoming ill, receive services that for which exorbitant costs were then required, driving up health cares for everybody:

> The failure of individuals to acquire insurance has other deleterious effects on the health-care market. Because those without insurance generally lack access to preventative care, they do not receive treatment for conditions—like hypertension and diabetes—that can be successfully and affordably treated if diagnosed early on. See Institute of Medicine, National Academies, Insuring America's Health . . . When sickness finally drives the uninsured to seek care, once treatable conditions have escalated into grave health problems, requiring more costly

> and extensive intervention. The extra time and resources providers spend serving the uninsured lessens the providers' ability to care for those who do have insurance. . . . Not only do those without insurance consume a large amount of health care each year; critically, as earlier explained, their inability to pay for a significant portion of that consumption drives up market prices, foists costs on other consumers, and reduces market efficiency and stability.[25]

Value of Social Welfare Outweighs Hypothetical Government Overreach

For Justice Ginsburg, the dint of the animating value of social welfare diminished the disvalue of governmental overreach:

> When contemplated in its extreme, almost any power looks dangerous. The commerce power, hypothetically, would enable Congress to prohibit the purchase and home production of all meat, fish, and dairy goods, effectively compelling Americans to eat only vegetables. . . . Yet no one would offer the "hypothetical and unreal possibilit[y] . . . of a vegetarian state as a credible reason to deny Congress the authority ever to ban the possession and sale of goods. The Chief Justice accepts just such specious logic when he cites the broccoli horrible as a reason to deny Congress the power to pass the individual mandate.[26]

Underlying the Chief Justice's view that the Commerce Clause must be confined to the regulation of active participants in a commercial market is a fear that the commerce power would otherwise know no limits.[27]

Value of Cyclicity

Beyond the obvious value of social welfare stood a worldview affirming the values of cyclicity. Life goes in cycles and the young become the old.

> In the fullness of time, moreover, today's young and healthy will become society's old and infirm.[28] Viewed over a lifespan, the costs and benefits even out: The young who pay more than their fair share currently will pay less than their fair share when they become senior citizens. And even if, as undoubtedly will be the case, some individuals, over their lifespans, will pay more for health insurance than they receive in health services, they have little to complain about, for that is how insurance works. Every insured person receives protection against a catastrophic loss, even though only a subset of the covered class will ultimately need that protection.

Value of Interdependence

Justice Ginsberg recognized and esteemed the value of interdependence. Commerce was intrinsically interconnected and the damage to one sector could cause damage to others. The uninsured were not out of the loop of commerce but also a negative factor, driving up health care costs:

> Straightforward application of these principles would require the Court to hold that the minimum coverage provision is proper Commerce Clause legislation. Beyond dispute, Congress had a rational basis for concluding that the uninsured, as a class, substantially affect interstate commerce. Those without insurance consume billions of dollars of health-care products and services each year... Those goods are produced, sold, and delivered largely by national and regional companies who routinely transact business across state lines. The uninsured also cross state lines to receive care. Some have medical emergencies while away from home. Others, when sick, go to a neighboring State that provides better care for those who have not prepaid for care.[29]

VALUE APPRAISAL

The values of social welfare, cyclicity, and interdependence drove Justice Ginsburg's concurrence and dissent. The Commerce Clause and the Necessary and Proper Clause were animated by these values and came to life in potent rather than enervated ways when it came to health care.

DISSENT BY JUSTICES ANTONIN SCALIA, ANTHONY KENNEDY, CLARENCE THOMAS, AND SAMUEL ALITO

In this dissent, the values were trumpeted, albeit at the conclusion and not at the outset, where people could have understood the lay of the land before traveling on it. Regardless, the values of caution, minimalism, limited power of the federal government were primary values. Second, according to the quartet, the value of the Constitution must not be overlooked and overshadowed by the Bill of Rights and Civil War Amendments, as this is the locus of the vital value of liberty. These four interlocked values define the scope of the dissent.

OPERATIVE VALUES

Values of Caution, Minimalism, and the Limitation of Federal Government Powers

In evaluating the ACA, the quartet of dissenters took a distinctive value path. They proceeded with caution when interpreting the Commerce Clause, which entailed minimalism. For how could one be cautious and then make major changes? The cautious tread lightly. Their minimalistic caution led them to view the Commerce Clause as extremely limited:

> The values that should have determined our course today are caution, minimalism, and the understanding that the Federal Government is one of limited powers. But the Court's ruling undermines those values at every turn. In the name of restraint, it overreaches. In the name of constitutional avoidance, it creates new constitutional questions. In the name of cooperative federalism, it undermines state sovereignty.[30]

Value of the Original Constitution as the Promotion of Liberty

For the quartet, it was vital to pay particular attention to the original Constitution and to not concentrate so much on the Bill of Rights or Civil War amendments. That was where the vital value of liberty was, a vital value that had been ignored:

> The Constitution, though it dates from the founding of the Republic, has powerful meaning and vital relevance to our own times. The constitutional protections that this case involves are protections of structure. Structural protections—notably, the restraints imposed by federalism and separation of powers—are less romantic and have less obvious a connection to personal freedom than the provisions of the Bill of Rights or the Civil War Amendments. Hence they tend to be undervalued or even forgotten by our citizens. It should be the responsibility of the Court to teach otherwise, to remind our people that the Framers considered structural protections of freedom the most important ones, for which reason they alone were embodied in the original Constitution and not left to later amendment. The fragmentation of power produced by the structure of our Government is central to liberty, and when we destroy it, we place liberty at peril. Today's decision should have vindicated, should have taught, this truth; instead, our judgment today has disregarded it.[31]

The quartet zenithed such liberty:

> The case is easy and straightforward, however, in another respect. What is absolutely clear, affirmed by the text of the 1789 Constitution, by the Tenth Amendment ratified in 1791, and by innumerable cases of ours in the 220 years since, is that there are structural limits upon federal power—upon what it can prescribe with respect to private conduct, and upon what it can impose upon the sovereign States. Whatever may be the conceptual limits upon the Commerce Clause and upon the power to tax and spend, they cannot be such as will enable the Federal Government to regulate all private conduct and to compel the States to function as administrators of federal programs.[32]

Value of States' Rights

The quartet of dissenters agreed with Chief Justice Roberts that that ACA coerced states to comply:

> When a heavy federal tax is levied to support a federal program that offers large grants to the States, States may, as a practical matter, be unable to refuse to participate in the federal program and to substitute a state alternative. Even if a State believes that the federal program is ineffective and inefficient, withdrawal would likely force the State to impose a huge tax increase on its residents, and this new state tax would come on top of the federal taxes already paid by residents to support subsidies to participating States.[33]

> The answer to the first of these questions—the meaning of coercion in the present context—is straightforward. As we have explained, the legitimacy of attaching conditions to federal grants to the States depends on the voluntariness of the States' choice to accept or decline the offered package. Therefore, if States really have no choice other than to accept the package, the offer is coercive, and the conditions cannot be sustained under the spending power.[34]

Diminishing Interdependence

In the dissent, the value of interdependence was explored and roundly rejected as an encroachment on individual liberty:

> In short, the Act attempts to achieve near-universal health insurance coverage by spreading its costs to individuals, insurers, governments, hospitals,

> and employers—while, at the same time, offsetting significant portions of those costs with new benefits to each group. . . . In summary, the Individual Mandate and Medicaid Expansion offset insurance regulations and taxes, which offset reduced reimbursements to hospitals, which offset increases in federal spending. So, the Act's major provisions are interdependent. . . . The Act then refers to these interdependencies as "shared responsibility."[35]

Devaluing of Social Welfare

While not explicitly disvaluing social welfare, the quartet diminished it in the following slight:

> The dissent's exposition of the wonderful things the Federal Government has achieved through exercise of its assigned powers, such as "the provision of old-age and survivors' benefits" in the Social Security Act . . . is quite beside the point.[36]

Value of the Liberty of the Individual

In contrast to the majority opinion, the quartet of dissenters contended that individual liberty was violated by being forced into a mandatory system:

> But as the discussion above makes clear, the decision to forgo participation in an interstate market is not itself commercial activity (or indeed any activity at all) within Congress' power to regulate. It is true that, at the end of the day, it is inevitable that each American will affect commerce and become a part of it, even if not by choice. But if every person comes within the Commerce Clause power of Congress to regulate by the simple reason that he will one day engage in commerce, the idea of a limited Government power is at an end.[37]

> Here, however, Congress has impressed into service third parties, healthy individuals who could be but are not customers of the relevant industry, to offset the undesirable consequences of the regulation. Congress' desire to force these individuals to purchase insurance is motivated by the fact that they are further removed from the market than unhealthy individuals with preexisting conditions, because they are less likely to need extensive care in the near future. If Congress can reach out and command even those furthest removed from an interstate market to

participate in the market, then the Commerce Clause becomes a font of unlimited power.[38]

Disvalue of Cyclicity

The commerce system was not viewed cyclically but disparately such that future commerce was denied:

> They are quite simply not participants in that market, and cannot be made so (and thereby subjected to regulation) by the simple device of defining participants to include all those who will, later in their lifetime, probably purchase the goods or services covered by the mandated insurance. Such a definition of market participants is unprecedented, and were it to be a premise for the exercise of national power, it would have no principled limits.[39]

VALUE VIGNETTE

The quartet of dissenters disabled the Commerce Clause by purposely devaluing the "general welfare" aspect. Their vision of strong state and individual rights eclipsed federal intervention. Their refusal to value the issue as any more than a succession of individual commercial ventures instead of an interlocking system further staked out their claim to denying health care for all.

RECKONING OF THE ROGUE JUSTICES

Human beings are vulnerable to disease, suffering, and death. These are viewed as negatives in most circles. If there can be ways to diminish disease and suffering and prolong life spans, that would seem to the Rogue Justices in the public welfare to do so. Like Justice Ginsberg, we view the Commerce Clause as promoting the general welfare. Health care as it becomes more and more expensive must be subsidized for most people, as even a regular checkup is often costly, much less birthing and even noninvasive procedures. Leaving millions of people without health insurance is hazardous to the whole health care system. The more sick people there are, the more chance of all of us to suffer not only financially but also in terms diseases being spread. The Commerce Clause is not value-free, but says that the government can spend for the general welfare of the people, a positive value. At this point in the history of the United States, health care is a part of that general welfare.

NOTES

1. Aziz Huq, "The Nation: Threats in the Health Care Ruling," NPR (July 2, 2012), https://www.npr.org/2012/07/02/156104486/the-nation-threats-in-the-health-care-ruling.
2. Robert J. Pushaw Jr., "The Paradox of the Obamacare Decision: How Can the Federal Government have Limited Unlimited Power?," *Florida Law Review* 65, 6 (October 2013): 1998.
3. David Loudon, "When Do the Ends Justify the Means?: The Role of the Necessary and Proper Clause in the Commerce Clause Analysis," *University of Massachusetts Law Review* 10, 2 (January 2015): 345.
4. Jack M. Beermann, "*NFIB v. Sebelius* and the Right to Health Care: Government's Obligation to Provide for the Health, Safety, and Welfare of Its Citizens," *New York University Journal of Legislation and Public Policy* 18 (2015): 277–330.
5. *National Federation of Independent Business v. Sebelius*, 567 U.S. 519, 588 (2012).
6. Ibid., 548.
7. Ibid., 538.
8. Ibid., 588.
9. Ibid., 653.
10. Ibid., 557.
11. Ibid., 578.
12. Ibid., 552.
13. Ibid., 549.
14. Ibid., 554.
15. Ibid., 556.
16. Ibid., 572.
17. Ibid., 583–584.
18. Ibid., 623.
19. Ibid., 600–601.
20. Ibid., 600.
21. Ibid., 590.
22. Ibid.
23. Ibid., 589.
24. Ibid., 596–597.
25. Ibid., 594.
26. Ibid., 616.
27. Ibid., 614.
28. Ibid., 511–12.

29. Ibid., 603.
30. Ibid., 572.
31. Ibid., 707.
32. Ibid., 647.
33. Ibid., 680.
34. Ibid., 678–679.
35. Ibid., 695–696.
36. Ibid., 659.
37. Ibid., 657.
38. Ibid., 652–653.
39. Ibid., 656.

Chapter 19

Venerated Objects v. Freedom of Speech

Texas v. Johnson

NARRATIVE IN A NUTSHELL

What did Gregory Lee Johnson do?

He burned an American flag.

Where?

In Dallas, Texas.

Any special reason for Dallas?

Dallas was the site of the 1984 Republican convention. Along with many others, Johnson protested the policies of President Ronald Reagan and Dallas-based corporations.

Where did Johnson obtain the flag?

Another protestor, who removed it from a flagpole on properties the protestors targeted.

Were Johnson's fellow protestors chanting anything while he burned the flag?

"America, the red, white, and blue, we spit on you."

Was anybody hurt by the flag-burning?

Nobody.

Were some people offended?

According to syllabus of this case, some people were "seriously offended."

What happened to the burned flag?

A witness buried the remains of the flag in his backyard.

VALUE-INFUSED SCHOLARSHIP

Those who value a safe harbor for dissent value the First Amendment.[1] Freedom of thought rises above the value of the government's absolute control over how its symbols like the flag are used.[2] Individual differences in our thinking rank higher than their suppression by the government.[3] While valuing the flag "proves noble and just," it pales in comparison to actually "nurturing and protecting" the freedoms for "which we raise our immortal flag."[4] The First Amendment accrues value as "a monument of safety" for free speech rarely found in the world.[5] Offending or even deeply offending a majority of citizens does not warrant an amendment criminalizing flag desecration.[6] This would devalue the Constitution by cluttering, trivializing, and denigrating it.[7] Banning "flag desecration would not be in accord with a liberal-democratic approach to civil liberties."[8] As one former armed forces member remarks:

> When I see an American burning a flag I am not provoked toward anger; rather, I feel pride in knowing that I (and my comrades in arms) have done our job protecting the Constitution [the higher value]. I need look no further than an individual's ability to freely desecrate the flag to see that my service to our country was not in vain.[9]

It could be argued that "the intangible dimension and symbolic significance of the American flag" take precedence over the First Amendment.[10] While diminishing the sacred value of the flag could disconnect people from the political community, this is outweighed by even higher values: the triumph of reason and by extension the Enlightenment the lessons learned about symbols including how politicians manipulate them and distinction between "symbols and truth."[11] This case spills over to the value of the substance over the dis-value of symbolism: "The Great 1989–1990 Flag Flap also suggests that the American political leadership is too often consumed with symbols rather than substance. Either out of inability or a reluctance to tackle real problems, much of the leadership seems to be more comfortable with unproductive and ultimately divisive public relations extravaganzas concerning purely symbolic issues."[12] From the viewpoint of axiological analysis, the First Amendment is a sacred zenith value allowing for the desecration of venerated objects in order to preserve itself.

TEXAS PENAL CODE ANN. § 42.09 (1989)

§ 42.09. Desecration of Venerated Object

(a) A person commits an offense if he intentionally or knowingly desecrates:
   (1) a public monument;
   (2) a place of worship or burial; or
   (3) a state or national flag.
(b) For purposes of this section, "desecrate" means deface, damage, or otherwise physically mistreat in a way that the actor knows will seriously offend one or more persons likely to observe or discover his action.
(c) An offense under this section is a Class A misdemeanor.

LEGAL FLASHPOINTS OF MAJORITY OPINION AND DISSENT

The majority opinion by Justice William J. Brennan called attention to different types of protest, for example, wearing pants with a small flag sewn into the seat; wearing of black armbands to protest American military involvement in Vietnam, a sit-in by blacks in a "whites only" area to protest segregation; and wearing of American military uniforms in a dramatic presentation criticizing American involvement in Vietnam. For him, flag-burning fit into the same category of legal protests in this country. As long as it didn't lead to violence, and in this case, it didn't, it was legal. In the dissent authored by Chief Justice Rehnquist, the American flag assumed the status of a venerated or sacred object and thus a sacred zenith value. Because of its venerated status, it was not subject to desecration of any kind. The flag unified the thirteen colonies during the American Revolution. It inspired Francis Scott Key to write the national anthem. When lowered at Fort Sumter, it signaled the beginning of the Civil. In World War II (WWII), it was raised at Iwo Jima. It was raised in Ichiron during the Korean War to mark the successful landing of American troops. On Memorial Day, flags are placed on the graves of soldiers who sacrificed their lives. Each day, countless Americans say "The Pledge of Allegiance to the Flag." Burning this venerated symbol is sure to incite violence, Chief Justice Rehnquist claimed—although it didn't in Dallas.

CHRONICLE OF AUTHORITIES WITH BRIEF COMMENTS

From the Majority Opinion by Justice William Brennan

Chaplinsky v. New Hampshire, 315 U.S. 568 (1942). Fighting words justify censorship, but not found in this instance

West Virginia Board of Education v. Barnette, 319 U.S. 624 (1943) The right to differ is the centerpiece of our First Amendment freedoms

Brandenburg v. Ohio, 395 U.S. 444, 395 U.S. 447 (1969) Determine whether provocative words have direct link to violence, which in *Johnson* they don't

Schacht v. United States, 398 U.S. 58 (1970) Federal statute permitting an actor portraying a military uniform if the portrayal likely not to discredit the military was invalidated, as a symbol can have multiple meanings

FROM THE DISSENT BY CHIEF JUSTICE WILLIAM REHNQUIST

Uniform Flag Act of 1917 § 3 "No person shall publicly mutilate, deface, defile, defy, trample upon, or by word or act cast contempt upon any such flag, standard, color, ensign or shield." All states except two have statutes prohibiting flag-burning

Chaplinsky v. New Hampshire, 315 U.S. 568 (1942). Right to free speech is not absolute and can be suppressed in certain well-defined instances

MAJORITY OPINION BY JUSTICE WILLIAM BRENNAN

OPERATIVE VALUES

Actual Freedom of Speech Preferred to Symbolic Freedom of Speech

Actual freedom of speech includes offensive and disagreeable ideas: "If there was a bedrock principle underlying the First Amendment, it was that the government may not prohibit the expression of an idea simply because society finds the idea itself offensive or disagreeable,"[13] Justice Brennan asserted.

The burning of a flag does not destroy the meaning of the flag:

> We can imagine no more appropriate response to burning a flag than waving one's own, no better way to counter a flag burner's message than by saluting the flag that burns, no surer means of preserving the dignity even of the flag that burned than by—as one witness here did—according its remains a respectful burial. We do not consecrate the flag by punishing its desecration, for in doing so we dilute the freedom that this cherished emblem represents.[14]

Affirmation of the Values of Freedom and Inclusiveness

Allowing flag-burning reinforced the values of freedom and inclusiveness symbolized by the American flag:

> We are tempted to say, in fact, that the flag's deservedly cherished place in our community will be strengthened, not weakened, by our holding today. Our decision is a reaffirmation of the principles of freedom and inclusiveness that the flag best reflects, and of the conviction that our toleration of criticism such as Johnson's is a sign and source of our strength. Indeed, one of the proudest images of our flag, the one immortalized in our own national anthem, is of the bombardment it survived at Fort McHenry. It is the Nation's resilience, not its rigidity, that Texas sees reflected in the flag—and it is that resilience that we reassert today.[15]

Part of actual freedom of speech is to punish people from burning the flag, but to convince them otherwise: "The way to preserve the flag's special role is not to punish those who feel differently about these matters. It is to persuade them that they are wrong."[16]

Value of Interpretation

Justice Brennan valued the interpretive faculty in each person and correspondingly devalued the state dictate a monolithic meaning for the American flag:

> In evaluating these choices under the First Amendment, how would we decide which symbols were sufficiently special to warrant this unique status? To do so, we would be forced to consult our own political preferences, and impose them on the citizenry, in the very way that the First Amendment forbids us to do.[17]

We never before have held that the government may ensure that a symbol be used to express only one view of that symbol or its referents.[18]

> *Rather, the State's claim is that it has an interest in preserving the flag as a symbol of nationhood and national unity, a symbol with a determinate range of meanings.*[19]

Texas could not dictate a monolithic meaning of the American flag:

> *According to Texas, if one physically treats the flag in a way that would tend to cast doubt on either the idea that nationhood and national unity are the flag's referents or that government, on this national unity actually exists, the message conveyed thereby is a harmful one, and therefore may be prohibited.*[20]

Value of Full Expression

Texas' focus on the precise nature of Johnson's expression, moreover, misses the point of our prior decisions: their enduring lesson, that the government may not prohibit expression simply because it disagrees with its message, is not dependent on the particular mode in which one chooses to express an idea.[21]

Government interferes with speech when it tells prohibits people how to express it.

The Disvalue of Venerated Objects above the First Amendment

If there are venerated objects above the First Amendment, then the First Amendment is nullified: Congress can make laws abridging free speech.

> Could the government, on this theory, prohibit the burning of state flags? Of copies of the Presidential seal? Of the Constitution? In evaluating these choices under the First Amendment, how would we decide which symbols were sufficiently special to warrant this unique status? To do so, we would be forced to consult our own political preferences and impose them on the citizenry, in the very way that the First Amendment forbids us to do.[22]

DISSENT BY JUSTICE WILLIAM REHNQUIST

OPERATIVE VALUES

The American Flag as Sacred Zenith Value

The American flag was held in the highest esteem, a sacred zenith value:

> The American flag, then, throughout more than 200 years of our history, has come to be the visible symbol embodying our Nation. It does not represent the views of any particular political party, and it does not represent any particular political philosophy. The flag is not simply another "idea" or "point of view" competing for recognition in the marketplace of ideas. Millions and millions of Americans regard it with an almost mystical reverence, regardless of what sort of social, political, or philosophical beliefs they may have. I cannot agree that the First Amendment invalidates the Act of Congress, and the laws of 48 of the 50 States, which make criminal the public burning of the flag.[23]

Almost all Americans share that reverence: The uniquely deep awe and respect for our flag felt by virtually all of us are bundled off under the rubric of "designated symbols." The majority opinion saw "the American flag is just another symbol, about which not only must opinions pro and con be tolerated, but for which the most minimal public respect may not be enjoined."

For Chief Justice Rehnquist, flag-burning was an evil, a profane nadir disvalue: "Surely one of the high purposes of a democratic society is to legislate against conduct that is regarded as evil and profoundly offensive to the majority of people—whether it be murder, embezzlement, pollution, or flagburning."[24] Because Justice Rehnquist valued the American flag as sacred and flag-burning was evil, it was an easy jump to conclude that Johnson's act "had a tendency to incite a breach of the peace."[25]

Value of Alternative Forms of Expression

For Chief Justice Rehnquist because Johnson had other avenues of protest open to him to make the same point, not being able to burn the flag did not infringe on his First Amendment rights:

> The Texas statute deprived Johnson of only one rather inarticulate symbolic form of protest—a form of protest that was profoundly offensive to many—and left him with a full panoply of other symbols and every conceivable form of verbal expression to express his deep disapproval of national policy. Thus, in no way can it be said that Texas is punishing him because his hearers—or any other group of people—were profoundly opposed to the message that he sought to convey.[26]

RECKONING OF ROGUE THE JUSTICES

Freedom of speech is a sacred zenith value of our society. It extends not only to what we say but also the manner in which we express it. If anything rose above this sacred zenith value, it would stand above criticism, which would be antithetical to the First Amendment. Second, when values live beyond the pale of criticism, this can only lead to division. You don't believe in this flag the way I do, there's only my way to believe, then you are wrong and evil. In trying to use the flag to unify the country, you divide it. When the symbol becomes more significant than the actions for which the symbol stands, the symbol is emptied of its original meaning and self-righteousness and hypocrisy ensue. Instead of bringing about unity and nationhood, the symbols sow the seeds of discontent.

What is offensive and what is evil don't necessarily occupy the same basket. A work of art could be considered offensive for foul language or nudity. Does that rise to the standard of evil, for example, premeditated murder or genocide? When the disvalue of the offensive becomes a sacred zenith value (as it does with venerated objects), it takes the value of the obscene with it for the ride in a typical Sacred Cow-Scapegoat value scheme.

Chief Justice Rehnquist also ignored how the flag was carried into ignoble causes, for example, the Trail of Tears and also how it flew over statehouses that supported suppression of Black people and internment of Japanese people during World War II. Although these could be considered a departure from American ideals, people who are historically oppressed might think differently about the American flag than those who are more privileged.

NOTES

1. William W. Van Alstyne, "Freedom of Speech and the Flag Anti-Desecration Amendment: Antinomies of Constitutional Choice," *Faculty Publications* (1991): 103. https://scholarship.law.wm.edu/facpubs/1622.
2. Deborah T. Eversole, "Texas v. Johnson, 109 S. Ct. 2533." *Florida State University Law Review* 17 (1990): 870.
3. Ibid., 898.
4. Troy Pieper, "Playing with Fire: The Proposed Flag Burning Amendment and the Perennial Attack on Freedom of Speech," *Journal of Civil Rights and Economic Development* 11, 3 (Summer 1996): 866.
5. William W. Van Alstyne, "Freedom of Speech and the Flag Anti-Desecration Amendment: Antinomies of Constitutional Choice," *Faculty Publications* (1991): 103, https://scholarship.law.wm.edu/facpubs/1622.
6. Geoffrey R. Stone, "Flag Burning and the Constitution," *Iowa Law Review* 75 (1990): 124.
7. Ibid.
8. Nicholas Barker, "The Constitutionality of Flag Burning: Hate or Free Speech? An Analysis of *Texas v. Johnson*," *Hinckley Journal of Politics* (Spring 2001): 54.
9. Tommy J. Lucas Jr., Whitney R. Linsenmeyer, and Elizabeth G. Finocchiaro, "The Impact of Flag Desecration on Social Justice Movements: The Case of Occupy SLU," *Jesuit Higher Education: A Journal* 6, 1 (May 2017): 42.
10. Patricia Lofton, "*Texas v. Johnson*: The Constitutional Protection of Flag Desecration," *Pepperdine Law Review* 17, 3 (1990): 791.
11. Sheldon H. Nahmod, "The Sacred Flag and the First Amendment," *Indiana Law Journal* 66, 2 (Spring 1991): 514.
12. Robert Justin Goldstein, "The Great 1989–1990 Flag Flap: An Historical, Political, and Legal Analysis," *Miami Law Review* 45, 1 (1990): 105.
13. *Texas v. Johnson*, 491 U.S. 397, 414 (1989).
14. Ibid., 420.
15. Ibid., 419.
16. Ibid.
17. Ibid.
18. Ibid., 417.
19. Ibid., 413.
20. Ibid.
21. Ibid., 416.

22. Ibid., 417.
23. Ibid., 429.
24. Ibid., 435.
25. Ibid., 430.
26. Ibid., 432.

Chapter 20

Functional Judiciary v. Executive Privilege as a Means to Secure National Security

United States v. Nixon

NARRATIVE IN A NUTSHELL

What did President Richard Nixon fail to produce in 1974 when he was under investigation?

Certain tape recordings and documents regarding seven indicted individuals who broke into the Democratic headquarters at the Watergate Hotel as well as another unindicted coconspirator (the president himself).

What was Nixon's strategy?

To argue for executive privilege on the grounds that the disclosure of such evidence would not be in the best interests of the public.

And what sayeth the Supreme Court?

That President Nixon wasn't airing this dirty laundry to the whole world, but to a prosecutor in private. Also, Nixon's refusal to turn over evidence threatened the whole system of law, founded as it was on producing evidence.

VALUE-INFUSED SCHOLARSHIP

The case is a question of tensions between two sacred zenith values rather than the assertion of zenith value and the removal of a nadir value. [M]embers of Congress, federal judges, Vice Presidents, cabinet officers, and governors can all be prosecuted,"[1] write two scholars. "But the presidency is unique and the Constitution does not view the President as it does these other officials."[2] The unique status of the presidency stems from, Alex Bickel asserts, the president being the embodiment of "the continuity and indestructibility of the state."[3] The uniqueness of the office[4] allows presidents to realize the higher value—the survival of the nation—and runs counter to value of fairness that no person is above the law. From this viewpoint, executive privilege is warranted. In contrast to the uniqueness premise, the relationship between the Congress can be based on mutual accommodation and good faith: "This long-standing practice is premised on a respect for Congress as a coordinate branch of government with legitimate needs for information that sometimes conflict with the executive branch's needs for confidentiality. Both branches have a constitutional obligation to work together in good faith to resolve such conflicts."[5] This is not valued in terms of wins and losses, but in terms of resolving conflicts, presumably to benefit the country. Yet secrecy can be valued as protecting national security interests, but it can also be used as a cloak for unconstitutional or destructive political ends and to avoid constitutional checks and balances.[6] The evil of "vast unchecked power in the hands of a single individual" justifies overriding executive privilege.[7] Finally, the decision can be valued for its expediency in solving a constitutional crisis and disvalued for creating more problems down the road by not clearing and defining executive privilege.[8]

MAJORITY OPINION BY CHIEF JUSTICE WARREN BURGER

Chronology of Flashpoint Authorities

1788

Federalist Papers (#47 by James Madison)—Each branch of the three branches of government possess powers the others do not possess, for example, the judicial power of the federal courts cannot be shared with the executive branch or the veto power of the executive branch shared with the judiciary.

1803

Marbury v. Madison, 5 U.S. 137—Supreme Court decision establishing judicial review: American courts can strike down laws, statutes, and some government should they violate the Constitution.

1940

Cobbledick v. United States, 309 U. S. 323, 309 U. S. 324–326 (1940).
Strong congressional policy against piecemeal reviews and against using interlocutory appeals to obstruct or impede an ongoing judicial proceeding.

1962

Baker v. Carr, 369 U.S. at 369 U.S. 211 (1940).
The Court is the ultimate interpreter of the Constitution in deciding whether measures by other branches of the government exceed their constitutional authority.

OPERATIVE VALUES

Absolute Power of the Supreme Court to Interpret the Law

Following *Marbury v. Madison*, 5 U.S. 137 (1803) the Supreme Court was deemed the final arbiter of what is or isn't constitutional.[9]

The Interdependence of the Three Branches of Government

None of the three branches of government was valued as independent:

> The impediment that an absolute, unqualified privilege would place in the way of the primary constitutional duty of the Judicial Branch to do justice in criminal prosecutions would plainly conflict with the function of the courts under Art. III. In designing the structure of our Government and dividing and allocating the sovereign power among three co-equal branches, the Framers of the Constitution sought to provide a comprehensive system, but the separate powers were not intended to operate with absolute independence.[10]

As a caveat to this pronouncement, the Supreme Court as the final arbiter of the rules of the country would appear to have absolute independence.

Zenith Value of a Functional Judiciary

Failure to disclose evidence (negative value), which interfered with the search for truth and the realization of justice, impeded a workable judiciary:

> The ends of criminal justice would be defeated if judgments were to be founded on a partial or speculative presentation of the facts. The very integrity of the judicial system and public confidence in the system depend on full disclosure of all the facts, within the framework of the rules of evidence. To ensure that justice is done, it is imperative to the function of courts that compulsory process be available for the production of evidence needed either by the prosecution or by the defense.[11]

A judiciary cannot function when justice cannot be done.

Specifically Applicable Eclipses the Vaguely General

The specific as it can be applied is preferred to the general that cannot be applied. The specific value of a functioning judiciary takes precedence over the general claim of presidential privilege:

> In this case, we must weigh the importance of the general privilege of confidentiality of Presidential communications in performance of the President's responsibilities against the inroads of such a privilege on the fair administration of criminal justice.[12]

The Court clearly stated that the value of the fundamental demands of justice eclipsed the general confidentiality:

> The President's broad interest in confidentiality of communications will not be vitiated by disclosure of a limited number of conversations preliminarily shown to have some bearing on the pending criminal cases.
>
> We conclude that, when the ground for asserting privilege as to subpoenaed materials sought for use in a criminal trial is based only on the generalized interest in confidentiality, it cannot prevail over the fundamental demands of due process of law in the fair administration of criminal justice. The generalized assertion of privilege must yield to the demonstrated, specific need for evidence in a pending criminal trial.[13]

LEGAL RATIONALE IN FIVE STEPS OR LESS

Through the lens of the leading values, the majority decision can be understood in a few short steps.

Step 1

The value of being completely candid and objective was deemed vital to the functioning of the executive branch and part and parcel of executive privilege and was appreciated by Chief Justice Burger:

> The expectation of a President to the confidentiality of his conversations and correspondence, like the claim of confidentiality of judicial deliberations, for example, has all the values to which we accord deference for the privacy of all citizens and, added to those values, is the necessity for protection of the public interest in candid, objective, and even blunt or harsh opinions in Presidential decisionmaking. A President and those who assist him must be free to explore alternatives in the process of shaping policies and making decisions, and to do so in a way many would be unwilling to express except privately. These are the considerations justifying a presumptive privilege for Presidential communications. The privilege is fundamental to the operation of Government, and inextricably rooted in the separation of powers under the Constitution.[14]

Moreover, a president's communications and activities encompass a vastly wider range of sensitive material than would be true of any "ordinary individual." It is therefore necessary in the interest of the public to afford presidential confidentiality the greatest protection consistent with the fair administration of justice.[15]

Step 2

Yet the value of an interdependent government laid the groundwork for denying executive privilege in some instances:

> The impediment that an absolute, unqualified privilege would place in the way of the primary constitutional duty of the Judicial Branch to do justice in criminal prosecutions would plainly conflict with the function of the courts under Art. III. In designing the structure of our Government and dividing and allocating the sovereign power among three co-equal branches, the Framers of the Constitution sought to provide a comprehensive system, but the separate powers were not intended to operate with absolute independence.[16]

Step 3

The value of relevant evidence required for a particular criminal case eclipsed the value of confidentiality of general presidential communications, especially since this evidence will only be shown in private:

> However, neither the doctrine of separation of powers nor the need for confidentiality of high-level communications, without more, can sustain an absolute, unqualified Presidential privilege of immunity from judicial process under all circumstances. The President's need for complete candor and objectivity from advisers calls for great deference from the courts. However, when the privilege depends solely on the broad, undifferentiated claim of public interest in the confidentiality of such conversations, a confrontation with other values arises. Absent a claim of need to protect military, diplomatic, or sensitive national security secrets, we find it difficult to accept the argument that even the very important interest in confidentiality of Presidential communications is significantly diminished by production of such material for *in camera* inspection with all the protection that a district court will be obliged to provide.[17]

A president's acknowledged need for confidentiality in the communications of his office is general in nature, whereas the constitutional need for the production of relevant evidence in a criminal proceeding is specific and central to the fair adjudication of a particular criminal case in the administration of justice. Without access to specific facts, a criminal prosecution may be totally frustrated. The president's broad interest in confidentiality of communications will not be vitiated by disclosure of a limited number of conversations preliminarily shown to have some bearing on the pending criminal cases.[18]

Step 4

In order for an adversarial criminal justice system to function and justice to be served, there must be a full disclosure of the facts and a search for truth, which absolute presidential confidentiality undermines:

> [W]hen a claim of Presidential privilege as to materials subpoenaed for use in a criminal trial is based, as it is here, not on the ground that military or diplomatic secrets are implicated, but merely on the ground of a generalized interest in confidentiality, the President's generalized assertion of privilege must yield to the demonstrated, specific need for evidence in a pending criminal trial and the fundamental demands of due process of law in the fair administration of criminal justice.[19]

VALUE VIGNETTE

The overarching value in Chief Justice Burger's majority opinion was the value of a functioning judiciary, which included the values of fairness and the search for truth. The legal rationale and authorities converged at this value. An overlooked value scheme in this case was the specifically applicable and the generally inapplicable. In this case, specific evidence was required to allow the judicial system to function while a general idea of absolute privacy was not necessary to ensure the national security. Bringing the wheels of justice to a grinding halt was valued more than saving the public from a remote possibility of harm when a prosecutor in private viewed evidence.

RECKONING OF THE ROGUE JUSTICES

President Richard Nixon conceived and valued the office of presidency as above the law and thus executive privilege as unlimited. This case concerned the zenith values of any society: the functioning of the judiciary as the means of securing a functioning society and executive privilege as a means to secure national security. To the extent that Richard Nixon prevented the judiciary from obtaining evidence, thwarting justice, and undermining the judiciary, his actions threatened national security much more than handing over documents to a special prosecutor in private.

AUTHORITIES

1788

Federalist Papers (#47 by James Madison)—Each branch of the three branches of the government possesses powers exclusive to them and only to them

1803

Marbury v. Madison, 5 U.S. 137—American courts have the power to strike down laws, statutes, and some governments should they violate the Constitution

1962

Baker v. Carr, 369 U.S. at 369 U.S. 211. The Court is the ultimate interpreter of the Constitution in deciding whether measures by other branches of the government exceed their constitutional authority.

OPERATIVE VALUES

Disvalue of Exemption of Justice

There is no exemption for any branch of government or any citizen from the process of the legal system.

Value of a Functional Judiciary

A society is unworkable without a functional judiciary.

Privacy as an Intrinsic versus an Instrumental Value

For the presidency to function and national security to be safeguarded to serve the interest of the public, conversations between the president and advisers must remain private and unavailable to the general public. Agreed as a general principle and held as sacred zenith value. But this does entail *all* such conservations disclose state secrets or that disclosure of state secrets in private to a special prosecutor will undermine national security and undermine the public interest. The end (national security) will not be jeopardized by the removal of absolute privacy. Second, to echo Chief Justice Burger, the specific directive for evidence supersedes the vague generality of executive privilege. Finally, President Nixon argued that his executive privilege ensured public interest.

VALUE FINALE

President Nixon and Chief Justice Burger ended up in the same place: the sacred zenith value of national security. While Nixon argued that presidential privilege lent itself to the public interest in terms of national security, Chief Justice Burger argued that presidential privilege lent itself to judicial dysfunction, itself certainly not in the public interest and not conducive to national security. It was more in the public interest to release those tapes and manuscripts than to bring the wheels of justice to a screeching halt. President Nixon's actions, if realized, proved more a national security threat than his tapes and transcripts could ever be.

However, the value of coequal branches of government and the value of the Supreme Court being the final arbiter of disputes cannot coexist. Those who interpret the laws and have lifetime appointments are superior to those branches that must live according to those laws interpreted by the judicial branch.

NOTES

1. Akhil Reed Amar and Brian C. Kalt, "The Presidential Privilege Against Prosecution," *Faculty Scholarship Series* (1967): 12.
2. Ibid., 12.
3. Alexander Bickel, "The Constitutional Tangle," *The New Republic* (Oct. 6, 1973), 14, 15, as quoted by Amar and Kalt, "The Presidential Privilege Against Prosecution," 12.
4. Akhil Reed Amar, "On Prosecuting Presidents," *Hofstra Law Review* 27, 4 (1999): 673.
5. Dawn E. Johnson, "Executive Privilege Since *United States v. Nixon*: Issues of Motivation and Accommodation," *Articles by Maurer Faculty* (1999): 1139, https://www.repository.law.indiana.edu/facpub/541.
6. Eric Lane, Frederick A.O. Schwarz Jr., and Emily Berman, "Too Big a Canon in the President's Arsenal: Another Look at *United States v. Nixon*," *George Mason Law Review* 17 (2010): 739–740.
7. William Pl Marshall, "Eleven Reasons Why Presidential Power Inevitably Expands and Why it Matters," *Boston University Law Review* 88 (2008): 522.
8. Philip B. Kurland, "*United States v. Nixon*: Who Killed Cock Robin," *UCLA Law Review* 22 (1974): 74, 75.
9. *United States v. Nixon*, 418 U.S. 683, 708 (1974).
10. Ibid., 707.
11. Ibid., 709.
12. Ibid., 711–712.
13. Ibid., 713.

14. Ibid., 703.
15. Ibid., 717.
16. Ibid., 707.
17. Ibid., 706.
18. Ibid., 712–713.
19. Ibid., 685.

Chapter 21

The First Amendment as a Means to Secure Corporate Dominance v. the First Amendment as a Means to Secure Democracy

Citizens United v. Federal Election Commission

NARRATIVE IN A NUTSHELL

The Bipartisan Campaign Reform Act of 2002 was a federal law prohibiting corporations and unions from exercising undue influence in elections.

How so?

General treasury funds could not be used to make independent expenditures for speech advocating the election or defeat of a candidate (electioneering communication).

What were the criteria for an electioneering communication?

An electioneering communication could be defined by its particular type of mass media delivery (broadcast, cable, or satellite communication); the identity of the political candidate (candidates clearly identified as running for Federal office); the timing (within thirty days of a primary election); and the breadth of distribution (publicly). When applied to presidential candidates in primary elections, the public distribution must be at least 50,000 persons in the state and the timing is within thirty days of the election. Political action committees (PACS), established by corporations or unions, advocate through these electioneering communications.

How did the Bipartisan Campaign Reform Act of 2002 end up in the Supreme Court?

In 2008, the PAC Citizens United wanted to air a documentary on video-on-command about presidential candidate Hillary Clinton within the thirty-day primary prohibition. Anticipating trouble from the Bipartisan Campaign Reform Act of 2002, Citizens United sought injunctive relief.

Which it did not receive?

Not only did the District Court deny Citizens United a preliminary injunction it also granted the Federal Election Commission summary judgment.

What happened when the case reached the Supreme Court?

The Supreme Court believed this case involved more than *Hillary* denied broadcast within the thirty-day period. This case could not be resolved on narrow grounds due to its *chilling* effect on free speech that was the crux of the First Amendment. The Supreme Court looked to fix this problem once and for all. First, overrule *Austin v. Michigan Chamber of Commerce*, which allowed the government to limit corporate independent expenditures. Second, by asserting that as persons corporations were covered by the First Amendment. Finally, distinguishing influence from corruption in terms of quid pro quo. Corruption was defined as an illegality of a specific quid-pro-quo transaction. Influence was vague, with no definite terms used for transactions.

VALUE-INFUSED SCHOLARSHIP

On one side of this ruling, people disvalue government control and thus herald the ruling. On the other side, people disvalue corporate control and thus depreciate the ruling. In this ruling, corruption takes the center stage, along with freedom of speech. In the majority decision, corruption is defined narrowly as quid pro quo.[1] This narrow definition values individual interactions over impacts on the larger society:

> Tobacco industry documents show that the industry's campaign contributions influenced individual legislators to be more favorable toward their industry. Corporate contributions to elections could similarly influence proposed or existing health policies concerning restrictions on taxation of unhealthful foods and beverages; advertising of unhealthful products such as sugar-sweetened drinks, high-fat foods, or alcohol to children or vulnerable communities; requirements for restaurant menu labeling; or issues of reproductive rights, air quality standards, global climate change, comprehensive school health education, worker health and safety, gun show background checks, and others.[2]

Maximizing information could go in two directions: "greater information about candidates and a more robust public debate [the value] or an outpouring of corporate funded communications that drown out other voices and unduly influence elected officials to favor corporate interests over the public interest [the disvalue]."[3] For those who eschew government control, this ruling is appreciated: "By removing limits on independent political speech—spending by people unconnected to candidates and parties—*Citizens United* weakened the government's control of who can speak, how much and on what subject. That's a good thing."[4] That's a good thing for those who have yet to grasp the distinction between the quantity and quality of speech with respect to the First Amendment—which our value analysis will shortly explore.

CHRONOLOGY OF CRUCIAL AUTHORITIES—WITH BRIEF COMMENTS

The First Amendment

> Congress shall make no law respecting an establishment of religion, or prohibiting the free exercise thereof; or abridging the freedom of speech, or of the press; or the right of the people peaceably to assemble, and to petition the Government for a redress of grievances.

Interpreted in majority opinion by Justice Kennedy to mean freedom of speech is chilled when corporations are prohibited from participating in electioneering.

Interpreted in concurrence-dissent by Justice Stevens to mean that the political speech of corporations can be regulated to prevent unfairness.

The Tillman Act of 1907 (34 Stat. 864) (January 26, 1907)

First U.S. law to ban corporations from making campaign donations

Referenced in concurrence-dissent by Justice Stevens as a warning sign of corporate-government corruption

Not referenced in majority opinion by Justice Kennedy nor by Justice Scalia in his dissent

Austin *v.* Michigan Chamber of Commerce, *494 U.S. 652 (1990)*

Referenced in majority opinion by Justice Kennedy, the government may not suppress political speech on the basis of the speaker's corporate identity.

Referenced by Justice Stevens to affirm that targeting communications does not entail corporations are being silenced

Bipartisan Campaign Reform Act of 2002

Within sixty days of general elections and thirty days of primaries, corporations are prohibited from electioneering to audiences.

Referenced by Justice Kennedy as ban on political speech hostile to First Amendment.

Referenced by Justice Stevens an appropriate measure to regulate corporate electioneering.

McConnell *v.* Federal Election Comm'n, *540 U. S. 93, 203–209 (2003)*

Referenced by Justice Kennedy as an overreach of government.
Referenced by Justice Stevens to affirm that targeting communications did not entail corporations are being silenced.

MAJORITY OPINION BY JUSTICE ANTHONY KENNEDY

Justice Kennedy ignored stare decisis and wiped away the *Bipartisan Campaign Reform Act of 2002 §441b* and *Austin* v. *Michigan Chamber of Commerce* with a facial review, stating they were never constitutional in the first place. Once those legal impediments were gone, then he could go about recreating the First Amendment in the image of pure liberty that served corporate leverage.

OPERATIVE VALUES

In the majority opinion, the First Amendment or free speech was upgraded to a zenith value. But that is not the only thing that is upgraded to a zenith value: corporations also received zenith standard gaining the legal status as persons. On the other hand, corruption was seen so narrowly its disvalue receded.

The Sacred-Zenith Value of the First Amendment

The majority opinion interpreted the First Amendment as purely in terms of the value of liberty. Reading around the rhetoric, the values become apparent.

Hands-off the First Amendment! Any changes in the sacred First Amendment could ruin it for everybody by "chilling protected speech":

> Courts, too, are bound by the First Amendment. We must decline to draw, and then redraw, constitutional lines based on the particular media or technology used to disseminate political speech from a particular speaker. It must be noted, moreover, that this undertaking would require substantial litigation over an extended time, all to interpret a law that beyond doubt discloses serious First Amendment flaws. The interpretive process itself would create an inevitable, pervasive, and serious risk of *chilling* [our emphasis] protected speech pending the drawing of fine distinctions that, in the end, would themselves be questionable.[5]

Too many laws "chill speech":

> The First Amendment does not permit laws that force speakers to retain a campaign finance attorney, conduct demographic marketing research, or seek declaratory rulings before discussing the most salient political issues of our day. Prolix laws chill speech for the same reason that vague laws *chill* [our emphasis] speech.[6]

This case had to be resolved broadly rather than narrowly to prevent a "chilling of political speech":

> As the foregoing analysis confirms, the Court cannot resolve this case on a narrower ground without *chilling* (our emphasis) political speech, speech that is central to the meaning and purpose of the First Amendment.[7]

> The ongoing *chill* [our emphasis] upon speech that is beyond all doubt protected makes it necessary in this case to invoke the earlier precedents that a statute which chills speech can and must be invalidated where its facial invalidity has been demonstrated.[8]

When something was considered a sacred zenith value, proposed changes to it were regarded as threats. The prohibition of electioneering in the mass media thirty days before the final primary is interpreted as a ban on freedom of speech:

> The law before us is an outright ban, backed by criminal sanctions. Section 441b makes it a felony for all corporations—including nonprofit advocacy corporations—either to expressly advocate the election or defeat of candidates or to broadcast electioneering communications within 30 days of a primary election and 60 days of a general election. Thus, the following acts would all be felonies under §441b: The Sierra Club runs an ad, within the crucial phase of 60 days before the general election, that exhorts the public to disapprove of a Congressman who favors logging in national forests; the National Rifle Association publishes a book urging the public to vote for the challenger because the incumbent U.S. Senator supports a handgun ban; and the American Civil Liberties Union creates a Web site telling the public to vote for a Presidential candidate in light of that candidate's defense of free speech. These prohibitions are classic examples of censorship.[9]

The First Amendment was violated when the identity of speaker's factored into the equation of whose speech is to be protected:

> Quite apart from the purpose or effect of regulating content, moreover, the Government may commit a constitutional wrong when by law it identifies

> certain preferred speakers. By taking the right to speak from some and giving it to others, the Government deprives the disadvantaged person or class of the right to use speech to strive to establish worth, standing, and respect for the speaker's voice. The Government may not by these means deprive the public of the right and privilege to determine for itself what speech and speakers are worthy of consideration. The First Amendment protects speech and speaker, and the ideas that flow from each.[10]
>
> If the First Amendment has any force, it prohibits Congress from fining or jailing citizens, or associations of citizens, for simply engaging in political speech. If the antidistortion rationale were to be accepted, however, it would permit Government to ban political speech simply because the speaker is an association that has taken on the corporate form.[11]

The First Amendment pushed back against governments disfavoring subjects or viewpoints and distinguishing between different speakers in order to suppress some and not others:

> Premised on mistrust of governmental power, the First Amendment stands against attempts to disfavor certain subjects or viewpoints. . . . Prohibited, too, are restrictions distinguishing among different speakers, allowing speech by some but not others. . . . As instruments to censor, these categories are interrelated: Speech restrictions based on the identity of the speaker are all too often simply a means to control content.[12]

Speech played a crucial role in democracies, allowing citizens to hear and question information in order to reach a consensus and self-govern:

> Because speech is an essential mechanism of democracy, for it is the means to hold officials accountable to the people. . . . The right of citizens to inquire, to hear, to speak, and to use information to reach consensus is a precondition to enlightened self-government and a necessary means to protect it.[13]

The First Amendment's protections did not depend on the speaker's "financial ability to engage in public discussion."[14] The government's equalizing the abilities of individuals and leveling electoral opportunities based on value judgments to impact elections[15] was seen as a disvalue.

At the founding of our country, three values characterized freedom of speech: its openness, comprehensiveness, and its vitality for societal self-definition: "At the founding, speech was open, comprehensive, and vital to society's definition of itself; there were no limits on the sources of speech and knowledge."[16] According to these values, it was contrary to the

First Amendment to make political speech a crime or else a wide range of political commentary of various forms can be censored within the thirty-day period:

> Modern day movies, television comedies, or skits on Youtube.com might portray public officials or public policies in unflattering ways. Yet if a covered transmission during the blackout period creates the background for candidate endorsement or opposition, a felony occurs solely because a corporation, other than an exempt media corporation, has made the "purchase, payment, distribution, loan, advance, deposit, or gift of money or anything of value" in order to engage in political speech. 2 U. S. C. §431(9)(A)(i). Speech would be suppressed in the realm where its necessity is most evident: in the public dialogue preceding a real election. Governments are often hostile to speech, but under our law and our tradition it seems stranger than fiction for our Government to make this political speech a crime. Yet this is the statute's purpose and design.[17]

Furthermore, this prohibition could conceivably be used to censor fiction and caricature:

> When word concerning the plot of the movie *Mr. Smith Goes to Washington* reached the circles of Government, some officials sought, by persuasion, to discourage its distribution. . . . Under *Austin*, though, officials could have done more than discourage its distribution—they could have banned the film. After all, it, like *Hillary*, was a speech funded by a corporation that was critical of Members of Congress. *Mr. Smith Goes to Washington* may be fiction and caricature; but fiction and caricature can be a powerful force.[18]

The Value of Corporations

Corporations were included in the class of flesh and blood human beings. Google the multinational possessed the same status as Carrie the supermarket cashier. Just as flesh and blood humans had different views, so did corporations.

> Our Nation's speech dynamic is changing, and informative voices should not have to circumvent onerous restrictions to exercise their First Amendment rights. Speakers have become adept at presenting citizens with sound bites, talking points, and scripted messages that dominate the 24-hour news cycle. Corporations, like individuals, do not have monolithic views.[19]

Just like flesh and blood humans, corporations had subjectivity owning a voice and viewpoint:

> By suppressing the speech of manifold corporations, both for-profit and nonprofit, the Government prevents their voices and viewpoints from reaching the public and advising voters on which persons or entities are hostile to their interests.[20]

Like flesh and blood humans, corporations could be victimized:

> By taking the right to speak from some and giving it to others, the Government deprives the disadvantaged person or class of the right to use speech to strive to establish worth, standing, and respect for the speaker's voice.[21]

Additionally, corporations were useful to voters because: "On certain topics corporations may possess valuable expertise, leaving them the best equipped to point out errors or fallacies in speech of all sorts, including the speech of candidates and elected officials."[22]

Low Bar for Corruption

The majority reinforced their views on corruption from *McConnell v. Federal Election Comm'n*, 540 U.S. 93 (2003):

> Favoritism and influence are not . . . avoidable in representative politics. It is in the nature of an elected representative to favor certain policies, and, by necessary corollary, to favor the voters and contributors who support those policies. It is well understood that a substantial and legitimate reason, if not the only reason, to cast a vote for, or to make a contribution to, one candidate over another is that the candidate will respond by producing those political outcomes the supporter favors. Democracy is premised on responsiveness.[23]

The majority took a narrow view on corruption: "independent expenditures, including those made by corporations, do not give rise to corruption or the appearance of corruption."[24] Corporate money did not have "ultimate influence over elected officials" and the electorate will not opt-out of democratic governance because of such influence. [25]

Unless there was quid pro quo and somebody is paying a politician x amount of money for an elected official to vote in a certain way, then no corruption is occurring.

CONCURRENCE AND DISSENT BY JUSTICE JOHN PAUL STEVENS

Justice Stevens did not see corporations as persons. This value judgment pervaded his concurrence and dissent.

OPERATIVE VALUES

Valuing the Equality Dimension of the First Amendment

The Founders, Justice Stevens contended, believed that for the sake of public welfare corporations could be "comprehensively regulated" and would have understood speech in terms of individual rather than corporate expression:

> The Framers thus took it as a given that corporations could be comprehensively regulated in the service of the public welfare. Unlike our colleagues, they had little trouble distinguishing corporations from human beings, and when they constitutionalized the right to free speech in the First Amendment, it was the free speech of individual Americans that they had in mind. While individuals might join together to exercise their speech rights, business corporations, at least, were plainly not seen as facilitating such associational or expressive ends.[26]

Also, it was clear that speech could be regulated on the basis of one's identity:

> Yet in a variety of contexts, we have held that speech can be regulated differentially on account of the speaker's identity, when identity is understood in categorical or institutional terms. The Government routinely places special restrictions on the speech rights of students, prisoners, members of the Armed Forces, foreigners, and its own employees. When such restrictions are justified by a legitimate governmental interest, they do not necessarily raise constitutional problem.[27]

If taken seriously, our colleagues' assumption that the identity of a speaker has no relevance to the government's ability to regulate political speech would lead to some remarkable conclusions. Such an assumption would have accorded the propaganda broadcasts to our troops by "Tokyo Rose" during World War II the same protection as speech by Allied commanders. More pertinently, it would appear to afford the same protection to multinational corporations controlled by foreigners as to individual Americans.[28]

Value of Democracy over the Value of Corporations

Justice Stevens understood the great value of corporations to society, but was wary of them as well, especially when it came to impacting elections:

> Although they make enormous contributions to our society, corporations are not actually members of it. They cannot vote or run for office. Because they

> may be managed and controlled by nonresidents, their interests may conflict in fundamental respects with the interests of eligible voters.[29]

We can understand Justice Stevens' depreciation of corporations by gathering his statements about them as well what he quoted. Words and phrases to describe corporations include "soulless," "subvert the Republic," "elevate corporations to a level of deference," "corporate power at the cost of the individual and collective self-expression," "majority's unwillingness to distinguish between corporations and humans," "corporate dominance of elections," "they can flood the market with advocacy that bears "little or no correlation" to the ideas of natural persons or to any broader notion of the public good," "created, supervised, and conceptualized as quasi-public entities," "corporations have no consciences, no beliefs, no feelings, no thoughts, no desires," and "they are not themselves members of "We the People."

Justice Stevens conferred a nadir value by associating them with the term "soulless":

> ("The word 'soulless' constantly recurs in debates over corporations . . . Corporations, it was feared, could concentrate the worst urges of whole groups of men.") Thomas Jefferson famously fretted that corporations would subvert the Republic.[30]

Personhood included human characteristics including conscience, beliefs, feelings, thoughts, and desire, none of which corporations possess. Corporations were depreciated for lacking these qualities.

> It might also be added that corporations have no consciences, no beliefs, no feelings, no thoughts, no desires. Corporations help structure and facilitate the activities of human beings, to be sure, and their "personhood" often serves as a useful legal fiction. But they are not themselves members of "We the People" by whom and for whom our Constitution was established.[31]

Justice Stevens refused to confer corporations an elevated social status such that deference was paid to them:

> The majority's rejection of this principle "elevate[s] corporations to a level of deference which has not been seen at least since the days when substantive due process was regularly used to invalidate regulatory legislation thought to unfairly impinge upon established economic interests." *Bellotti*, 435 U. S., at 817, n. 13 (White, J., dissenting)[32]

For Justice Stevens, individual and collective self-expression was preferred to corporate power and corporations were seen as instruments to serving the state:

> The Court's blinkered and aphoristic approach to the First Amendment may well promote corporate power at the cost of the individual and collective self-expression the Amendment was meant to serve.[33]

Corporations were created, supervised, and conceptualized as quasi-public entities, "designed to serve a social function for the state."[34]

When society considered corporations considered persons, it overlooked their special advantages:

> The majority's unwillingness to distinguish between corporations and humans similarly blinds it to the possibility that corporations' "war chests" and their special "advantages" in the legal realm . . . may translate into special advantages in the market for legislation.[35]

Corporate electioneering undermined citizens' faith to change public policy:

> When citizens turn on their televisions and radios before an election and hear only corporate electioneering, they may lose faith in their capacity, as citizens, to influence public policy. A Government captured by corporate interests, they may come to believe, will be neither responsive to their needs nor willing to give their views a fair hearing.[36]

Corporate electioneering replaced the ideas of ordinary citizens of ordinary with corporate agendas:

> Consequently, when corporations grab up the prime broadcasting slots on the eve of an election, they can flood the market with advocacy that bears "little or no correlation" to the ideas of natural persons or to any broader notion of the public good.[37]

In summation, Justice Stevens worried that this new interpretation of the First Amendment "threatens to undermine the integrity of elected institutions across the Nation. The path it has taken to reach its outcome will, I fear, do damage to this institution."[38]

Corruption

While the majority opinion separated influence from corruption, Justice Stevens saw them as the same kettle of fish. Corporations had the resources to employ lobbyists to do their bidding, which ordinary citizens didn't have at their disposal.

> Corporations, as a class, tend to be more attuned to the complexities of the legislative process and more directly affected by tax and appropriations measures that receive little public scrutiny; they also have vastly more money with which to try to buy access and votes. . . . Business corporations must engage the political process in instrumental terms if they are to maximize shareholder value. The unparalleled resources, professional lobbyists, and single-minded focus they bring to this effort, I believed, make quid pro quo corruption and its appearance inherently more likely when they (or their conduits or trade groups) spend unrestricted sums on elections.[39]
>
> There are threats of corruption that are far more destructive to a democratic society than the odd bribe. Yet the majority's understanding of corruption would leave lawmakers impotent to address all but the most discrete abuses.[40]

Corruption was not so easily folded into quid pro quo. Money for favors was one form of corruption, but so was money for access, especially when that access was inaccessible to those without money or influence:

> Corruption can take many forms. Bribery may be the paradigm case. But the difference between selling a vote and selling access is a matter of degree, not kind. And selling access is not qualitatively different from giving special preference to those who spent money on one's behalf. Corruption operates along a spectrum, and the majority's apparent belief that quid pro quo arrangements can be neatly demarcated from other improper influences does not accord with the theory or reality of politics.[41]

Justice Stevens identified many forms of corruption that ran the gamut from quid pro quo to other more subtle types.

Because nonresidents of the United States could run corporations, the interests of those corporations might run counter to the interests of the American people. Allowing corporations carte blanche in electioneering invites disruption of American interests both home and abroad:

> In the context of election to public office, the distinction between corporate and human speakers is significant. Although they make enormous contributions to our society, corporations are not actually members of it. They cannot vote or run for office. Because they may be managed and controlled by nonresidents, their interests may conflict in fundamental respects with the interests of eligible voters. The financial resources, legal structure, and instrumental orientation of corporations raise legitimate concerns about their role in the electoral process. Our lawmakers have a compelling constitutional basis, if not also a democratic duty, to take measures designed to guard against the potentially deleterious effects of corporate spending in local and national races.[42]

Corruption was viewed as systemic rather than on a one-to-one basis. When foreign corporations influence elections, they corrupt our democratic system. Because corporations have more money, which allows them to hire lobbyists and gives them access to politicians, they corrupt our democratic system.

RECKONING OF THE ROGUE JUSTICES

In some quarters, *Citizens United* represents a victory for freedom of speech and the First Amendment. A closer axiological look discloses other dimensions. Free speech was valued according to its quantity. The more units of free speech in the marketplace of ideas, the more closely the First Amendment was being followed, according to the majority opinion. This type of thinking was analogous to those who judge the best economic system as one that produced the overall amount of wealth, even if allowed a dominant group to suppress other groups. In the realm of freedom of speech, some speech was so amplified that other speeches were not heard. In terms of the total amount of free speech, allowing corporate speech added more units, but that sum total of speech like the sum total of happiness in utilitarianism could justify silencing others.

However, how can free speech be fully actualized when those without the means to participate repetitively will never have their voices heard? How can it be open when those voices are muted by the sheer quantity from wealthy corporations? If only the voices capable of endlessly replicating themselves can be heard, those incapable of replication will be muted in the big picture. Was the First Amendment designed to maximize participation or maximize democracy?

Not increasing, but decreasing political speech was the goal of *Citizens United.* The din from the wealthiest corporations drowned out voices of the dispossessed. In the final analysis, Justice Kennedy and Justice Stevens were not talking about free speech in the same way. For Justice Kennedy, free speech was everyone getting a chance to speak; for Justice Stevens, free speech was everyone being heard. The identity of the speaker does matter if that person is capable of subverting the principle of free speech!

The real agenda behind the majority opinion was corporate hegemony. The First Amendment was simply an instrument to achieve that objective, allowing the most powerful corporations to spread their agendas more pervasively. At this time unions that protect working people were on a steep decline and have been on a steep decline for decades. Would the majority be so willing to pursue this course if unions had the upper hand as they did in the middle of the twentieth century?

Elections are races and those races must appear above reproach or else trust in democracy erodes. When these "races" are influenced by corporations such that a candidate can flood the airways and control the message and optics, that is one aspect of the *influence*. Second, politicians are public servants charged with improving lots of lives of their constituents in a fair manner. If we contend it's inappropriate for judges who also must act fairly to accept gifts from lawyers, why would it be any different for politicians? This is another aspect of *influence*.

The contention that corporations are on the side of the people is misguided. Corporations care about their profits, and to increase their profits, they need friendly laws. Elected officials will make those friendly laws and thus become targets of corporate *influence*.

NOTES

1. Richard Briffault, "Corporations, Corruption, and Complexity: Campaign Finance after *Citizens United*," *Cornell Journal Law and Public Policy* 20, 3 (Spring 2011): 644.
2. William H Wiist, "*Citizens United*, Public Health, and Democracy: the Supreme Court Ruling, Its Implications, and Proposed Action," *American Journal Public Health* 101, 7 (July 2007). 10.2105/AJPH.2010.300043.
3. Lloyd H. Mayer, "Breaching a Leaking Dam?: Corporate Money and Elections, *Charleston Law Review* 91 (2009–2010): 94–95.
4. Ilya Shapiro, "Citizens United Misunderstood," Cato Institute (January 20, 2015) https://www.cato.org/commentary/citizens-united-misunderstood.
5. Ibid., 326–327.
6. Ibid., 324.
7. Ibid., 329.
8. Ibid., 312.
9. Ibid., 337.
10. Ibid., 340–341.
11. Ibid., 349.
12. Ibid., 312.
13. Ibid., 312.
14. Ibid., 313.
15. Ibid., 350.
16. Ibid., 353.
17. Ibid., 371–372.
18. Ibid., 371.
19. Ibid., 364.
20. Ibid., 354.
21. Ibid., 340–341.
22. Ibid., 364.
23. Ibid., 359.
24. Ibid., 357.

25. Ibid., 360.
26. Ibid., 428.
27. Ibid., 420–421.
28. Ibid., 424.
29. Ibid., 394.
30. Ibid., 427.
31. Ibid., 466.
32. Ibid., 479.
33. Ibid., 475.
34. Ibid., 427.
35. Ibid., 471.
36. Ibid., 470.
37. Ibid.
38. Ibid., 396.
39. Ibid., 454.
40. Ibid., 449.
41. Ibid., 447–448.
42. Ibid., 394.

Conclusion

One Hundred and Six Mic Drop Takeaways, Conversation Starters & Stuff That Can Startle the Stymied into Writing Creatively

Conclusions are primarily perfunctory and infrequently fecund. They offer something between little and nothing. Our conclusion sends readers off with ideational gems rather than bales of bromides. A few are positively perspicacious, blue diamonds, or C B (trace). Others are passably perspicacious, aquamarine, or $Be_3Al_2Si_6O_{18.}$ Some are merely pedestrianly perspicacious, jasper, or SiO_2.

1. Herding authorities into logical proofs rather than allowing them to roam free-range makes them much easier for readers to follow, helps writers to grasp and assess patterns, and adds more transparency. Rating: SiO_2
2. The reintroduction and reinvention of *e*s*s*e*n*t*i*a*l*i*s*m* into mainstream philosophy. Excommunicated *e*s*s*e*n*t*i*a*l*i*s*m* returns in a new form. Rating: C B (trace)
3. The graphic description of *e*s*s*e*n*t*i*a*l*i*s*m* captures its new meaning. Rating: C B (trace)
4. Husserl's bracketing is redefined in terms of value such that the bracket's contents are predetermined by value. This throws into question the basis of all phenomenology and establishes value as the foundational basis. Rating: C B (trace)
5. Sacred Cow-Scapegoat Value Scheme—sacred values versus profane values embodied in sacred cows that are exalted and scapegoats that are reviled. The relationship between sacred cows and scapegoats in a value scheme requires a traversal between multiple ideas. Rating: C B (trace)
6. Contempt as a looking down from a zenith value at a lesser but often nadir value. Rating: C B (trace)

7. Bubba's Beard is a countermeasure to Ockham's Razor, which has been indiscriminately applied to prematurely and proactively preventing ideas from emerging and burgeoning. Listen, let's grow out ideas to see what they are before shaving them. Rating: $Be_3Al_2Si_6O_{18}$
8. The Contempt Continuum declares that the height of contempt is determined by the degree to which the higher value is esteemed and the lower value depreciated. Rating: $Be_3Al_2Si_6O_{18}$
9. The distinction between the Near Other and the Remote Other introduces a nuance that distinguishes degrees of alienation from others and puts alienation on a spectrum. Putting the others on a spectrum of otherness reveals their distinct differences. Rating: $Be_3Al_2Si_6O_{18}$
10. The distinction between the Near Other and the Remote Other emerges from degrees of contempt: the Remote Other from extreme contempt in which the Other is a nadir value and the Near Other from a lesser contempt in which the Other is beneath one but not nadirized. High marks for its long and deep ideational traversal. Rating: $Be_3Al_2Si_6O_{18}$
11. Zenithed and nadirized are new verbs. Please welcome them to the language! Rating: SiO_2
12. In his *Enquiry Concerning Human Understanding*, Hume values moderate skepticism, but actually practices extreme skepticism by doubting the necessary connection between cause and effect. The level of extreme skepticism Hume disvalues, epitomized by doubting the existence of an outer world, is equivalent to the extreme skepticism involved in believing cause and effect are not necessarily connected. Axiological analysis throws light on this disparity. Rating: $Be_3Al_2Si_6O_{18}$
13. Embracing the view that cause and effect are not loose separate and their connection arbitrary and the result of custom impacts the distinction between impressions and ideas. Valuing the absence of a necessary connection between cause and effect devalues the connection between impressions and ideas. Rating: SiO_2
14. Even articles of speech express value! Rating: C B (trace)
15. The Ambiguity Paradox states: as clearly understood ambiguity is not ambiguous. Rating: SiO_2
16. Conglomerates of values rather than single values frequently appear and buttress a single primary value or each other. Rating: $Be_3Al_2Si_6O_{18}$
17. Values are the sharp edge of meaning. You can't touch meaning without feeling value. Shout-out to the much-overlooked tactile sensation as a metaphor in philosophy. Rating:
18. The removal of the Is-Ought distinction, tattooed on the corpus of philosophy, is long overdue. Rating: C B (trace)
19. For the Sunday matinee Is-Ought will be replaced by Is-Value. Rating: $Be_3Al_2Si_6O_{18}$

20. But for opening and closing nights, Value-Is will take the role. Rating: $Be_3Al_2Si_6O_{18}$
21. The experience of oughtness increases to the extent it approaches sacred zenith values. Rating: C B (trace)
22. When the value of cosmopolitanism vitalizes the value of justice, justice is experienced as pervasive rather than local. Rating: $Be_3Al_2Si_6O_{18}$
23. Axiological Law Theory elaborates on values that necessarily nurture our being. Rating: $Be_3Al_2Si_6O_{18}$
24. When necessity and probability are a duality, they are valued as exclusive and different in kind. However, if necessity and probability are on a possibility continuum, they are valued in terms of degrees of possibility. For the sheer ideational traversal, high marks. Rating: C B (trace)
25. Necessity can be both positive and negative. It is positive when there is no possibility that something cannot be. It is negative when there is no possibility that something can be. Rating: C B (trace)
26. Near necessities approach the border of positive necessity as the possibility for their reversal remote. Rating: C B (trace)
27. Far necessities approach the border of negative necessity and the possibility for their reversal is certain. Rating: C B (trace)
28. The felt necessity of values is the experience of absolute values: what we experience as absolute, we believe is necessary. Rating: $Be_3Al_2Si_6O_{18}$
29. Natural Law Theory points to sacred zenith values and profane sacred disvalues and misses out on a spectrum of values. Rating: C B (trace)
30. For Legal Positivism, the empirically verifiable law text serves as its prime matter; for Formalism, the coherent text serves in the same capacity. "What you see is what you get" (sense perception) versus "what you conceive is what you get" (rationality). Rating: SiO_2
31. Legal Positivism leads us to the texts, but with its value illiteracy cannot read them. This is like taking illiterate people to the library. Rating: $Be_3Al_2Si_6O_{18}$
32. The expansion and contraction of the net of implication depends upon the degree to which expansion is valued or disvalued for the originalist. Rating: SiO_2
33. Originalism overvalues the human intellect in its attempt to recreate the past. Rating: SiO_2
34. The very act of originalism is intellectual overreach, which cannot be a good thing for judicial restraint, one of the hallmarks of originalism. Rating: $Be_3Al_2Si_6O_{18}$
35. The arrogance of originalism includes its failure to acknowledge the ambiguity at the heart of all interpretive exercises. Rating: $Be_3Al_2Si_6O_{18}$

36. The broader the interpretive exercise, the more it involves the recesses of the past and requires implications to tie together those recesses, the more ambiguity involved. Rating: $Be_3Al_2Si_6O_{18}$
37. Fluidity, holism, subjectivity, prediction, and the common good are the leading values of Legal Realism. Legal Realism also values fluidity over stability, subjectivity over objectivity, holism over insularity, prediction of legal consequences over ratiocination of legal texts, and the common good over law for law's sake. This description shows the power of axiological analysis. Rating: SiO_2
38. Efficiency is the value on the basis of economics and law theory. Rating: SiO_2
39. Fundamental questions of value ripple through economic theory. How do we value poverty? As a necessary evil? An evil? Do we value private property over the commons? Do we value economies that create a permanent underclass over economies that offer upward mobility? Rating: SiO_2
40. Egalitarianism emerges as the leading value of Critical Legal Studies and as such the diminishment and demise of oppression become disvalues. Rating: SiO_2
41. Critical Legal Theory does a great service by demystifying jurisprudence. Yet Critical Legal Studies exposes a narrow sphere of values that pertain to hierarchy and oppression. But when it comes to its own value scheme, it proves unreflective. Its "pure negativity" obscures the vast landscape of values. Its pure negativity narrows rather than expands the inquiry of values. Rating: $Be_3Al_2Si_6O_{18}$
42. Deconstruction values undecidability as much as Economic Theory values efficiency. We find undecidability no less an imperative than the ten famous imperatives of Moses, all of which protrude with values. Rating: $Be_3Al_2Si_6O_{18}$
43. Ultimately, the sacred zenith value of personhood protrudes as the leading value in Critical Race Theory. Rating: $Be_3Al_2Si_6O_{18}$
44. Gay legal narratives challenge the conventional and alleged neutral values embedded in the law and serving dominant classes. Rating: SiO_2
45. Feminist Legal Theories values diversity and embraces anti-essentialism. Like Critical Race Theory, Legal Realism, and Queer Law Studies, the goal becomes a reorientation of jurisprudence, diversifying it and making it accountable to people who are not served by it. Each of these theories prefers concrete experience to abstract theories. For each of these theories, the goal is to break law out of a prison of orthodoxy, rigidity, unfairness, abstraction, and concentration of power into a wider world where a wider variety of people can partner to create, adjudicate, and administer it. Law, as an instrument of torture, must be disassembled.

Each unwittingly employs values and partakes of value essentialism. Rating: C B (trace)

46. By adding a literary component to jurisprudence, the artistic dimension of jurisprudence appreciates and takes a place beside the strictly rationalistic aspect of rulemaking. Rather than the narrow faculty of reasoning, a broader use of the human intellect is appreciated. Rating: SiO_2

BELL V. BUCK

47. Not eugenics but efficiency was the overarching value of *Buck*. Eugenics was just another form of efficiency. Rating: C B (trace)
48. Compassion could contribute to an efficient society by leading people to help each other, forge social bonds, and cooperate more effectively. Rating: SiO_2
49. For Justice Holmes, efficiency was a zenith value and inefficiency a nadir disvalue. In his Contempt Continuum, the efficient were regarded as sacred cows, the inefficient in this case, the mentally challenged, whom he regarded as scapegoats. Rating: C B (trace)
50. Sacrifices for one's country functioned on a value spectrum. The most sacred were those in which people fought for the country and put themselves in harm's way. Other sacrifices did not reach this standard and were considered minimal, for example, relinquishing one's procreativity. Rating: $Be_3Al_2Si_6O_{18}$
51. Axiological analysis presents possibilities other than moral outrage and sanctimoniousness and a eugenics-centered approach. It focuses on the protuberant value of efficiency as the greater value in contrast to the lesser value of self-determination. Rating: SiO_2
52. Axiological analysis introduces a wide variety of disvalues such as crude utilitarianism, lifeboat ethics, or any version of hierarchy featuring an underappreciated underclass disvalued as inefficient that hurls the eugenics into a broader context. Rating: C B (trace)

YICK WO V. SULLIVAN

53. The sacred zenith value of freedom was animated by a specific value conglomerate grounding Chinese launderers as both members of the community and breadwinners for their families, as particular persons. Rating: C B (trace)
54. In the majority opinion, the Chinese were valued as everymen instead of aliens. Rating: C B (trace)

55. The exploitation of the Chinese was not simply on the level of racism, but more importantly classism. As poor and vulnerable members of society, they easily fell prey to legal oppression. For those who value the larger picture of exploitation, this is the takeaway from the case, as it is this oppressive mechanism that remains in place to harm the next vulnerable group. Rating: SiO_2

ABRAMS V. UNITED STATES

56. Truth works itself out in the process of experimentation in the form of free speech and the First Amendment safeguards that process. Rating: SiO_2
57. Experimentation implies the value of human fallibility in seeking truth. The First Amendment implicitly values such fallibility. Rating: $Be_3Al_2Si_6O_{18}$
58. The swing value in Justice Clarke's opinion was his disvalue of the Abrams and Co. as remote others, whereas in Justice Holmes's dissent the defendants were characterized as bumbling and benign fools, as near others. Near others receive protection from the Constitution, while remote others like Abrams do not. Rating: C B (trace)
59. Justice Holmes's "clear and present danger" stipulation was not a full-throated protection of the First Amendment, merely approaching the sacred zenith value of the First Amendment. Rating: SiO_2
60. The First Amendment in using absolute language—NO—is sacred among zenith values. Rating: SiO_2

DRED SCOTT V. SANDFORD

61. Dred Scott was a classic example of how judicial oppression functions via value. First, disvalue a group of people as property. Devalue any type of new knowledge or awareness that might challenge that view while hyper-valuing past practices and morality that support it; deify ancestors and hyper-value their ideas and written works to irreproachable gospel; value justice as a past act instead of a present construction; value fate over responsibility (as if it was cruel fate that Negroes ended up as slaves); and value safety concerns and fear of "free" Negroes. Rating: C B (trace)
62. Pigeon-holed personhood dependent upon the laws of nations stands against universal personhood regardless of nations. Rating: C B (trace)

PLESSY V. FERGUSON

63. Segregation and integration (co-mingling) fail to capture the social realities in the United States. They are overused, outdated, and misleading terms. Rating: C B (trace)
64. The social reality in the United States can be better understood in terms of parallelism and exploitative tangents. White Supremacy eschews all contact with people of color and endorses parallel paths except at tangents of exploitation (labor, sex). Rating: C B (trace)
65. Purity is maintained in these parallel paths. Rating: C B (trace)
66. White supremacy means two things: at the tangents being superior to people of color and in a parallel world being rid of them. Rating: C B (trace)
67. "The badge of inferiority" references, humanizes, and concretizes the Fourteenth Amendment. It casts African Americans in full personhood. Rating: C B (trace)

LOCHNER V. NEW YORK

68. Three distinct value schemes emerge. The majority opinion valued liberty over state interventions in all but extreme health matters; one rejected the liberty side; a third recognized the tension between the two, but sided with health over liberty. This adds a third view in the mix instead of the usual libertarian-communitarian value scheme. Rating: C B (trace)
69. Justice Peckham held state intervention in contempt as much as Justice Holmes held liberty in contempt, in opposition to the zenith values of majority rule and of actual implementation (compared to past implementation). Rating: $Be_3Al_2Si_6O_{18}$
70. On the other hand Justice Harlan took a middle course that leaned toward state intervention, but maintained the tension between the two extremes. He came down on the side of judicious state intervention. Rating: $Be_3Al_2Si_6O_{18}$

WICKARD V. FILBURN

71. Economic life possessed sacred zenith value by virtue of the fact that all economic encounters are interdependent. Rating: C B (trace)
72. Economic self-determination even with the confines of the home was depreciated and nullified. Rating: C B (trace)
73. A private economic sphere in which farmers could make the best use of their resources for their own personal needs was eliminated. Rating: $Be_3Al_2Si_6O_{18}$

GRISWOLD V. CONNECTICUT

74. The sacred value of the intimacy of marriage deeply woven into the tradition of American culture and perhaps even beyond that into the human condition eclipsed the value of a state law interfering in it. In one sense, this was a case of catching up with the times and in another it wasn't. The catching up with the times aspect of the case concerned including the new technologies of birth control into the intimacy of married life and of professionals who could guide married couples to use this new technologies. On the other hand, *Griswold* was an affirmation of a sacred zenith value that practically transcended time. Thus, the case was about changing times and timeless truths. Rating: C B (trace)
75. Invasion of privacy was a profane nadir disvalue, akin to invading a sovereign country. Working within the penumbra metaphor, the penumbras give the specific guarantees of the Bill of Rights "life and substance" in the same way that the exercise and good nutrition make bodies strong and alive. Those specific guarantees are better seen by the penumbras. Thus, the interconnectivity between the specific guarantees of the Bill of Rights and the penumbras was valued. Rating: C B (trace)
76. The relationship between the specific guarantees of the Bill of Rights could be seen as lifeless abstractions, gaining "life and substance" only when applied to vital societal issues. Rating: C B (trace)
77. There is a multiple-penumbra approach in the majority opinion versus a single-penumbra approach in the concurrence by Justice Goldberg. The multiple penumbras arise from specific Amendments of the Bill of Rights while the single penumbra arises from the Bill of Rights as a whole. Rating: $Be_3Al_2Si_6O_{18}$

NEW YORK TIMES CO. V. SULLIVAN

78. The value of freedom of speech was deemed so important that collateral damage was accepted for its maintenance. That collateral damage includes falsehoods, half-truths, misinformation, and vilification. Free speech comes at a price, but its value is so important that price must be paid. Public officials are forewarned that being at the center of this war of words is a central element of their job descriptions. Rating: $Be_3Al_2Si_6O_{18}$
79. Freedom of speech placed a premium value on the speechmaker and much less value on the speech recipient. Freedom of speech protected the speechmaker and left the recipient of speech vulnerable to speech. The First Amendment as articulated by Justice Brennan spoke to citizens

protecting themselves with speech rather than be prey to the speech of others. Rating: $Be_3Al_2Si_6O_{18}$

80. The First Amendment valued action and activity on the part of people and not passivity. It promoted an attitude of engagement rather than disengagement. It was all about people finding their voices not in an echo chamber or in a silent meditation but with or against others. Resistance was inherent in freedom of speech and compliance was never coerced. Rating: $Be_3Al_2Si_6O_{18}$

BROWN V. BOARD OF EDUCATION

81. Education was treated as a sacred zenith value for its transformative role in human beings. Rating: C B (trace)
82. Sociological and psychological findings were the basis for valuing the perspectives of those who were negatively impacted by segregation. This represented the subjective turn of the Fourteenth Amendment. Rating: C B (trace)
83. The badge of servitude was now understood not as simply objective, but as how Black people saw themselves, their self-image. Rating: C B (trace)

DISTRICT OF COLUMBIA V. HELLER

84. For Justices Breyer and Stevens, safety was seen from a communitarian perspective and represented a shared societal responsibility. The communitarian position was stopping violence before it could be started—by limiting access to weapons. The individualistic perspective meant taking on violence one bad guy at a time. Rating: C B (trace)
85. As a riddle the Second Amendment is value. As a law, it is disvalue. Its disvalue consists of offering little direction about its general meaning. Accordingly, it must be approached as nothing more than an amorphous mass used by each side of the ideological divide. Rating: C B (trace)

ENGEL V. VITALE

86. The government needed to stay out of the business of religion as much as the mother-in-law needed to stay out of her son's marital business with his wife. In delicate situations, even the best of intentions lead to havoc. Rating: SiO_2

LAWRENCE V. TEXAS

87. "Lifestyle" was a nadir disvalue inherently condemning gay people for their sexual promiscuity and socially and morally unacceptable practices. Rating: C B (trace)
88. Justice Scalia participated in the culture war by invoking the nadir disvalue "lifestyle." This was his weapon of choice in the war of words and imbroglio of ideologies. Rating: $Be_3Al_2Si_6O_{18}$
89. Heterosexualism impacted Justice Scalia's valuations as much as white supremacy impacted Justice Taney, ableism impacted Justice Homes, and xenophobia impacted Justice Clarke. Rating: C B (trace)
90. Preferring traditional morality to emerging understanding trapped Justice Scalia in replicating multi-tentacled heterosexualism. Rating: $Be_3Al_2Si_6O_{18}$
91. The omission of rape and age-inappropriate relationships in Justice Scalia's list of horribles prevented an understanding of a new sexual morality in which coercion and age appropriateness stood as distinguishing moral characteristics of a new sexual morality. Rating: C B (trace)
92. Justice Scalia valued gay people as individuals acting out sexually instead of a group that had been oppressed in systemic ways. Rating: C B (trace)
93. For Justice Kennedy, sexuality between consenting adults was a sacred act and the home was sanctuary for such acts. Rating: $Be_3Al_2Si_6O_{18}$

BRANDENBURG V. OHIO

94. When considering freedom of speech as a sacred value, we were led to see its full potential, its genesis in thought and conscience, its articulation in words, and its connection to action. Sacred valuations eschewed containment and are prone to universalization or full actualization. According to this value framework, both words and actions are expressions of and as sacred as thought and conscience. The curtailment of speech and action was tantamount to a curtailment of conscience. Content doesn't matter; the exercise of it does. Rating: C B (trace)

LOVING V. VIRGINIA

95. Anti-miscegenation was an effective means to maintain this social, political, ideological, and psychological parallelism. Marriage was not only

a union of two people, but of families as well, where religion, culture, and ideas could be united. Rating: C B (trace)

96. Also, if marriage as a sacred zenith value included interracial relationships, one of the most sacred institutions of the civilization would be corrupted. Rating: C B (trace)
97. Invidious racism caused direct harm to people. It was a profane nadir disvalue. Racism rose to the level of unconstitutionality when declared invidious. However, it must be wondered whether there are other forms of racism, not invidious, that do not rise to the level of being unconstitutional. Rating: C B (trace)

NATIONAL FEDERATION OF INDEPENDENT BUSINESS V. SEBELIUS

98. The dissenters disvalued the interdependence of health systems and that disvalue cloistered with the disvalue of shared responsibility. When interdependence was affirmed, so were connections between people and from these connections a shared responsibility. Rating: C B (trace)

TEXAS V. JOHNSON

99. Unless the First Amendment was regarded as a sacred zenith value, innumerable objects could be put above it, claiming sacredness for themselves and eventually diminishing and finally denying the First Amendment. Rating: $Be_3Al_2Si_6O_{18}$
100. The same symbol can be regarded as sacred or profane. This includes the American flag and numerous other symbols. The First Amendment allows people to determine what is sacred or profane according to their own judgment. Rating: $Be_3Al_2Si_6O_{18}$

UNITED STATES V. NIXON

101. President Nixon conceived and valued the office of presidency as above the law. This case concerned the sacred zenith value of any society: the functioning of the judiciary as the means of securing a functioning society. To the extent that President Nixon prevented the judiciary from obtaining evidence, his actions could be considered profane nadir disvalues. Rating: SiO_2

CITIZENS UNITED V. FEDERAL ELECTION COMMISSION

102. Freedom of speech can be valued for both its quality and quantity. Rating: C B (trace)
103. Libertarians value its quantity; communitarians value its quality. Rating: C B (trace)
104. Does the mere quantity of speech ensure freedom of speech? Rating: C B (trace)
105. The value of being heard was essential to freedom of speech, according to Justice Stevens. Rating: C B (trace)
106. Was the First Amendment designed to maximize participation or maximize democracy? This question alone justifies the cost of this book. Rating: C B (trace)

Bibliography

"Cato Institute Scholar Reviews "Worst" Supreme Court decisions." Duke Law (September 15, 2008). https://law.duke.edu/news/cato-institute-scholar-reviews-worst-supreme-court-decisions/.

Akhil Reed, Amar "On Prosecuting Presidents." *Hofstra Law Review* 27, 4 (1999): 671–676.

Akhil Reed, Amar and Brian C. Kalt. "The Presidential Privilege Against Prosecution." *NEXUS* 2 (1997): 11–23.

Alfieri, Anthony V. "Reconstructive Poverty Law Practice: Learning Lessons in Client Narrative." *Yale Law Journal* 100 (1991): 2107–2147.

Amar, Akhil Reed. "*Plessy v. Ferguson* and the Anti-Canon." *Pepperdine Law Review* (2013): 75–89.

Aquinas, Thomas. *Summa Theologica*. Project, Guttenberg, March 1, 2006. https://www.gutenberg.org/cache/epub/17897/pg17897.html.

Aristotle, *Nicomachean Ethics of Aristotle*. Project Gutenberg. July 10, 2003. https://www.gutenberg.org/files/8438/8438-h/8438-h.htm.

Aristotle, *The Art of Rhetoric*. London and New York: William Heineman and J.P. Putnam's Sons, 1926. https://ryanfb.github.io/loebolus-data/L193.pdf.

Balkin, Jack M. "Tradition, Betrayal, and the Politics of Deconstruction." Yale Law School Repository, May 20, 2021. https://digitalcommons.law.yale.edu/cgi/viewcontent.cgi?article=1282&context=fss_papers.

Barker, Nicholas. "The Constitutionality of Flag Burning: Hate or Free Speech? An Analysis of Texas v. Johnson." *Hinckley Journal of Politics* [Online] 3 (24 February 23, 2017): 49–56.

Barnett, Randy E. "Justice Kennedy's Libertarian Revolution: *Lawrence v. Texas*." *Georgetown Law Faculty Publications and Other Works* 838 (2003): 21–41 https://scholarship.law.georgetown.edu/facpub/838.

Baron, Jane. "Law, Literature, and the Problems of Interdisciplinarity." *Yale Law Journal* 108 (March 1999): 1059–1085.

Bartholet, Elizabeth. "Race Separatism in the Family: More on the Transracial Adoption Debate." *Duke Journal of Gender Law & Policy* 2 (Spring 1995): 99–105.

Beermann, Jack M. "*NFIB v. Sebelius and the Right to Health Care:* Government's Obligation to Provide for the Health, Safety, and Welfare of Its Citizens." *New York University Journal of Legislation and Public Policy* 18 (2015): 277–330.

Bell Jr., Derrick A. "The Unintended Lessons in Brown v. Board of Education." *New York Law School Law Review* 49, 4 (2004–2005): 1053–1057.

Bernstein, David E. "*Lochner v. New York*: A Centennial Retrospective." *Washington University Law Quarterly* 83 (2005): 1469–1527.

Bernstein, David E. "*Lochner*, Parity, and the Chinese Laundry Cases." *William and Mary Law Review* 41 (1999): 211–294.

Berry, Roberta M. "From Involuntary Sterilization to Genetic Enhancement: The Unsettled Legacy of *Buck v. Bell.*" *Notre Dame Journal of Law, Ethics & Public Policy* 12, 2 (1998): 401–448.

Blocher, Joseph. "Institutions in the Marketplace of Ideas." *Duke Law Journal*, 54, 4, (2008): 822–889.

Bloustein, Edward J. "Criminal Attempts and the Clear and Present Danger Theory of the First Amendment." *Cornell Law Review* 74 (1989): 1118–1150.

Bobertz, Bradley C. "The Brandeis Gambit: The Making of America's 'First Freedom,' 1909–1931." *William and Mary Law Review* 40 (1999): 557–651.

Burt, Robert A. "What Was Wrong with Dred Scott, What's Right About Brown." *Washington and Lee Law Review* 42, 1 (1985): 1–25.

Butler, P. "Racially Based Jury Nullification: Black Power in the Criminal Social System." *Yale Law Journal* 105 (1995): 677–725.

Calabresi, Steve G. "On Originalism in Constitutional Interpretation." National Constitution Center. https://constitutioncenter.org/interactive-constitution/white-papers/on-originalism-in-constitutional-interpretation.

Calabresi, Steven G. and Hannah B. Begley. "Justice Oliver Wendell Holmes and Chief Justice John Roberts's Dissent in *Obergfell v. Hodges.*" *Elon Law Review* 8 (2016): 1–39.

Carpenter, Dale. "The Unknown Past of *Lawrence v. Texas.*" *Michigan Law Review* 102 (2004): 1464–1527.

Chafee, Jr., Zechariah. "A Contemporary State Trial: The United States versus Jacob Abrams et al." *Harvard Law Review* 33, 6 (April 1920): 9–14.

Chambers, Jr., Henry L. "*Dred Scott*: Tiered Citizenship and Tiered Personhood." *Chicago-Kent Law Review* 82 (2007): 209–232.

Chen, James Meng. "The Story of *Wickard v. Filburn*: Agriculture, Aggregation, and Commerce." (September 15, 2008): 1–37. *Constitutional Law Stories*. 2nd ed. Edited by Michael C. Dorf. Foundation Press, 2008. University of Louisville School of Law Legal Studies Research Paper Series No. 2008-40. https://ssrn.com/abstract=1268162.

Chin, Gabriel. "Unexplainable on Grounds of Race: Doubts about *Yo Wick.*" *University of Illinois Law Review* (2008): 1359–1391.

Cicero, Marcus Tullius. *The Republic of Cicero*. New York, 1829, Project Gutenberg, February 12, 2017. https://www.gutenberg.org/files/54161/54161-h/54161-h.htm.

Clay, Calvert. "First Amendment Envelope Pushers: Revisiting the Incitement-to-Violence Test with Messrs. Brandenburg, Trump, & Spencer." *Connecticut Law Review* 411 (2019): 117–144.

Cohen, Felix S. "Transcendental Nonsense and the Functional Approach." *Columbia Law Review* 35 (1935): 809–849.

Cohen, Morris R. "On Absolutism in Legal Thought." *University of Pennsylvania Law Review* 84 (1936): 681–715.

Cohen, Morris R. "On Absolutism in Legal Thought." *University Pennsylvania Law Review* 84 (1936): 681–715.

Colby, Thomas and Peter J. Smith. "The Return of *Lochner*." *Cornell Law Review* 100 (2015): 527–602.

Coles, Matt. "*Lawrence v. Texas* and the Refinement of Substantive Due Process." *Stanford Law and Policy Review* 16 (2005): 23–56.

Combs, Michael W. and Gwendolyn M. Combs. "Revisiting *Brown v. Board of Education*: A Cultural, Historical Legal, and Political Perspective." *Management Department Faculty Publications* 48 (Spring 2005): 627–678. https://digitalcommons.unl.edu/managementfacpub/48.

Cooter, Richard D. "The Best Right Value Foundations of the Economic Analysis of the Law." *Notre Dame Law Review* 64 (1989): 817–837.

Culbertson, Tucker. "Arguments Against Marriage Equality: Commemorating & Reconstructing Loving v. Virginia." *Washington University Law Review* 85 (2007): 575–609.

Curtis, Michael Kent. "Albion Tourgée: Remembering Plessy's Lawyer on the 100th Anniversary of *Plessy v. Ferguson*." *Constitutional Commentary* 13, 2 (Summer 1996): 187–199.

Dallin, Lewis. "Flaws and Repercussions of Engel v. Vitale." *Brigham Young University Prelaw Review* 21, 1 (2007): 53–65.

Davis, Thomas J. "More Than Segregation, Racial Identity: The Neglected Question in *Plessy v. Ferguson*." *Washington and Lee Race & Ethnic Ancestry Law Journal* 10, 1 (2004): 2–41.

Delgado, Richard. "The Ethereal Scholar: Does Critical Legal Studies Have What Minorities Need?" *Harvard Civil Rights-Civil Liberties Law Review* 22 (1987): 301–322.

———. "Story-Telling for Oppositionists and Others: A Plea for Narrative." *Michigan Law Review* 87 (1989): 2410–2441.

Derrick Bell, *Faces at the Bottom of the Well*. Internet Archive. https://www.archive.org/stream/facesatbottomofw00bellrich/facesatbottomofw00bellrich_djvu.txt. Last visited November 18, 2018.

———. "Racial Realism." *Connecticut Law Review* 24, 2 (Winter 1992): 363–379.

Dery III, George M. "Unintended Consequences: The Supreme Court's Interpretation of the Second Amendment in *District of Columbia v. Heller* Could Water-Down Fourth Amendment Rights." *University Pennsylvania Journal of Law and Social Change* 13 (2009): 1–45.

Destro, Robert A. "Law and the Politics of Marriage: *Loving v. Virginia* after 30 Years Introduction." *Catholic University Law Review* 47 (1998): 1207–1230.

Dworkin, Ronald. *Law's Empire*. Cambridge and London: The Belknap Press of Harvard University Press, 1986. http://www.filosoficas.unam.mx/~cruzparc/empire.pdf.

———. "The Model of Rules." *University of. Chicago Law Review* 35 (1967): 14–46.

Ellis, James W. "Disability Advocacy and Atkins." *DePaul Law Review* 57, 3 (2008): 653–666.

Epstein, Richard A. "Was New York Times v. Sullivan Wrong?" *University of Chicago Law Review* 53 (1986): 782–818.

Eskridge, Jr., William N. "Body Politics: *Lawrence v. Texas* and the Constitution of Disgust and Contagion." *Florida Law Review* 57, 5 (December 2005): 1011–1064.

Eskridge, Jr., William N. "Gaylegal Narratives." *Stanford Law Review* 46 (1994): 607–646.

Failinger, Marie A. "*Yick Wo* at 125: Four Simple Lessons for the Contemporary Supreme Court." *Michigan Journal of Race and Law* 17 (2012): 217–268.

Field, Martha. "*Brandenburg v. Ohio* and its Relationship to *Masses Publishing Co. v. Patten.*" *Arizona State Law Journal* 50 (2018): 791–801.

Fineman, Jay "Critical Approaches to Contract Law." *UCLA Law Review* 30 (1983): 829–860.

Finkelman, Paul. "Slavery in the United States: Persons or Property?" In *The Legal Understanding of Slavery: From the Historical to the Contemporary*. Edited by Jean Allain. Oxford Scholarship Online (January 2013): 105–134.

Fiss, Owen M. "The Death of the Law." *Cornell Law Review* 72 (1986): 1–16.

———. "Objectivity and Interpretation." *Stanford Law Review* 34 (1982): 739–763.

Flanagan, Fintan M., George Lorinczi and Frank Schlax. "Constitutional Problems Under the Alien Land Laws." *Marquette Law Review* 36 (1953): 267–278.

Freeman, Alan and Elizabeth Mensch. "The Public-Private Distinction in American Law and Life." *Buffalo Law Review* 36 (1987): 237–257.

Fuller, Lon. "Positivism and Fidelity to the Law—A Reply to Professor Hart." *Harvard Law Review* 71 (1958): 630–672.

Geoffrey Bennett and Russell L. Weaver. "Is The New York Times 'Actual Malice' Standard Really Necessary? A Comparative Perspective." *Louisiana Law Review* 53 (1993): 1153–1190.

Gilmore, Grant. "Legal Realism: Its Cause and Cure." *Yale Law Journal* 70 (1961): 1037–1048.

Goldstein, Robert Justine. "The Great 1989-1990 Flag Flap: An Historical, Political, and Legal Analysis." *University Miami Law Review* 45 (1990): 19–106.

Gombrich, E.H. *Art and Illusion*, 2nd ed. Princeton, NJ: Princeton University Press, 1972.

Gould, Andrew R. "The Hidden Second Amendment Framework within *District of Columbia v. Heller.*" *Vanderbilt Law Review* 62 (2019): 1535–1576.

Graber, Mark A. "Desperately Ducking Slavery: Dred Scott and Contemporary Constitutional Theory." *Constitutional Commentary* 14, 2 (Summer 1997): 271–318.

Greely, Henry T. "A Footnote to 'Penumbra' in Griswold V. Connecticut." *Constitutional Commentary* 6 (1989): 251–265.

Greene, Jamal. "The Anticanon." *Harvard Law Review* 125 (2011): 380–475.

Grey, Thomas C. "Modern American Legal Thought." *Yale Law Journal* 106 (1996): 493–517.

Grossman, Joanna L. "*Griswold v. Connecticut*: The Start of the Revolution Verdict." Hofstra Law Faculty Scholarship (2015): 1–6. https://scholarlycommons.law.hofstra.edu/cgi/viewcontent.cgi?article=1776&context=faculty_scholarship.

Grossman, Joanna L. and John DeWitt Gregory. "The Legacy of *Loving*." *Howard Law Journal* 51 (2007): 15–52.

Hall, Davin J. "Not So Landmark After All? *Lawrence v. Texas*: Classical Liberalism and Due Process Jurisprudence." *William and Mary Bill of Rights Journal* 13, 2 (2004): 617–650.

Hariharan, Abhishek. "Implications of *Lochner v. New York* 2019 *Columbia University Undergraduate Law Review*." January 6, 2019.

Harris, Angela R. "Race and Essentialism in Feminist Legal Theory." *Stanford Law Review* 42, 3 (Feb, 1990): 581–616.

Hayman, Jr., Robert L., Nancy Leavit, Richard Delgado. *Jurisprudence Contemporary and Classical*. 2nd ed. St. Paul, MN: West Group 2002.

Healy, Thomas. "Brandenburg in a Time of Terror." *Notre Dame Law Review* 84 (2009): 655–731.

Henly, Burr. "Penumbra: The Roots of a Legal Metaphor." *Hastings Constitutional Law Quarterly* 15, 81 (1987): 251–265.

Holmes, Oliver Wendell. "The Path of the Law." *Harvard Law Review* 10 (1897): 1–20.

Huberfeld, Nicole. "Heed Not the Umpire (Justice Ginsburg Called NFIB)." (January 29, 2013). *University of Pennsylvania Journal of Constitutional Law Heightened Scrutiny* 15 (2013): 43–55.

Hume, David. *A Treatise of Human Nature*. Project Gutenberg, February 13, 2010. https://www.gutenberg.org/files/4705/4705-h/4705-h.htm.

Huq, Aziz. "The Nation: Threats in the Health Care Ruling." NPR. (July 2, 2012) https://www.npr.org/2012/07/02/156104486/the-nation-threats-in-the-health-care-rulin.

Huq, Aziz. "Judging Discriminatory Intent." *Public Law and Legal Theory Working Papers* (2017): 1–61. https://chicagounbound.uchicago.edu/public_law_and_legal_theory/662.

Hutchinson, Alan C. "Identity Crisis: The Politics of Interpretation." *New England Law Review* 26, 4 (1992): 1173–1219.

Inazu, John. "Holmes, Humility, and How Not to Kill Each Other." *Notre Dame Law Review* 94 (2019): 1631–1652.

Jackson, Faith J. "*Dred Scott v. Sandford*: A Prelude to the Civil War." *Richmond Journal Law and Public Interest* 15 (2011): 377–401.

James, William. *The Will to Believe and Other Essays in Popular Philosophy*. London, Bombay, Calcutta, 1912; Project Guttenberg, May 9, 2009. https://www.gutenberg.org/files/26659/26659-h/26659-h.htm.

Janz, James F. "Church and State: Prayer in Public Schools." *Marquette. Law Review* 46 (1962): 233–237.

Johnson, Dawn E. "Executive Privilege Since *United States v. Nixon*: Issues of Motivation and Accommodation." *Minnesota Law Review* 83 (1999): 1127–1141.

Johnson, Maureen. "Separate But (Un)Equal: Why Institutionalized Anti-Racism is the Answer to the Never-Ending Cycle of *Plessy v. Ferguson*." *University of University of Richmond Law Review* 52, 2 (2018): 327–386.

Kaminski, Margot. "Incitement to Riot in the Age of Flash Mobs." *University Cincinnati Law Review* 81 (2013): 1–84.

Kant, Immanuel. *Critique of Pure Reason*. Translated by Norman Kemp Smith New York: St. Martin's Press, 1965.

Katherine M. Franke, Katherine M. *The Domesticated Liberty of Lawrence v. Texas. Columbia Law Review* 104 (2004): 1399.

Katin, Ernest. "*Griswold v. Connecticut*: The Justices and Connecticut's Uncommonly Silly Law." *Notre Dame Law Review* 42 (1967): 680–706.

Kay, Richard. "The Equal Protection Clause in the Supreme Court, 1873–1903." *Buffalo Law Review* 29 (1980): 667–725.

Kendall Thomas, "Beyond the Privacy Principle." *Columbia Law Review* 92 (1992): 1431–1516.

Kendrick, Leslie. "On 'Clear and Present Danger.'" *Notre Dame Law Review* 94 (2019): 1653–1669.

Kennedy, Duncan "Legal Education and the Reproduction of Hierarchy." *Journal of Legal Education* 32 (1982): 591–615.

Kens, Paul. "*Lochner v. New York*: Tradition or Change in Constitutional Law." *New York University Journal of Law and Liberty* 1, 1 (2005): 404–431.

King, Jr. Martin Luther, "Letter from Birmingham City Jail." African Studies Center-University of Pennsylvania. https://www.africa.upenn.edu/Articles_Gen/Letter_Birmingham.html.

Kuhn, Thomas. "Objectivity, Value Judgment, and Theory Choice," http://shamiller.net/phi031/readings.d/kuhn.pdf (last visited January 7, 2019).

Kurland, Philip B. "*United States v. Nixon*: Who Killed Cock Robin." *UCLA Law Review* 22 (1974): 68–85.

Lain, Corinna Barrett "God, Civic Virtue, and the American Way: Reconstructing *Engel*." *Stanford Law Review* 67 (2015): 479.

Lane, Eric, Frederick A.O. Schwarz Jr. and Emily Berman. "Too Big a Canon in the President's Arsenal: Another Look at *United States v. Nixon*." *George Mason Law Review* 17 (2010): 737–788.

Larson, Edward J. "Putting *Buck v. Bell* in Scientific and Historical Context: A Response to Victoria Nourse." *Pepperdine Law Review* 39, 1 (2011): 119–128.

Lawrence III, Charles R. "The Id, the Ego, and Equal Protection: Reckoning with Unconscious Racism." *Stanford Law Review* 39 (1987): 317–388.

Levinson, Sanford. "United States: Assessing *Heller*." *International Journal of Constitutional Law* 7, 2 (April 2009): 316–328, https://doi.org/10.1093/icon/mop002.

Lewis, John B. and Bruce L. Ottley. "*New York Times v. Sullivan* at 50: Despite Criticism, the Actual Malice Standard Still Provides 'Breathing Space' for Communications in the Public Interest." *DePaul Law Review* 64 (2014): 1–64.

Lieter, Brian. "Positivism, Formalism, Realism." *Colorado Law Review* 99 (1999): 1138–1164.

———. "Rethinking Legal realism: Toward a Naturalized Jurisprudence." *Texas Legal Review* 76 (1997): 267–315.

Llewellyn, Karl N. "A Realistic Jurisprudence—The Next Step." 30 *Columbia Law. Review* 30 (1930): 431–465.

Lofton, Patricia. "*Texas v. Johnson:* The Constitutional Protection of Flag Desecration." *Pepperdine Law Review* 17, 3 (1990): 757–792.

Logan, David Andrew. "Rescuing Our Democracy by Rethinking" *New York Times Co. v. Sullivan. Ohio State Law Journal* 81 (2020): 759–814.

Longinus, *On the Sublime*. London and New York, 1890; Project Guttenberg, March 10, 2006. https://www.gutenberg.org/files/17957/17957-h/17957-h.htm.

Lopez, Geraldo and Rebecca Burciago. "The Troublesome Legacy of Brown v. Board of Education." *Educational Administration Quarterly* 50, 5 (December 2014): 796–811.

Loudon, David. "When Do the Ends Justify the Means?: The Role of the Necessary and Proper Clause in the Commerce Clause Analysis." *University of Massachusetts Law Review* 10, 2 (January 2015): 296–345.

Lucas Jr., Tommy J., Whitney R. Linsenmeyer , and Elizabeth G. Finocchiaro. "The Impact of Flag Desecration on Social Justice Movements: The Case of Occupy SLU." *Jesuit Higher Education: A Journal* 6, 1 (2017): 33–43.

Machiavelli, Nicolo. *The Prince*. Project Guttenberg, March 1998. https://www.gutenberg.org/files/1232/1232-h/1232-h.htm.

MacKinnon, Catherine. "*Points Against Postmodernism*." *Chicago Kent Law Review* 75 (2000): 687–712.

Marshall, William P. "Eleven Reasons Why Presidential Power Inevitably Expands and Why it Matters." *Boston University Law Review* 88 (2008): 505–522.

Schwartz, Martin A. "*Lawrence v. Texas*: The Decision and Its Implications for the Future." *Touro Law Review* 20 (2004): 221–249.

Mayer, Lloyd H. *Breaching a Leaking Dam?: Corporate Money and Elections, Charleston Law Review* 4 (2009–2010): 91–148.

McClain, Linda. "Prejudice, Constitutional Moral Progress, and Being on the Right Side of History: Reflections on *Loving v. Virginia* at Fifty." *Fordham Law Review* 86, 6 (2018): 2701–2715.

Meacham, Jon *Thomas Jefferson: The Art of Power*. New York: Random House, 2012.

Mendelson, Wallace. "Dred Scott's Case—Reconsidered." *Minnesota Law Review* 38 (1953): 16–28.

Merin, Jerome Lawrence. "Libel and the Supreme Court." *William and Mary Law Review* 11, 2 (1969): 371–423.

Messenger, Ashley. "The Problem with *New York Times Co. v. Sullivan*: An Argument for Moving from a Falsity Model of Libel Law to a Speech Act Model." *First Amendment Law Review* 11 (2012): 172–234.

Mill, John Stuart. *On Liberty*, London, Felling-on-Tyne, New York, Melbourne; Project Gutenberg, January 10, 2011. http://www.gutenberg.org/files/34901/34901-h/34901-h.htm.

Mills, Jon L. "The Meaning of "Equal": Evolution of Racial Equality in the United States." *Florida Journal of International Law* 29, 1 (2017): 285–298.

Montgomery, Montgomery. "Can *Brandenburg v. Ohio* Survive the Internet and the Age of Terrorism?: The Secret Weakening of a Venerable Doctrine." *Ohio State Law Journal* 70, 1 (2009): 141–193.

Moore, Michael "Moral Reality." *Wisconsin Law Review* 6 (1982): 1061–1156.

Motley, Candace Baker. "Symposium: *Brown v. Board of Education* and Its Legacy: A Tribute to Justice Thurgood Marshall, The Historical Setting of Brown and Its Impact on the Supreme Court's Decision." *Fordham Law Review* 61 (1992): 9–17.

Nahmod, Sheldon H. "The Sacred Flag and the First Amendment." *Indiana Law Journal* 66, 2 (Spring 1991): 511–548.

Nourse, Victoria "*Buck v. Bell*: A Constitutional Tragedy from a Lost World." *Pepperdine Law Review* 39, 1 (2011) 101–117.

Nourse, Victoria. "A Tale of Two *Lochners*: The Untold History of Substantive Due Process and the Idea of Fundamental Rights." *California Law Review* 97 (2009): 751–799.

Novick, Sheldon. "Homer Plessy's Forgotten Plea for Inclusion: Seeing Color, Erasing Color-Lines." *West Virginia Law Review* 118 (2016): 1181–1210.

Ottley, Bruce L., John B. Lewis, and Younghee J. Ottley. "*New York Times v. Sullivan*: A Retrospective Examination." *DePaul Law Review* 33 (1984): 741–781.

Patterson, Dennis M. "Law's Pragmatism and Practice and Narrative." *Virginia Law Review* 76, 5 (1990): 937–996.

Patterson, James T. "*Brown v. Board* of Education and the Civil Rights Movement." *Stetson Law Review* 34, 2 (Winter 2005): 413–421.

Paul, Ellen Frankel. "Freedom of Contract and the "Political Economy" of *Lochner v. New York*." *NYU Journal of Law and Liberty* 1, 1 (2005): 515–569.

Pedrioli, Carlo A. "*New York Times v. Sullivan* and the Rhetorics of Race: A Look at the Briefs, Oral Arguments, and Opinions." *Georgetown Journal Literature and Modern Critical Race Perspectives* 7 (2015): 109–136.

Penaro, Steven. "Reconciling Morse with Brandenburg." *Fordham Law Review* 77 (2008): 251–286.

Pierce Jr., Samuel R. "The Anatomy of an Historic Decision: *New York Times Co. v. Sullivan*." *North Carolina Law Review* 43 (1965): 315–363.

Pihos, Deanna N. "Assuming Maturity Matters: The Limited Reach of the Establishment Clause at Public Universities." *Cornell Law Review* 90, 5 (July 2005): 1349–1376.

Plato, *Crito*. In *Political Philosophy*, 3rd ed. Ed. Steven M. Cahn. New York and Oxford: Oxford University Press, 2015.

Popper, Karl. "*Conjectures and Refutations*." In *Scientific Knowledge: Basic Issues in Philosophy of Science*. Edited by Janet Kourany. Belmont: CA: Wadsworth, 1987.

Pound, Roscoe. "The Scope and Purpose of Sociological Jurisprudence." *Harvard Law Review* 24 (1911): 489–516.

Powell, John. A. "The Law and Significance of *Plessy*." *The Russell Sage Foundation Journal of the Social Sciences* 7, 1 (February 2021): 20–31; https://doi.org/10.7758/RSF.2021.7.1.02.

Pushaw Jr., Robert J. "The Paradox of the Obamacare Decision: How Can the Federal Government Have Limited Unlimited Power?" *Florida Law Review* 65 (2013): 1993–2053.

Radin, Margaret J. "The Pragmatist and the Feminist." *California Law Review* 63 (1990): 1699–1726.

———. "Reconsidering the Rule of Law." *Boston University Law Review* 69 (1989): 781–819.

Rawls, John *A Theory of Justice*. Cambridge, MA: The Belknap Press of Harvard University Press, 1971.

Richard Briffault, "Corporations, Corruption, and Complexity: Campaign Finance after *Citizens United*." *Cornell Law and Public Policy* 20 (2011): 643–671.

Rideout, Chris. "Penumbral Thinking Revisited: Metaphor in Legal Argumentation." *Legal Communication & Rhetoric: JALWD* 7 (2010): 155–191.

Roberts, Dorothy. "*Loving v. Virginia* as a Civil Rights Decision." *New York Law Scholarly Law Review* 59 (2014–2015): 175.

Roche, John P. *Plessy v. Ferguson*: Requiescat in Pace." *University Pennsylvania Law Review* 103 (1954): 44–58.

Rodes, Robert E. "The Passing of Nonsectarianism—Some Reflections on the School Prayer Case." *Notre Dame Lawyer* 38 (1962–1963): 115–137.

Rorty, Richard. "What You Can Expect from Anti-Foundationalist Philosophers: A Reply to Lynn Baker." *Virginia Law Review* 78, 3 (1992): 710–727.

Schaerer, Enrique. "What the Heller?: An Originalist Critique of Justice Scalia's Second Amendment Jurisprudence." *University Cincinnati Law Review* 82 (2018): 795–830.

Schauer, Frederick. "Formalism." *Yale Law Journal* 97 (1988): 509–548.

Schauer, Frederick. "Towards an Institutional First Amendment." *Minnesota Law Review* 89 (2005): 1278–1279.

Scheler, Max. *Formalism in Ethics and Non-Formalism in Values*. Translated by Manfred S. Frings and Roger L. Funk. Evanston, IL: Northwestern University Press, 1973.

———. *Selected Philosophical Essays*. Translated by David Lacterman. Evanston, IL: Northwestern University Press, 1973.

Scott, Rebecca J. "Public Rights, Social Equality, and the Conceptual Roots of the Plessy Challenge." *Michigan Law Review* 106, 5 (2008): 777–804.

Sears (Ret.), Justice Leah Ward and Greenberg, Sasha N. "The Love in Loving: Overcoming Artificial Racial Barriers." *Notre Dame Law Review Online* 94, 1 (2018): 28–31.

Segal, Revi. "Dead or Alive: Originalism as Popular Constitutionalism in Heller." *Harvard Law Review* 122, 1 (November 2008): 191–245.

Shapiro, Ilya. "Citizens United Misunderstood." Cato Institute. (January 20, 2015) https://www.cato.org/commentary/citizens-united-misunderstood.

Siegel, Stephen A. "Justice Holmes, *Buck v. Bell*, and the History of Equal Protection." *Minnesota Law Review* 90 (2005): 106–143.

Singer, Joseph William, "The Player and the Cards: Nihilism and Legal Theory." *Yale Law Journal* 94 (1984): 1–70.

Spindelman, Marc. "Some Early Views on *District of Columbia v. Heller*." *Louisiana Law Review* 69 (2009): 603–608.

Spindelman, Marc. "Surviving *Lawrence v. Texas*." *Michigan Law Review* 102 (2004): 1615–1667.

Stephenson Jr., D.G. "The Supreme Court and Constitutional Change: *Lochner v. New York* Revisited." *Villanova Law Review* 21, 2 (1976): 217–243.

Stone, Geoffrey R. "Flag Burning and the Constitution." *Iowa Law Review* 75 (1990): 111–124.

Strauss, David A. (2003) "Why Was Lochner Wrong?" *University of Chicago Law Review* 70, 1 (2003): 373–386.

Sykes, Emerson J. "In Defense of *Brandenburg*: The ACLU and Incitement Doctrine in 1919, 1969, and 2019." *Brook. Law Review* 85 (2019): 15–36.

Teitelbaum, Joel and Erica Spector. "*District of Columbia v. Heller*: Implications for Public Health Policy and Practice." *Public Health Reports* 124, 5 (Sep-Oct 2009): 758–760.

Colby, T.B. and Peter J. Smith. "The Return of *Lochner*." *Cornell Law Review* 100 (2015): 527–602.

Thompson, Phillip "Silent Protest: A Catholic Justice Dissents in *Buck v. Bell*." *The Catholic Lawyer* 43, 1 (Spring 2004): 125–148.

Thoreau, Henry David. *On the Duty of Civil Disobedience* (1849; Project Gutenberg, June 1993.

Travis, Thomas E. "*Horne v. USDA*: The Takings Clause, the Commerce Clause, and the 'World's Most Outdated Law.'" *Kentucky Journal of Equine, Agriculture, & Natural Resources Law* 7, 2 (2015): 399–422.

Trubek, David M. "Back to the Future: Happy Life of the Law and Society Movement." *Florida State University Law Review* 18 (1990): 1–55.

Van Alstyne, William W. "Constitutional Separation of Church and State: The Quest for a Coherent Position." *Faculty Publications* 775 (1963): 865–882.

Van Alstyne, William W. "Freedom of Speech and the Flag Anti-Desecration Amendment: Antinomies of Constitutional Choice." *Free Speech Yearbook* 29, 1 (1991): 96–105. 10.1080/08997225.1991.10556133.

Weinrib, Ernest J. "Legal Formalism: On the Immanent Rationality of Law." *Yale Law Journal* 97 (1988): 949–1016.

Wells, Christiana E. "Discussing the First Amendment Eternally Vigilant: Free Speech in the Modern Era." *Michigan Law Review* 101 (2003): 1566–1588.

Wells, Christina E. "Assumptions about Terrorism and the Brandenburg Incitement Test." *Brooklyn Law Review* 85 (2019): 111–147.

Wendy Williams, Wendy. "Equality's Riddle: Pregnancy and the Equal Treatment/ Special Treatment Debate." *Review Law and Social Change* 13 (1984–1985): 325–380.

Werham, Keith. "Checking Congress and Balancing Federalism: A Lesson from Separation-of-Powers Jurisprudence." *Washington and Lee Law Review* 57 (2000): 1213–1284.

West, Robin. "Jurisprudence and Gender." *Chicago Law Review* 55, 1 (1988): 1–72.

———. "Three Positivisms." *Boston University Law Review* 78 (1998): 791–834.

Westover, Casey L. "Structural Interpretation and the New Federalism: Finding the Proper Balance Between State Sovereignty and Federal Supremacy." *Marquette Law Review* 88 (2005): 693–750.

Wiist, William H. "*Citizens United*, Public Health, and Democracy: the Supreme Court Ruling, Its Implications, and Proposed Action." *American Journal of Public Health* 101, 7 (July 2011): 1172–1179.

Wildman, Stephanie M. and Adrienne D. Davis. "Language and Silence: Making Systems of Privilege Visible," *Santa Clara Law Review* 35 (1995): 881–906.

Williams, Joan C. "Culture and Certainty: Legal History and the Reconstructive Project." *Virginia Law Review* 76 (1990): 713–746.

Williams, Neil G. "*Brown v. Board* of Education Fifty Years Later: What Makes for Greatness in a Legal Opinion?" *Loyola University Chicago Law Journal* 36 (2004): 177–199.

Wisdom, Hon John Minor. "*Plessy v. Ferguson*—100 Years Later." *Washington and Lee Law Review* 53, 1 (Winter January 1, 1996): 9–20.

Wright, Danaya C. "The Logic and Experience of Law: *Lawrence v. Texas* and the Politics of Privacy." *University of Florida. Journal of Law and Public Policy* 15 (2003): 403–422.

Wright, R.G. "Equal Protection and the Idea of Equality." *Law and Inequality* 34, 1 (2016): 1–53.

Zinn, Howard. *A People's History of the United States*. libcom.org, https://libcom.org/files/A%20People's%20History%20of%20the%20Unite%20-%20Howard%20Zinn.pdf. If professional historians value as they do history, so do jurists.

Zrkel, Sabrina. "Ongoing Issues of Racial and Ethnic Stigma in Education 50 Years after *Brown v. Board*." *The Urban Review* 37, 2 (June 2005): 107–126.

Index

About the Authors

George David Miller has garnered national and international accolades for his teaching, page and performance poetry, plays, short stories, mixed media art, and treatises. These accolades include Illinois Professor of the Year, the Soka University Award of Honor, cowinner of the Value Inquiry Book Series book of the Year, and many stints as an artist-in-residence and keynote speaker. Over the last twenty years through his company, Before I Read This Poem, he has delivered over 1,000 writing and performance workshops and shows to over 50,000 students. Dr. Miller taught philosophy for thirty-seven years, articulating an interactive teaching style that integrated intellectual and physical elements of the human experience. He is a certified yogi who has studied in India and taught professionally and also hiker-journalist, who during his 184.5-mile, nine-day trek on the Chesapeake and Ohio Towpath shared his narrative on social media.

Laura Brown is a PhD candidate in philosophy at the University of Iowa. She earned a JD from the University of Illinois, and graduate certificates in African American Studies and Gender, Women's and Sexuality Studies from the University of Iowa. Brown has made scholarly contributions in political philosophy, with a focus on the intersection of theoretical constructions and burdened communities. As an instructor at the University of Illinois College of Law, she developed three-week programming to teach intricacies of the American legal system to international law students. She has also counseled corporations and individuals about developing and maintaining socially responsible web presences at the cutting-edge of their industries and created SEO and UX-optimized web content for legal and business organizations. Her publications include "Surviving the Indifferents" (*University of Iowa Digital Scholarship and Publishing Studio*) and "Hate Crime and Punishment: Why Typical Punishment Does Not Fit the Crime" (*University of Illinois Law Review*).

www.ingramcontent.com/pod-product-compliance
Lightning Source LLC
LaVergne TN
LVHW091525200926
848483LV00002B/310